INESSENTIAL WOMAN

INESSENTIAL WOMAN

Problems of Exclusion in Feminist Thought

ELIZABETH V. SPELMAN

BEACON PRESS BOSTON

Beacon Press
25 Beacon Street
Boston, Massachusetts 02108

Beacon Press books
are published under the auspices of
the Unitarian Universalist Association of Congregations.

95 94 93 92 91   8 7 6 5 4

Text design by Joanna Steinkeller

Library of Congress Cataloging-in-Publication Data
Spelman, Elizabeth V.
   Inessential woman : problems of exclusion in feminist
thought / Elizabeth V. Spelman.
   Includes index.
   ISBN 0-8070-6744-X
   ISBN 0-8070-6745-8 (pbk.)
   1. Feminism—Philosophy.   I. Title.
HQ1206.S666   1988
305.4'2'01—dc19   87-47878

For Roo and Nordy

Contents

Preface

The word "inessential" in the title of this book is ambiguous on purpose. On the one hand, it is intended as a reminder that women have been said by many Western philosophers to lack what is essentially human and to be inessential to whatever is most important about human life. On the other hand, it is meant to point to and undermine a tendency in dominant Western feminist thought to posit an essential "womanness" that all women have and share in common despite the racial, class, religious, ethnic, and cultural differences among us. I try to show that the notion of a generic "woman" functions in feminist thought much the way the notion of generic "man" has functioned in Western philosophy: it obscures the heterogeneity of women and cuts off examination of the significance of such heterogeneity for feminist theory and political activity.

It is not news that dominant Western feminist thought has taken the experiences of white middle-class women to be representative of, indeed normative for, the experiences of all women. Much of such thought, it is now common to say, expresses and reinforces the privilege of white middle-class women: their lives and works, their griefs and joys constitute the norm in relation to which other women's lives—if they are mentioned at all—are described as "different." This book came to have the particular shape it does out of the conviction that those of us who think such privilege damages (albeit in different ways) both the women who have it and those who do not must do much more than simply note its presence. For if we really think it can disfigure and distort feminist thought—and few of us doubt that masculine privilege has done that in many fields of human inquiry—then we'll want both to understand how such privilege works and to examine how deeply it has informed and deformed feminist thought.

If you get very far into what follows you'll soon see that I think that white middle-class privilege has found friendly places to lodge at the very root of much feminist thinking—for example, in the assumption that gender identity exists in isolation from race and class identity; in the assumption behind contrasting the situation of "women" with (for example) the situation of "Blacks" or "Jews"; in the assumption that the meaning of gender identity and the experience of sexism are the same for all women "as women." Throughout the book I try to describe ways in which certain apparently innocent concepts and methodological strategies in much feminist inquiry lead quietly but inexorably to putting the lives of white middle-class women at the logical center of such inquiry. Indeed, I have come to think even of the phrase "as a woman" as the Trojan horse of feminist ethnocentrism.

But the book is not finally, or even initially, a counsel of despair. In fact, as I describe in more detail in the last chapter, it may well be an expression of white middle-class privilege for those of us with it to think that because we have produced theories reeking with our own privilege, then anybody's theories must be similarly and fatally redolent. Moreover, as I also suggest, the fact that many women have cared enough about certain feminist writings and activities to challenge being excluded from them opens up the possibility of impassioned debates about what "feminism" is, or rather, what "feminisms" are; about what we mean by "women," "women's issues," "women's viewpoint," and other concepts at the heart of feminist inquiries. Any version of feminism which has closed the books on such questions has to have made most women's voices inessential.

Some indulgent old friends are expecting a book called *Out of Their Minds: Philosophers on Women, Slaves, Emotions, and the Body*. They'll find distant relatives of what would have been early chapters of that book in chapters 1 and 2 of this one. What I now think about Plato's and Aristotle's views about women is quite different from what I used to think. The difference is perhaps worth remarking upon briefly, since it has much to do with the book that emerges here. Thanks to the many writers whose work is referred to and echoed in what follows, I finally began to take notice of the ways in which so much of Western feminist theory has referred to women as if all women were white and middle-class. Then I began to wonder to what extent such theory implicitly endorses forms of hierarchy it explicitly critiques in the writings of figures such as Plato and Aristotle. I turned back to my own analyses of these philosophers to see whether I was replicating some undesirable aspects of their thought even while undertaking to criticize and distance myself from specific positions they held. Though I had in other places examined how thinking about "women and Blacks" in fact typically obscures the existence of women who are Black, I had written (to take just one example) about how Aristotle's treatment of "women" was similar to his treatment of "slaves," never thinking to ask about his treatment of women who were slaves. As I hope chapter 2 of this book makes clear, once I asked that question I had to rethink everything I and many other feminists had written about Aristotle; for we in effect had decided that in order to get at Aristotle's account of "women" we would explore the lives of free women rather than slave women. We didn't pause to think about where such a decision came from or what it meant. And yet we might have learned from the best of Western philosophy and feminism that how one starts, in thinking as in acting, has everything to do with where one might go. I feel confident that despite its shortcomings, *Inessential Woman* provides a richer path alongside women's lives than *Out of Their Minds* ever could have.

It is notoriously difficult to know when to stop fussing and fuming over a manuscript. The only reason I finally stopped putting off publication was to reach the moment at which I get to thank in print those who have given me so many different kinds of encouragement and help.

In a number of ways this book is an elaboration on themes I first discussed in "Theories of Race and Gender: The Erasure of Black Women," which more or less constitutes chapter 5. That essay came into existence at the prodding and nudging of many people, especially Sharon Pollack, who was my student research assistant while I was a 1980 summer fellow of Smith College's Project on Women and Social Change; Alison Jaggar, who invited me to give an early version of the essay at the conference Philosophical Issues in Feminist Theory at the University of Cincinnati in late 1980; and to Sarah Begus, who asked me to send the essay to *Quest: a feminist quarterly*, where it received superb editing from Lisa Hoogstra and Jackie MacMillan.

In the spring of 1981 the Smith College Government Department's invitation to teach "Sex and Politics" provided the first occasion to see how this new turn in my research would affect the way in which I discussed feminist theory with my students. I wish that group of students, along with those in feminist theory courses I've taught since then in the philosophy departments at Carleton College and at Smith, might know how important our ongoing conversations were to my growing understanding of the issues we discussed.

While I was visiting at Carleton the 1981–82 school year, María Lugones and I began to write together. The courage and passion of her thinking continues to sustain and inspire me. Those who know our joint projects will see the many ways this book is a working out of some of the problems María and I have discussed and written about together in recent years. *Gracias, querida mujer, amiga juguetona.*

The philosophy department at Smith has provided an extraordinary home for my work. Among the genial qualities of my colleagues is their continued enthusiasm for my regularly teaching "Philosophy and Women" with Johnnella Butler of the Afro-American Studies Department. This book would be quite different if I had not known the power of collaborating with Johnnella and the great fun of our friendship. I know she joins me in thanking our students over the years for their questioning, their humor, and their desire to put the discomfort they often feel in our class to good use.

I am very grateful to many other Smith colleagues, in particular those associated with the Advisory Committee on the Study of Women. I wish also to thank the Committee on Faculty Compensation and Development for their generous and timely award of Mellon II funds.

A year in heaven to complete this project was provided by the Mary Ingraham Bunting Institute of Radcliffe College. The pleasure I associate with the writing of this book is inseparable from the sense of warm and friendly enthusiasm I felt from the Bunting staff and my fellow, uh, fellows. They might recognize portions of the talk I gave at the Institute in parts of the Introduction and chapter 7.

Joanne Wyckoff, my editor at Beacon, has been wonderfully patient with me; I want to thank her here for knowing just when and how to push. Marie Cantlon, Spencer Carr, and Mary Vetterling-Braggin offered crucial editorial inspiration along the way. I wish my lurches toward grace did not obscure the inspired copyediting of Carlisle Rex-Waller.

The friendship of Helen Longino has been essential to my coming to understand philosophy in the way that I do, and loving certain of its possibilities.

I hope this work has even a little of the spirited love and passionate energy I admire so in Barbara Cottle Johnson. And I will be happy if it reflects in any way the kind of care and thoughtfulness which characterize Martha Ackelsberg's presence in this crazy world. Conversations with Barbara and Martha over many years have given shape and purpose to much of this book.

Friends, colleagues, and family members have been part of ongoing discussions about many of the issues raised here, and I have learned much from them. In particular I thank Arlene Avakian, John Bollard, Ann Ferguson, Jean Grossholtz, Liz Lerman, Margaret Lloyd, Jon Spelman, John Walter, and Mary Ruth Warner.

For their timely and thoughtful encouragement over the years, I am grateful to Kathy Addelson, Peggy Antrobus, Sandra Bartky, Lee Bowie, Sarah Franklin, Marilyn Frye, Sandra Harding, Hilde Hein, Alison Jaggar, Annie Jones, Evelyn Keller, Frédérique Marglin, Jane Martin, Meredith Michaels, Fi Mithoefer, Sally Ruddick, Richard Schmidt, Joe Singer, Bob Solomon, Cornelia Spelman, Ingrid Stadler, Fran Volkmann, Mary Helen Washington, Caroline Whitbeck, Deborah Wolf-Spelman.

More than a few stalwart readers have plowed through one or more drafts of one or more chapters; the dross that remains is entirely of my making. Many thanks, with promises to return the favor, to Martha Ackelsberg, Kathy Addelson, the Boston area Femcrits, Ann Congleton, John Connolly, Jill de Villiers, Reg Gibbons, Barbara Houston, Alison Jaggar, Murray Kiteley, Jan Krawitz, Helen Longino, María Lugones, Gary Matthews, Valerie Miner, Judith Plaskow, Amélie Rorty, Sally Ruddick, Celeste Schenck, Marilyn Schuster, Molly Shanley, Barry Smith, Janet Farrell Smith, Ruth Solie, Peter Stallybrass, Sharon Strom, Tom Tymoczko, Iris Young. Special thanks to Martha Minow for loving the pebbles even while feeling the pull of pebblehood. And a tweak on the old MPU to Mama Tandy, for her uninterrupted and never disapproving hum.

This book is dedicated to the memory of my parents, Elizabeth Schneider Spelman and Norman Leslie Spelman, in hopes that it reflects even a little what I learned from them about the necessary and playful embrace of loyalty and irreverence. I wish I'd known to thank them for that in their lifetimes.

Introduction

In one of the typically theory-drenched chapters of Iris Murdoch's novel *The Nice and the Good,* an elderly gentleman, Uncle Theo, sits with his twin niece and nephew while they play on the seashore. The beach is a source of acute discomfort to Uncle Theo. While the children's noise and exuberance bother him, what really seems to make him most anxious is the multiplicity of *things.* As if twinness weren't already enough of an ontological disturbance, there are on the beach all those pebbles, each clamoring in its particularity, the totality of them threatening the intelligibility, the tractability, the manageability of the world. Theo is a man who can only negotiate the possibility of plurality if the many can be reduced to a few or, best of all, to one. The horror of the manyness of the pebbles could then be stilled by the awareness that they are all instances of a single thing, pebblehood.

In describing this man's preoccupation with perceptual and conceptual tidiness, Murdoch presents, with a twist of existential angst, the throes of a problem that appeared in Western philosophical literature long before Plato: what is the world *really* made of? Do we get closer to an answer to this question by noting the manyness of the pebbles, or by reflecting on the fact that though there are *many* pebbles, there is only *one* kind of thing, the kind of thing that they all are, namely, a pebble? Does their significance stem from their distinctness from one another, despite the fact that all are pebbles, or does it reside in what they share in common as pebbles, despite the fact that in other ways they are distinct from one another?

1

How one answers all these questions depends of course on one's scheme for ranking things according to some "reality" scale and some "significance" scale. To the extent that the Murdoch character echoes Plato, he might answer these questions in the following way: The pebbles that we see and touch aren't really "real"; as material things, they are mere appearances of the Form "pebblehood," which is singular and "real." The pebbles, in their multiplicity, physicality, and changeability, are significant only insofar as they are instantiations of the single, nonphysical, and unchanging Form of pebblehood.[1] At least, according to Plato, this is what the true *philosopher* would say, even though the man in the street, and surely almost any woman anywhere, will most likely be drawn to the pebbles they can see and touch, and will think that what they can see and touch is what is most real. Uncle Theo exhibits not merely a Platonic disdain for the physical things of the world, but a plethoraphobic distaste for and discomfort with their manyness; the twins, on the other hand, display a childlike delight in multiplicity and physicality, which Plato would regard as antithetical to philosophical inquiry. Real philosophers, Plato tells us, don't "lose themselves and wander amid the multiplicities of multifarious things" (*Republic* 454b). Uncle Theo is thus overwhelmed by the multitude of colors, shapes, and sizes that confront him:

Uncle Theo . . . fingered the mauve and white pebbles on the beach. These stones, which brought such pleasure to the twins, were a nightmare to Theo. Their multiplicity and randomness appalled him. . . . The pebbles . . . looked at closely . . . exhibited almost every intermediate colour and also varied considerably in size and shape. All were rounded, but some were flattish, some oblong, some spherical; some were almost transparent, others more or less copiously speckled, others close-textured and nearly black, a few of a brownish-red, some of a pale grey, others of a purple which was almost blue.[2]

I wish to suggest that much of Western feminist theory has been written from a viewpoint not unlike that of Uncle Theo: that is, as if not just the manyness of women but also all the differences among us are disturbing, threatening to the sweet intelligibility of the tidy and irrefutable fact that all women are women.[3] From the Uncle Theo view, the theocratic view, the view of the ultimate purveyor of intelligibility, this fact about women is more important than those facts about us that distinguish us from one another.

This book is in large part an exploration of why the Uncle Theo view may seem essential to the possibility of any feminist theory and any feminist political activity focused on and intending to change the condition of women as women. It is not at all difficult to understand why many theorists might find what differentiates one woman from another irrelevant to our concerns as feminists (whether it also gives us ontological queasiness is another, though not unrelated, matter). First of all, it might be thought that as feminists, our motivation for thinking, talking, and writing about any particular woman is that she is a *woman;* at the same time, the point is not to talk only about *one* woman, but about *women*—any and all women. So the logic of our inquiry and concern seems to lead us to focus on the "womanness" or womanhood of any or all women, just as the Platonist's interest directs his explorations: If I'm studying pebbles, and want to learn the truth about them, I want to focus on what can be said about any and all pebbles, not just about some. I want to focus on what can be said about pebbles as pebbles, and not about, say, pebbles as found art objects or pebbles as slingshot ammunition. Just so, the apparent logic of feminist inquiry directs me to disregard what differentiates one woman from another, to see beyond what is peculiar to a woman or to a group of women who can also be identified as middle-class or working class, or Jewish or Catholic, or white or Black, or lesbian or heterosexual. After all, if I am interested in pebbles as pebbles, then I best not be distracted by the flatness of some or the roundness of others, the beige of one or the rosiness of another. For it is their pebbleness I said I was interested in, not their shape or their color.

On the other hand, if I am interested in knowing about all the pebbles, how can I disregard those features of each pebble that may distinguish it from others? This leads us to the paradox at the heart of feminism: Any attempt to talk about all women in terms of something we have in common undermines attempts to talk about the differences among us, and vice versa. Is it possible to give the things women have in common their full significance without thereby implying that the differences among us are less important?[4] How can we describe those things that differentiate women without eclipsing what we share in common?

The Uncle Theo version of feminism responds to the paradox with a paradox: The way to give proper significance to differences among women is to say that such differences simply are less significant than what women have in common. This solution is very neat, for it acknowledges differences among women only enough to bury them. But it doesn't bury them very effectively. For as we shall see, the focus on women "as women" has addressed only one group of women—namely, white middle-class women of Western industrialized countries. So the solution has not been to talk about what women have in common as women; it has been to conflate the condition of one group of women with the condition of all and to treat the differences of white middle-class women from all other women as if they were not differences.

It is not as if, in the history of feminist theory, just any group of women

3

has been taken to stand for all women—for example, no one has ever tried to say that the situation of Hispanas in the southwestern United States is applicable to all women as women; no one has conflated their case with the case of women in general. And the "problem of difference" within feminist theory is not the problem of, say, Black women in the United States trying to make their theories take into account the ways in which white women in the United States are different from them.

This should tell us that the "problem of difference" for feminist theory has never been a general one about how to weigh the importance of what we have in common against the importance of our differences. To put it that way hides two crucial facts: First, the description of what we have in common "as women" has almost always been a description of white middle-class women. Second, the "difference" of this group of women— that is, their being white and middle-class—has never had to be "brought into" feminist theory. To bring in "difference" is to bring in women who aren't white and middle-class.

This is where the analogy between dominant Western feminism and Uncle Theo's view is misleading. There is no history of the color and shape of one pebble being mistaken for all in an attempt (which many would regard as ill-conceived) to get at the pebblehood of all pebbles as pebbles.[5] The analogy to pebbles suggests that for feminism the problem has been how we weigh what we have in common against what differentiates us. But the real problem has been how feminist theory has confused the condition of one group of women with the condition of all.

What I hope to show is how easily that conflation takes place, how it can happen without anybody even trying to make it happen; indeed, how it happens despite the desire that it not happen. A measure of the depth of white middle-class privilege is that the apparently straightforward and logical points and axioms at the heart of much of feminist theory guarantee the direction of its attention to the concerns of white middle-class women. I also hope that revealing the extent to which feminist theory provides a friendly home for white middle-class privilege will help to undermine that privilege—not ignoring, of course, the necessity of great economic and political changes. If we think of privilege simply as appearing in individuals rather than being lodged in ways of thinking, we focus on what privilege feeds but not on what sustains it.

Feminists have long been aware of the levels at which male privilege operates to erase women's lives and concerns and perspectives from view. (As will become clear in the following chapters, such privilege has belonged only to *some* males.) We examine the many devices men have manufactured to make it a matter of course that their own needs and deeds will be attended to. Among such devices are theories of "human nature" that in the guise of apolitical metaphysical inquiry tell us why it is quite rational that men should dominate women. Feminists have rightly criticized these theories (reviewed briefly below and at length in chapters 1 and 2). Nevertheless, our distancing ourselves from the views of blatant sexists keeps us from recognizing the extent to which we may in fact share elements of their views. It is always easier to see how privilege works in others than in ourselves, but the insights so gained may be entirely lost if we can't imagine that we are anything like those others. Feminist theory may come to be more aware of the extent of the privilege it expresses, and of the depths at which such privilege works, by thinking about its similarities to theories of human nature that it has justifiably condemned.

At the same time our inquiry can benefit from something consumer watchdogs call "antiredeposition": the property of detergents that prevents the dirt taken out of concentrated spots from being redeposited more generally over the whole load. Those of us with privilege may find it very handy to parlay our embarrassment at having it into a prodigious preoccupation with revealing and exterminating it. We should keep in mind the pleasure flagellants may take in revealing their sins, especially the sin of self-adoration. We make our sins the most interesting and most pressing thing to talk about: so we are still center stage. Maybe the best thing we can do in light of this danger is to remind ourselves that the kind of privilege we are discussing here will only have ended when a book like this is unnecessary.

But there is another danger, perhaps even more insidious than the first: that those who would be happy to find any fault they can with feminism will relish yet another opportunity to see some of its shortcomings exposed. In the event that any such readers have gotten even this far into the text, please heed this: you have no right to take comfort in what follows. The extent to which you gloat is a perfect measure of your satisfaction with the sexual status quo.

I

What philosophers have had to say about women typically has been nasty, brutish, and short. Except for those resolved to keep women in their place—or rather, in their places, since a woman's race and class, for example, will influence her "place" along with her gender—thoughtful readers who seek enlightenment in the canonical texts of Western philosophy will have learned not to expect to find it on the subject of women.

Nevertheless, in the first two chapters of this book I turn to the progenitors of Western philosophy—Plato and Aristotle—and explain the arguments and devices they use to effect the banishment of women from the class of fully human beings. The views of Plato and Aristotle have been amply and well critiqued,[6] and surely, it would seem, we need alternatives to their views, not a rehashing of the problems with them. Why, then, should we direct still more attention to them?

I would be more enthusiastic about leaving Plato and Aristotle on the library shelves (on the matter of women, anyway) if I had not come to believe that too many of the critiques of their inherent sexism are equally exclusionary in their focus and concerns. Most philosophical accounts of "man's nature" are not about women at all. But neither are most feminist accounts of "woman's nature," or "women's experiences" about all women. There are startling parallels between what feminists find disappointing and insulting in Western philosophical thought and what many women have found troubling in much of Western feminism.

Here I begin by describing those parallel disappointments, then I examine how feminist thought has generated accounts of women's lives in their own way as deeply inegalitarian as the views of Plato and Aristotle. Finally, I want to consider what we might learn from such an ironic and painful comparison.

II

Rehearsing the history of Western philosophical thought about women is for the most part a gloomy business. First of all, even if the entire body of a philosopher's work is readily available, there may be no or only very scattered references to women.[7] Moreover, given what most philosophers who have written about women have had to say, we might be tempted to think that the less we find about women in a philosopher's work the less disappointed we'll be. We have only to turn to Nietzsche for an example:

Woman wants to become self-reliant—and for that reason she is beginning to enlighten men about "woman as such": *this* is one of the worst developments of the general *uglification* of Europe. . . . Woman has much reason for shame; so much pedantry, superficiality, schoolmarmishness, petty presumption, petty licentiousness and immodesty lies concealed in woman.[8]

Kant is less scurrilous, more quietly abusive:

Women will avoid the wicked not because it is unright, but because it is ugly. . . . Nothing of duty, nothing of compulsion, nothing of obligation! They do something only because it pleases them, and the art consists in making only that please them which is good. I hardly believe that the fair sex is capable of principles.[9]

Charity, if not wisdom, suggests the following response: It would be extraordinary if philosophers were immune to misogyny.[10] Perhaps we might also grant them a distinction between on-the-record and off-the-record remarks, or between good days and curmudgeonly days—distinctions we may invoke sometimes in our own behalf. But such generosity surely runs the risk of letting people off the hook, insofar as it dismisses as a quirk of disposition what may be a sign of a much deeper problem. For example, what should one do with the fact that Kant not only thought that acting out of duty was essential to acting rightly, but that women were incapable of acting out of duty?

Well, perhaps matters are not so hopeless, if we can construct what philosophers like Nietzsche and Kant would have said if they had not been subject to the prejudices of their times. Had they been able to shake off at least some of the effects of living in a sexist society, so the argument goes, they wouldn't have made such invidious distinctions between women and men. Surely what these reconstructed philosophers would say about women is just what they said about men. And thus when philosophers talk about "man's nature," we might assume that they really are talking about woman's nature as well.

I have several caveats about this reconstruction. At best, of course, it will only tell us what these philosophers have said about women, not getting us any closer to what the women might say themselves.[11] Moreover, the suggested reconstruction doesn't consider whether the philosophers in question excluded not only women from those having "man's nature," but a lot of men as well. For example, it leaves out what Kant said about racial differences and what he thought such differences implied about the capacity of all men to be guided by the dictates of reason in their moral behavior: what are we to make of his belief that one can tell from the color of a man's skin whether or not he is stupid?[12] It thus also ignores whether Kant thought that women of different races had different natures or capacities.

Finally, such reupholstering of a philosophical position doesn't require us to ask this crucial question: Does the existence of those who can be defined as complete persons demand the existence of others who cannot be granted personhood? For example, does the full flowering of a person's rationality require that he or she be surrounded by other human beings who will gather or cultivate or shop for or cook food, make shoes, clean up, raise children? As Plato so often reminds us, those engaged in contemplation of eternal truths can't be bothered with menial tasks.[13]

In short, we have learned to expect from philosophers sometimes facile, sometimes carefully sculpted invective about women, and it is not at all clear that there is any easy way around this state of affairs. Because John Stuart Mill is such a notable exception to what is otherwise a litany of abuse, some of us may be tempted to ignore the fact that the women whose subjection concerned him were the women of his own social class, that the men whose violence toward women was most apparent to him were not of his own social class. But there is much to learn from his short-sightedness as well as from the views of more venomous philosophers whom we are justified in putting on misogyny row.

III

There are startling similarities between the disappointment, not to say the anger, of feminists about Western philosophy and responses to much of their own theory. Many women who have turned to the history of mainstream feminist thought for enlightenment about the conditions of their lives have found that there was no mention of women like themselves, a silence that extends their exile from humanity as defined by the philosophers. To take a shopworn but not atypical example, Betty Friedan thought that a large part of the solution to "the problem that has no name" would be for women to get out of the house.[14] She couldn't have been thinking of the millions of women who always have worked "outside the house," for example, as domestic labor for the very women about whom Friedan was concerned. Lest anyone think that everything has changed since 1963, listen to the words of a white feminist at an international conference on women's history held in 1986 in Amsterdam. In response to questions about why "women's history" in Western countries still is "white women's history," she replies: "We have enough of a burden trying to get a feminist viewpoint across, why do we have to take on this extra burden?"[15] This attitude, as we shall see throughout this book, is but the tip of a very slow-melting iceberg.

Similarly, just as philosophers such as Nietzsche and Kant reproduced and further entrenched the misogyny of their time, feminist theorists may unthinkingly sustain demeaning images and stereotypes. For example, Audre Lorde wonders why non-European women are mentioned only as victims in Mary Daly's *Gyn/Ecology,* and not included among the women whose power Daly celebrates.[16] Can we assume that feminist accounts of "women's" lives, or of the social, economic, and political conditions under which "women" live, have been about all women? Elizabeth Cady Stanton was certainly not speaking of all women when she argued that "women" should get the vote before or at the same time as "the lower orders of Chinese, Africans, Germans and Irish."[17] Indeed, as I shall argue in chapters 2 and 5, the more universal the claim one might hope to make about women—"women have been put on a pedestal" or "women have been treated like slaves"—the more likely it is to be false. If we think of women who were part of slave populations, their problem surely was not that they were put on a pedestal; and it would be very odd to say that they were "treated like slaves" if they *were* slaves. All too often feminists have been as sloppy in our descriptions of "the woman's condition" as philosophers have been in their descriptions of "the human condition."

Moreover, versions of women's liberation—of what conditions would have to prevail in order for women to be free of oppression and have the opportunity to flourish—may involve in practice if not in principle the impoverishment of others, as, for example, when a woman's career is predicated upon her paying unconscionably low wages to the other women (or men) who do her housework or if the company of which she is an executive exploits the women (and men) who labor for it.[18]

Finally, if it is important in looking at the history of Western philosophy to ask whether women had any part in the formulation of accounts of "woman's nature" or of "human nature," it surely is important in looking at the history of Western feminist thought to ask who has participated in the formulation of its accounts of what it means to be a woman and in the description of the conditions of women's lives.[19] Who has been heard from? Perhaps more to the point, who has been listened to? Feminists have argued persuasively that we can't get adequate accounts of women's lives through theories constructed by men that are geared to direct us to the lives of men and away from the lives of women. But by the same token we should be sceptical about any claim that theories constructed by and for one group of women will automatically enlighten (rather than deeply mislead) us about all women's lives. Have we thought enough about what kind of knowledge and skill are necessary in order for one woman to speak about another? In order to speak in behalf of another?

IV

The parallels between the legacy of Western philosophy and the operation of much of modern feminism are troubling, since the impetus of feminism has been to undermine various forms of privilege and domination. This becomes especially clear when we remind ourselves what Plato and Aristotle were up to.

First of all, Plato and Aristotle were inegalitarian to the core: they unapologetically wanted to justify the domination of men over women, masters over slaves, philosophers or intellectuals over manual workers.[20]

9

They maintained that such domination served not simply the interests of those who were to rule but the best interests of everyone and the highest interests of the state.

For both Plato and Aristotle, the politics of domination are grounded in the facts of human nature. As we shall see, despite apparent references to a common human essence, neither Plato nor Aristotle believed in a nature shared by all humans. Rather, there are several different kinds of nature possessed by different kinds of humans: in particular, some humans are of the kind that are to rule, others of the kind that are to be ruled. They thus assert a variety of human natures, hierarchically arranged.

According to a central if not exclusive strand of thought in Plato, the souls of humans are separable, in concept and in existence, from the bodies of humans. It is by virtue of what our bodies are that we have a particular sexual identity; it is by virtue of the kind of work our bodies do that we have something like a class identity.[21] But our souls, which are what we *really* are, are distinct from our bodies. So there would seem to be no way to distinguish among people or to rank them, as long as we focus on what is most important about them: their souls. However, it turns out in Plato that souls really aren't all alike. They aren't alike insofar as there are kinds of souls: we come to know what kind of soul a person has by knowing what kind of body she or he has or by what they do with their body. If you have a female body (unless you are among the small number of women who might be philosopher-rulers) or a body that engages in manual tasks, you have a different kind of soul than that found in a male body that cannot be bothered with physical labor. Souls also aren't alike insofar as they have parts, for how the parts are related differs among different kinds of people: only in some people does the higher, rational part of the soul rule the lower appetitive and emotional parts, and these people ought to rule those in whom the lower parts predominate.

Aristotle appears to hold some positions quite at odds with Plato's. He thinks of soul and body as inseparable, and he cautions us against thinking that the soul has "parts" in anything but a metaphorical sense. Aristotle holds that all humans have reason and recognizes that this works against his claim that some humans are more rational than others and thus ought to rule those others. He dissolves the tension, however, by stating that reason, which might appear to be the same in all humans, is not the same after all. As in Plato, the important issue becomes the distribution of powers within the soul: Aristotle says that in some people, the rational part (his language ceases to be metaphorical) prevails over the irrational part, in others it doesn't (indeed in them it can't).[22] Ultimately, according to Plato and Aristotle, the idea that all humans have souls, or that all humans have reason, is no argument for a common human "essence."

Now feminists have not wanted to have anything to do with such Platonic and Aristotelian positions. Though feminists differ about the nature and causes of oppression, no version of feminism has had as its central aim the justification of the domination of one group over another. And while feminism may seem by definition to be dedicated to dismantling sex oppression rather than any other form of oppression, the emergence of women's movements in the nineteenth and twentieth centuries in the United States is linked historically and conceptually to abolitionist and civil rights activity.[23] Moreover there are versions of feminism, such as socialist feminism, according to which we cannot account for gender oppression without reference to class oppression.

For the most part, feminists have been eager to postulate a kind of sameness among women that Plato and Aristotle denied existed among humans. We have felt the need to speak of women as in crucial respects constituting a unitary group, sharing something very important in common. There are at least two apparently very good reasons for thinking it is not necessary and indeed undesirable to highlight differences among women: (1) Though feminism shares concerns with other liberation movements, what distinguishes it is its central focus on sexism; and sexism, it is argued, affects all women alike, no matter what other forms of oppression they are subject to. (2) Focusing on differences among women is only likely to lead to invidious hierarchical rankings of the sort we see so clearly in Plato and Aristotle.

However, our views can function to assert or express domination without explicitly or consciously intending to justify it. Feminist theory does that wherever it implicitly holds that some women really are more complete examples of "woman" than others are. How does this happen, given our desire to avoid it?

We saw that in Plato and Aristotle it is the insistence on the importance of differences among humans, the reliance on a theory of multiple "human natures" (in particular the view that some humans really are more human than others), that serves as the metaphysical foundation for a politics of domination. Paradoxically, in feminist theory it is a *refusal* to take differences among women seriously that lies at the heart of feminism's implicit politics of domination. The paradox dissolves when we consider that both the assertion of difference and the denial of difference can operate on behalf of domination.[24] The assertion of differences among women can operate oppressively if one marks the differences and then suggests that one of the groups so differentiated is more important or

11

more human or in some sense better than the others.[25] But on the other hand, to stress the unity of women is no guarantee against hierarchical ranking, if what one says is true or characteristic of women as a class is only true or characteristic of some women: for then women who cannot be so characterized are in effect not counted as women. When Stanton said that women should get the vote before Africans, Chinese, Germans, and Irish, she obviously was relying on a concept of "woman" that blinded her to the "womanness" of many women.

The fact that hierarchical rankings are compatible with both the postulation of difference and the insistence on some kind of root similarity is closely linked to the promises and the pitfalls of any attempt to provide an ahistorical, acultural description of "human nature" or "man's nature" or "woman's nature." Many differences among us are linked to our being historical beings, living in particular places at particular times, subject to particular interpretations of our physical characteristics and activities. Our differences have been invoked to justify claims that some of us are superior to others and by virtue of this superiority are entitled, perhaps obliged, to dominate others. Under such circumstances, efforts to mute our differences, or to show how irrelevant they are in light of a shared humanity (or manhood or womanhood) that transcends them, can be and have been used to attack unjust political institutions predicated on inequalities. Nevertheless, whatever advances such attempts might achieve, the difficulties involved in "transcending" historical differences usually are painfully obvious. The 1956 preface to Kenneth Stampp's book about U.S. slavery, *The Peculiar Institution: Slavery in the Ante-Bellum South,* provides a case in point. Waxing enthusiastic about how much we can learn "from the natural and social sciences about the Negro's potentialities and about the basic irrelevance of race," Stampp describes a guiding belief of his study:

I have assumed that the slaves were merely ordinary human beings, that innately Negroes *are,* after all, only white men with black skins, nothing more, nothing less.[26]

Stampp goes on to say that the fact that Black men really are white underneath gives "their story a relevance to men of all races."

Though Stampp's view was progressive for its time, and though in later printings of the book he indicates his regret at having put his point the way he did, it is a fine example of what might be called boomerang perception: I look at you and come right back to myself.[27] In the United States white children like me got early training in boomerang perception when we were told by well-meaning white adults that Black people were just like us—never, however, that we were just like Blacks.

Herein lies a cautionary tale for feminists who insist that underneath or beyond the differences among women there must be some shared identity—as if commonality were a metaphysical given, as if a shared viewpoint were not a difficult political achievement. "We're the same," Stampp was saying, "because underneath that black skin is a white man." Western feminist theory has in effect used Stampp's argument whenever it has implicitly demanded that Afro-American, Asian-American, or Latin American women separate their "woman's voice" from their racial or ethnic voice without also requiring white women to distinguish being a "woman" from being white.[28] This double standard implies that while on the one hand there is a seamless web of whiteness and womanness, on the other hand, Blackness and womanness, say, or Indianness and womanness, are discrete and separable elements of identity. If, like Stampp, I believe that the woman in every woman is a woman just like me, and if I also assume that there is no difference between being white and being a woman, then seeing another woman "as a woman" will involve seeing her as fundamentally like the woman I am. In other words, the womanness underneath the Black woman's skin is a white woman's, and deep down inside the Latina woman is an Anglo woman waiting to burst through an obscuring cultural shroud.[29] As Barbara Omolade has said, "Black women are not white women with color."[30]

Thus the phrase "as a woman" is the Trojan horse of feminist ethnocentrism. Whatever else one does, or tries to do, when one is thinking of a woman "as a woman," one is performing a feat of abstraction as sophisticated as the one Plato asks us to perform in thinking of a person not as her body but as her soul. What is it to think of a woman "as a woman"? Is it really possible for us to think of a woman's "womanness" in abstraction from the fact that she is a particular woman, whether she is a middle-class Black woman living in North America in the twentieth century or a poor white woman living in France in the seventeenth century?

V

There is a powerful combination of logical and political assumptions found in most versions of feminism that makes the use of "as a woman" appear logically unexceptionable and politically necessary. In order to speak of someone as a victim of sexism, as being oppressed on account of her being a woman, she has to be identifiable as a woman. Any and all women can be identified as women, however else they can be identified—as Black, brown, white, left-handed, right-handed, carpenter, housewife, professor, weight-lifter. Furthermore, in order to justify the claim in any particular case that it is sexism that has harmed a woman, one must be able to show that the harm comes to her because she is a woman and not because of some other fact about her. Thus if she is subject to other forms of oppression, this must be because of other facts about her, her race or class, sexual orientation, religious or cultural heritage. But do we exclude crucial dimensions of her being a woman if we don't talk about these elements of her identity?

Here we have to distinguish between sex and gender.[31] When talking about a woman as a woman, do we refer to the physiological properties of femaleness or do we mean the ways in which she is expected in her culture to think, feel, and act? To identify a person as a female is one thing, to identify her as a woman is another. If this weren't true, no one could ever talk about a female having or lacking womanly qualities, or not acting the way women are supposed to act. If we did not distinguish between being a female and being a woman, it would be impossible to make the anthropological point that different societies have different constructions of womanhood for their females. Indeed, within any single society the definitions and expectations of what it means to be a woman will vary greatly. This is often a bitter truth, as we reflect, for example, on the lot of a white slaveowner's wife "as a woman" and on the condition of a slave woman "as a woman." Sojourner Truth's question, "Ain't I a Woman?" would not have arisen or made sense otherwise.

Moreover, if being oppressed by sexism depends on the particular construction that is made of womanhood, then even if we say all women are oppressed by sexism we cannot automatically conclude that the sexism all women experience is the same. We have to understand what one's oppression "as a woman" means in each case. The sexism most Black women have experienced has not typically included being put on a pedestal. Moreover, we cannot describe what it is to be subject to several forms of oppression, say, sexism and racism and classism, by adding together their separate accounts. For example, we surely cannot produce an accurate picture of Latina women's lives simply by combining an account of Anglo women's lives and one of Latino men's lives. Or as a recent article in the *New York Times* unwittingly made clear, we can't generate a picture of the place of Black women in the United States armed forces by talking about how "women and Blacks transform the military."[32]

Examples like this might suggest that we can get the clearest picture of how women are oppressed "as women" if we focus on the lives of women who are subject only to sexism and not to any other form of oppression. We then don't have to look at a woman's race or class in order to understand how she is being treated as a woman. But this idea is preposterous: while a woman's being white, for example, is not the cause of or occasion for her being systematically subject to violence, it has everything to do with how she is treated.[33] In short, and as I will argue in detail throughout the following pages, the fact that a woman is not oppressed on account of her racial identity hardly leads to the conclusion that the sexist oppression to which she is subject can be understood without reference to her racial identity. One's gender identity is not related to one's racial and class identity as the parts of pop-bead necklaces are related, separable and insertable in other "strands" with different racial and class "parts."

Nevertheless, there seem to be imperative political reasons for speaking of women as sharing some very important identity "as women." At the heart of anything that can coherently be called a "women's movement" is the shared experience of being oppressed as women. The movement is, as it has to be, grounded in and justified by the fact of this shared experience: without it there would be neither the impulse nor the rationale for the political movement (whatever else is true of the movement). That is, unless in some important sense women speak in a single voice, the voice each has as a woman, there are no solid grounds for a "women's movement." Speaking of differences among women seems politically dangerous; it can only lead to factions and hence to struggles to give priority to some women's concerns over others.

These responses perhaps rightly protest that political movements cannot be fussy about every fine logical point. And these claims about the very possibility of a coherent political movement have to be taken seriously. But let us suppose that it is true that a coherent women's movement, like any other political movement with any hope of being heard and making change, requires that a group speak in a single voice, that is, requires that its demands and hopes be stated on behalf of a number of people in agreement about those demands and hopes. This doesn't tell us how such a voice is to be achieved. We can't simply brush aside the possibility, indeed as I have just argued the inevitability, of there being differences between how one group of women understand themselves "as women" and how others do. How, from the multiplicity of voices, will a single one be shaped? Are some people, as Plato argued, supposed to know better than others how to find the one voice among the many? If so, who are they? If not, how is the decision to be made?

Finally, given our discussion above of the perils of trying to "transcend" differences, can we confidently affirm that it is any less politically dangerous *not* to focus on them? For whom is it less politically dangerous? Will "not focusing" on differences among women guarantee that no woman's concerns will take priority over another's?

VI

Feminist theory always has had to make decisions about how to weigh the significance of differences among women, even when it has not been self-conscious about doing so. We shall examine in the next seven chapters how those decisions are made and the extent to which they have functioned, for the most part unintentionally, to preserve the privileged status of some women over others.

In chapters 1 and 2 we shall be reminded of the fact that as far back as Plato and Aristotle, male thinkers differentiated among women: all women together did not constitute a simple Other for them. We will then have to ask how such views ought to be investigated and examine why for the most part feminists have taken men's views about just one group of women to be their entire account of women.

In chapter 3, we look at a landmark text in twentieth-century Western feminism: Simone de Beauvoir's *The Second Sex*. We will trace what led her to describe the case of white middle- and upper-class women as the case of "women in general" despite the many rich clues in her own account that speak otherwise.

By the time we reach chapter 4, it will have become evident that in some way the attempt to isolate gender from other elements of human identity such as race and class, along with the parallel attempt to isolate sexism from other forms of oppression such as racism and classism, has been instrumental in the preservation of white middle-class privilege in feminist theory. We turn to the very influential work of Nancy Chodorow to see why such attempts seem both possible and necessary for feminist inquiry, and how at the same time they keep race and class, racism and classism, at the periphery of feminist thought. We also begin to see Chodorow's linking of sexism, racism, and classism work to obscure the race and class privilege of white middle-class women in feminist theory.

In chapter 5, we examine "additive analyses" of the situation of those women subject not only to sexism but also to other forms of oppression such as racism. Paradoxically, such analyses end up erasing from view the very women meant to be under consideration.

In chapter 6, we return to a question at the heart of feminist theory and practice: how are women alike, and how are we different from one another? What is significant about such similarities and differences? Are some women in a better position, politically or epistemologically, to answer such questions? How are conflicting claims about these questions to be adjudicated?

In chapter 7, we finally face up to inevitable questions: Will feminist theory be recognizable if it doesn't talk about women as women? If it doesn't focus on gender in isolation from the other elements of identity? If it doesn't try to describe the situation of "women in general"? How will removing its current focus on white middle-class concerns affect what "feminism" means and what its projects are?

Although these questions are difficult ones, we should not despair. Feminist theory and practice at their best do not founder on struggles over the definition of "woman" or on heated debates about the significance of differences among women. On the contrary, they are constituted by and thrive on such struggles. So despair over what follows isn't appropriate, except for those who fear losing the power to control single-handedly the outcome of such struggles.

> *and what*
> *pure happiness to know*
> *all our high-toned questions*
> *breed in a lively animal.*
>
> ADRIENNE RICH

Hairy Cobblers and Philosopher—Queens

In book 5 of Plato's *Republic,* Socrates proposes that women are poten-
tially just as good guardians or philosopher-rulers of the state as men.
The notion of the equality of men and women must have been startling to
Plato's contemporaries, since it went so much against the grain of Athenian society and its history.[1] But it should also be startling to modern
readers of Plato who know how deeply undemocratic and antiegalitarian
his views in general are.

In this chapter, I will describe what made it possible for Plato to imagine women in roles quite other than those defined by their society, and I
also hope to make clear how he must have perceived their equality to men
in light of his otherwise inegalitarian politics. Plato's notion of the equality of the sexes is carefully sculpted so as not to be inconsistent with his
thinking of one class of people as the superiors of other classes.[2] If we can
understand why it is not inconsistent, then perhaps we can gain some insight into troubling features of contemporary feminist thought: that is,
perhaps we can see how one can argue against sexism in a way that leaves
other forms of oppression intact; how one can argue for views that support, or at least leave unexamined, the domination of some women over
others. We will see the sad irony in the description of Plato as the first
feminist philosopher.[3]

I

Let us turn to the *Republic* for Plato's views about women. This central
dialogue of the Platonic corpus is an examination of the nature of justice,

19

and it becomes perforce a prescription for the best society: we can come to understand what justice in the individual is, Socrates urges, if we look at justice "writ large" in the state. What is justice in a state or society? Plato assumes the following as general principles of construction of that society in which we can find justice: (1) different kinds of people have different natures, and (2) both individuals and the state are best served if people perform the functions for which their natures, complemented by the appropriate education, best suit them.[4] The ideal state is based on the recognition of the mutuality of need among people who do different things. People stand in need of each other because not everybody does everything well; indeed, no one does everything well; in fact, everyone does only one thing well. People will lead the best and most flourishing lives of which they are capable, and the state will be the best and the happiest possible state, if each person fulfills his or her "natural" role. Justice consists in the harmony that prevails under these conditions. Individuals will enjoy the harmony that is justice if their reason, aided by the spirited part of their souls, rules their appetites; the state will enjoy the harmony that is justice if those individuals in whom the power of reasoning is strongest rule, with the aid of high-spirited soldiers, over the multitudes. That is, justice will prevail to the extent that a guardian class of philosophers, aided by the class of "auxiliaries" whom they command, rules over the class of artisans or producers. (Plato appears to assume that in addition to these three classes there will be the underclass of slaves.)[5]

It follows from Plato's argument that if women and men have different natures, they ought not to have the same pursuits, they ought not to perform the same functions in the state. Indeed, given Plato's definition of justice, it would be unjust for them to be delegated the same functions and responsibilities.

In book 5 of the *Republic* Socrates insists that there is no reason women ought not to be included among the philosopher-rulers. He manages to do so without giving up the principle that we ought to assign "different pursuits to different natures and the same to the same" (454b) and without giving up entirely the notion that men and women have different natures. He points out to Glaucon that if one is careful enough to "apply the proper divisions and distinctions to the subject under consideration" (454a) one will think not simply about whether two natures are different or the same but whether they are different or the same *with respect to a particular pursuit*. In this connection, Socrates insists that just as whether a person is bald or long-haired is irrelevant to whether he has the kind of nature that makes him a good cobbler, so whether a person is male or female is irrelevant to whether he or she is suited to a task—indeed, a male and a female physician are more alike than a male physician and a male carpenter (454d–e). The two cases suggest that a difference in bodily features is not necessarily a sign of a difference in nature; what is crucial is whether two people have the same mind or soul: "A man and a woman who have a physician's mind[6] have the same nature" (454d). Yes, male and female differ in that "the female bears and the male begets," but this does nothing to show that "the woman differs from the man for our purposes" (454e). While the body can be a hindrance to performing a task well (455c)—that is, in cases in which "bodily faculties" do not adequately serve the mind—whether the body is or is not a hindrance doesn't depend on whether it is male or female.

So not all men will do the same things because they are men; not all women will do the same things because they are women. Some men will be suited to being carpenters, others suited to being guardians; similarly, "one woman has the qualities of a guardian and another not. . . . The women and the men, then, have the same nature in respect to the guardianship of the state, save in so far as the one is weaker, the other stronger" (456a).

In short, Socrates says, people ought to engage in different pursuits only when their differences are relevant to the capacity to carry out the task. He does not challenge the idea that men and women are different in some respects—specifically, in terms of their role in reproduction—but says that there are other respects in which they are or might be the same. Similarly, he does not challenge the idea that two men may be alike in some respect, or that two women may be the same in some respect, but argues that there may be other respects in which they are different. What is visible about you does not tell the whole story, or maybe any of the story, of who you are. Plato wants us to see that it takes the skill of a real philosopher to see which differences and similarities are relevant to which pursuits. Part of what enables Socrates to imagine women engaged in the same pursuits as men is this capacity.

The importance of being able to know what differences make a difference appears in another dialogue in which the significance of apparent differences between men and women is discussed. When Socrates asks young Meno, in the dialogue of that name, if he knows what virtue is, he replies by telling Socrates about the virtue of men and the virtue of women:

The virtue of a man consists in managing the city's affairs capably . . . a woman's virtue . . . is easily described. She must be a good housewife, careful with her stores and obedient to her husband. (71e)

Socrates responds by getting Meno to acknowledge that bees don't differ from one another as bees, even though they differ in size and beauty; he then leads Meno into considering by analogy whether "even if [virtues] are many and various, . . . they all have some common character which makes them virtues" (72c). He wants Meno to see that virtue will not "differ, in its character as virtue, whether it be in a child or an old man, a woman or a man" (73a).

Thus a man's having virtue doesn't mean the virtue he has is manly—that it belongs to him by virtue of his being male—and a woman's having virtue doesn't mean that her virtue is womanly. Just as a bee *qua* bee is neither big nor small, beautiful nor ugly, so virtue *qua* virtue is neither manly nor womanly—it is just virtue. Virtue itself cannot be various, even though there may be a variety of virtues. Again, it is Socrates' capacity to note similarities and to know their significance that is presented as crucial to his ability to see beyond the physical differences that exist between people or things.

Finally, Socrates is able to argue that sexual identity is irrelevant to the capacities required for the philosopher-ruler because he thought of those capacities as being of the soul and distinct from the qualities of the body. Whether or not you have the capacity to rule is determined by your soul and not your body; no inferences can be drawn from the fact that someone has a particular kind of body about what kind of soul they have.

Someone might well agree with Socrates that we can't simply note physical differences between people and conclude that they must have different natures. As Socrates makes us see, it would be absurd to think that because the excellent cobbler one knows has a full head of hair, no bald man could be a good cobbler; the presence or absence of hair is irrelevant to whether or not one might be a cobbler "by nature." But how, Socrates' critic might ask, could sexual identity *not* make a difference to one's ability? Young Meno easily grants Socrates the point about bees all being essentially the same, and about health being the same, as health, in men and women; but about whether virtue can be the same in men and women he expresses some reservations: "I somehow feel that this is not on the same level as the other cases" (73a).

There are at least two ways Plato could silence such doubts. He could argue that *no* facts about a person's body entail facts about that person's nature, or soul.[7] Or he could maintain that while some bodily facts entail something about people's natures, their sexual identities aren't among such facts. There is much in Plato's treatment of the soul/body distinction that suggests that his holding the former view enabled him to "see beyond" a person's sex. But we need to remind ourselves of the way, or ways, in which Plato described the soul and the body and the relation between them.

II

Plato took soul and body to be distinctly different kinds of things. The distinction hums continuously throughout the dialogues. According to Plato, souls are invisible, not observable by the senses; they are subject neither to generation or decay. Bodies, to the contrary, are quite visible, apprehendable by the senses, and they are entirely subject to generation and decay. In the *Phaedo,* Socrates summarizes a discussion with Cebes about the distinction between soul and body:

[The soul is] most like that which is divine, immortal, intelligible, uniform, indissoluble, and ever self-consistent and invariable, whereas [the] body is most like that which is human, mortal, multiform, unintelligible, dissoluble, and never self-consistent. (80b)

Precisely because the soul is not visible and is unchanging, it can "see" the invisible and unchanging things the senses never can (*Republic* 510e, 527e, 532a). Soul and body each have a kind of beauty, health, pleasure, and good and evil distinct from the qualities of the other (*Phaedo* 114e; *Gorgias* 464a, 477b–c, 501b; *Philebus* 33c). There are concerns peculiar to the soul and those specific to the body (*Republic* 535b; *Laws* 673a, 795d).

The soul not only is different in kind from the body; it can exist without it. At death, the invisible, indissoluble soul separates from the visible decaying body (*Phaedo* 64c, 67d; *Gorgias* 524b; *Laws* 828e, 927a). The soul thus *is* the person; immortality is the continued existence of the person, the soul, after the death of the body.[8] The connection to the body is so contingent as to allow the soul to inhabit an entirely different body: for example, a soul that was in a man's body in one lifetime might inhabit a woman's body in another (*Timaeus* 42b–c, 76e, 91a; *Laws* 944e; *Republic* 614–21).

Finally, those who really care about the state of their souls (i.e., those who are or aspire to being philosophers) will do everything they can to keep the body from interfering with the proper work of the soul. In the *Apology,* this is portrayed as the central concern of Socrates' life:

[I have spent] all my time going about trying to persuade you, young and old, to make your first and chief concern not for your bodies nor for your possessions, but for the highest welfare of your souls. (30a–b)

It is only through the soul that a person can come to have any real knowledge, for it is only through the soul that one can "see" what is real—the invisible, eternal, unchanging Forms. The body, with its deceptive senses, keeps us from real knowledge, insofar as it rivets us in a world

23

of material things far removed from the world of reality. We are mistaken if we think that what we can touch or see or otherwise sense are real: the beautiful things we can hold in our hands are not Beauty itself, which is

an everlasting loveliness which neither comes nor goes, which neither flowers nor fades, for such beauty is the same on every hand, the same then as now, here as there, this way as that way, the same to every worshipper as it is to every other. (*Symposium* 221a)

Only the soul can know the Forms, those eternal and unchanging denizens of reality; our changing, decaying bodies can put us in touch only with changing, decaying pieces of the material world. The philosophers who will rule the ideal state

are those who are capable of apprehending that which is eternal and unchanging, while those who are incapable of this, but lose themselves and wander amid the multiplicities of multifarious things, are not philosophers. (*Republic* 484b)

Our bodies (or sometimes, the lower parts of the soul) also are the source of temptations that must be resisted if we are to lead lives of virtue. "Enjoyment of flesh by flesh" is "wanton shame," while desire of soul for soul is at the heart of a relationship that "reverences, aye, and worships, chastity and manhood, greatness and wisdom" (*Laws* 837c–d). At a less anxious moment in the dialogues, Plato isn't so worried about the enjoyment of flesh by flesh as long as the enjoyment doesn't get in the way of the spiritual development of both lovers.[9]

The body is not without use, however: for example, appreciation of the physical beauty of another can lead to an understanding of Beauty itself. One can begin to learn about Beauty in the contemplation of those who are beautiful, which leads to the realization that Beauty is something beyond any particular beautiful body or thing.[10] We also learn from the dialogues that one shouldn't neglect the body: an ill-tuned body can prevent the proper functioning of the soul; and one ought to understand as well that the well-tuned body can serve certain epistemological ends, albeit severely limited ones.

But in general the dialogues tell us that one has no hope of understanding Knowledge, Reality, Goodness, Love, or Beauty unless one recognizes the distinction between soul and body; and one has no hope of attaining or comprehending any of these essential Forms unless one works hard on freeing the soul from the lazy, vulgar, beguiling body. The person is not only distinct from the body but is much better off finally without it.

These lessons from the dialogues about the relation of soul and body enable us to see, then, why Plato could see beyond someone's sex: What difference can having a male or female body make to whether one can be a philosopher-ruler, if it is the state of one's soul that determines whether or not one is a philosopher, and if the soul not only is distinct from the body but can exist without it? What kind of inference about someone's soul could possibly be based on whether their body is male or female, if the same soul could be in either a male or female body, or in no body at all? While one's body can be an obstacle to the proper functioning of the soul of a philosopher, a woman who is a philosopher will by her nature avoid the ensnarements of her body; and her education, which is the same as that of her male equals, will strengthen her natural resolve. Thus whatever differences there are between men and women are irrelevant in terms of their eligibility for guardianship of the state.

III

This was for the most part a startling political position: not even the democrats of Athens were proposing that women ought to share in the governance of the polis. But the arguments Plato relied on were not so clearly political as they were logical and metaphysical: he was trying to get his companions to see that it is irrational to differentiate between people on the basis of sex if sex is irrelevant to the point at hand.

What is particularly important here is that he does not appeal to existing arguments or institutions about equality—for example, he didn't turn to the democrats and try to convince them that on their own grounds women ought to have the chance to shape the policies of the state.[11] Paradoxically, his case rests on a metaphysical argument that establishes *inequality* in two ways: (1) People have different natures and in light of that ought to be educated differently to play different roles in the polis (as opposed to being given the opportunity to do anything they want). (2) It takes a special skill to see which differences and similarities are relevant to which pursuits; only people with this skill should be leaders. That is, the very same arguments meant to establish the equality of some women to some men are also meant to establish or reflect the inequality of some groups of women and men to other groups of women and men.

Now we must look more closely at the relation between the equality Plato appears to posit between men and women who are philosopher-rulers and the inequality he posits between the class of philosopher-rulers and all the other members of the state.

Plato's inegalitarianism—his view that some people are by nature meant to rule, others to assist them, and still others to be ruled—requires that there are different natures, rooted in different kinds of souls. His egalitarianism—his view that some women are as fit to rule as some men

25

are—requires that whatever else might differentiate souls, being male or female does not. His inegalitarianism and egalitarianism thus seem to go neatly together: while the natures of men and women as philosophers do not differ, the natures of philosophers and cobblers do. In other words, the claim that souls are distinct from bodies—which is crucial to the idea that it doesn't matter whether you have a male or female body—does not mean that there cannot be different kinds of souls. All it means is that we can't tell from the kind of body a person has, what kind of soul she or he has. Some souls are of the kind to rule, some are of the kind to be ruled— but the body does not reveal, simply on the basis of whether it is male or female, what kind of soul is inside it.

Now as we've just seen, Plato seems to say not only that being male or female is irrelevant to the kind of soul you have, but that no aspect of the physical self can tell us anything about the kind of soul someone has. If that is the case, then given that souls are not visible, how are we to decide where the ruling and where the ruled souls reside?

When we ask this question, we end up wondering whether Plato can after all sustain the grounds for both his arguments. For it begins to look as if those he uses to establish a kind of equality of men and women among the rulers will finally undermine his description of the inequality among philosopher-rulers, auxiliaries, and the "multitude." Any argument strong enough to show that sexual identity is irrelevant must undermine attempts to make crucial distinctions between any people or groups of people.

The dialogues provide us with at least two ways to get around the dilemma. First of all, among the special skills of the philosopher-kings and -queens is the ability to tell what kind of nature a person has. Their nature and their training enable them to "distinguish the baseborn from the trueborn" (*Republic* 536a), and the well-being of the state depends on this ability:

For when the knowledge necessary to make such discriminations is lacking in individual or state, they unawares employ at random for any of these purposes the crippled and baseborn natures, as their friends or rulers. (*Republic* 536a)

The rulers' responsibility for "assign[ing] to each the status due to his nature" is described as one they must address with the greatest care.[12] In fact they must be prepared to "thrust [their own sons] out among the artisans or the farmers" in the unlikely but possible case that they do not inherit their parent's nature (*Republic* 415b–c).

Second, we find in the dialogues that while Plato is at pains to argue that we can't tell, simply from the fact of someone's having a female body, what kind of soul she has, he is very concerned about how one behaves, since what happens in or to the body has profound effects on what happens in and to the soul, and vice versa. Thus although one's nature is not revealed through the kind of body one has, it is revealed through the activities one engages in. Plato is concerned about how philosophers comport themselves and what kind of activities they engage in. He thinks it crucial that those with philosophers' souls behave in certain ways rather than others—this is why education is so important in the *Republic*. The living conditions of philosopher-rulers resembles what in our time Erving Goffmann has called a "total institution": every aspect of their lives is controlled, for every action, every gesture, Plato thinks, has an effect on the state of their souls.[13] For example, since philosophers ought not to give in to grief when afflicted in their own lives, they should not give in to it in the theater either (*Republic* 604a–b): there are no occasions on which what we do does not seriously affect the quality of our souls. Philosophers-in-training thus have to be tested again and again to see if their souls are up to par—for example, to see if rather than being overcome by fear or by pleasure they remain "immune to such witchcraft and preserve [their] composure throughout," thereby showing themselves to be "good guardian[s] of [themselves] and the culture [they have] received" (*Republic* 413e). All children will receive the same initial education (there is no sure way of telling at birth what kind of nature a person has, so all should be educated up to the point at which differences among them emerge), but only those who pass such tests can be established as philosopher-rulers (*Republic* 414a, 503a).

Although the life of philosopher-rulers requires a kind of constant vigilance, it also requires a particular leisure. As Socrates said to his judges in the *Apology* (36d), anyone whose appointed task is to care for people's souls must be free of the need to earn a living. Wage-earning is suitable only for those

servitors who in the things of the mind are not altogether worthy of our fellowship, but whose strength of body is sufficient for toil; so they, selling the use of this strength and calling the price wages, are designated, I believe, "wage earners," are they not? (*Republic* 371e)

Indeed, some commentators have insisted that "the whole of Plato's political philosophy is grounded in the conviction that to earn a livelihood, and especially by means of manual labour, corrupts the soul and disqualifies a man for politics, making it not only justifiable but necessary for him to subject himself to the command of others."[14]

We see now why Plato's example of the carpenter (*Republic* 454d−e; see p. 21 above) is so telling: Socrates is trying to get Glaucon to understand that if we think carefully about who is fit to be a ruler of the state, what matters is not whether you are male or female but what kinds of pursuits you are suited for, what kinds of activities you can do well, and how you respond to challenges to self-control. What matters is not what kind of body you have, but what you do with it, and how well you can control it. If you have the kind of soul that a carpenter does, you don't have the kind of soul a ruler does; both rulers and ruled might be male or female. We can only tell that some women have the souls of philosopher-rulers if they do what philosopher-rulers do and not what carpenters, say, or male or female slaves do.[15]

IV

Our rendering of Plato's account of the significance of being male or female becomes more complicated if we move beyond the fifth book of the *Republic*, the *Meno*, and aspects of the *Laws*. For the dialogues are very liberally peppered with misogynistic remarks of the most casual and off-hand kind. We realize that Plato's proposals in book 5 of the *Republic* are surprising not only in light of the sexism of fifth-century Athens, and his inegalitarianism, but especially in light of the sexism otherwise rampant in his own work. So even if Plato's account of the potential equality of men and women is one we could heartily embrace (a point to which we shall return), we nevertheless must admit that his vision of equality is hardly the whole story about women to be found in the dialogues.

Plato routinely tosses off what might appear to be gratuitous remarks about the foibles of womanhood. But these comments almost always function to clarify or make vivid an important philosophical point. As we saw earlier, for the most part he wants to convince us that the soul is much more important than the body: it is to our peril that we let ourselves be beckoned by the rumblings of the body at the expense of the soul. Plato sets out to convince us of this by holding up for our inspection the silly and sordid lives of those who pay too much attention to their bodies and do not care enough for their souls; he wants to remind us of how unruly, how without direction, are the lives of those in whom the lower part of the soul holds sway over the higher part.

Because he can't point to an adulterated soul—they are invisible—he points instead to those embodied beings whose lives are in such disarray that we can be sure their souls are corrupted. And whose lives exemplify the proper soul/body relationship gone haywire? Well, says Plato, look at the lives of women.[16] It is women who get hysterical at the thought of death; obviously, their emotions have overpowered their reason, and they can't control themselves (*Phaedo* 60a, 112d; *Apology* 356). "A woman, young or old or wrangling with her husband, defying heaven, loudly boasting, fortunate in her own conceit, or involved in misfortune or possessed by grief and lamentation" is a dreadful model for a young man— still worse is "a woman that is sick, in love, or in labor" (*Republic* 395d–e).

> When in our own lives some affliction comes to us you are aware that we plume ourselves . . . on our ability to remain calm and endure, in the belief that this is the conduct of a man, and [giving in to grief] that of a woman. (*Republic* 605c–d)

To have more concern for your body than your soul is to act just like a woman; hence, the most proper penalty for a soldier who surrenders to save his body, when he should be willing to die out of the courage of his soul, is for him to be turned into a woman (*Laws* 944c).[17] Plato sometimes expresses the belief that souls can go through many different embodied lifetimes. There will be certain indications, in one's life, of the kind of life one is leading; and unless a man lives righteously, he will as his next incarnation "pass into a woman," and if he doesn't live rightly then, he'll become a brute (*Timaeus* 42b–c, 76e, 91a).[18]

The message is that in matters of knowledge, reality, and beauty, don't follow the example of women. They can only be mistaken about those things. In matters of love, women's lives serve as negative examples also. Those men who are drawn by "vulgar" love, that is, love of body for body, "turn to women as the object of their love, and raise a family" (*Symposium* 208e); those men drawn by a more "heavenly" kind of love, that is, love of soul for soul, turn to other men. But there are strong sanctions against physical love between men: physical unions, especially between older and younger men, are "unmanly." The older man isn't strong enough to resist his lust (as in women, the irrational part of the soul has overtaken the rational part), and the younger man, "the impersonator of the female," is reproached for this "likeness to the model" (*Laws* 836e). The problem with physical love between men, then, is that men are acting like women.[19]

It is true that Socrates apparently held at least one woman in very high regard: Diotima.[20] In the *Symposium*, Socrates describes her as being "deeply versed in this [love] and many other fields of knowledge" (201d). But this praise occurs in the context of a discussion from which women have been excluded in order to keep matters on a serious note, in the inquiry in the *Symposium* in which the love of men for women has been referred to—by Diotima among others—without challenge as vulgar and unmanly.

Socrates' reference to Diotima is perhaps of a piece with what he says in book 5 of the *Republic* about women who would be philosopher-rulers; it stands in stark contrast to the generous scattering of misogynistic remarks throughout the dialogues. Misogyny has always been compatible with having high regard for "exceptional" (and surely for imaginary) women.

V

It is clear that the contradictory sides of Plato's views about women are in part tied to the distinction he makes between soul and body and the somatophobic lessons he hopes to teach his readers about their relative value. When preaching about the overwhelming importance of the soul, he can't but regard the kind of body one has as of no final significance, so there is no way for him to assess differentially the lives of women and men. But when making gloomy pronouncements about the worth of the body, he points an accusing finger at a class of people with a certain kind of body—a female body—because he regards them as embodying the very traits he wishes no one to have. In this way, women constitute a deviant class in Plato's philosophy. They live the kinds of lives that no one, especially philosophers, ought to live. It is true that Plato chastises certain kinds of men: sophists, tyrants, and cowards, for example. But he frequently puts them in their place by comparing them to women. We've already seen some examples of this, such as the ridicule of homosexuals for their likeness to women. There is a highly polished moral gloss to the soul/body distinction in Plato. A device that brings this moral gloss to a high luster is his holding up, for our contempt and ridicule, the lives of women in order to demonstrate that it makes no small difference whether you lead a soul-directed or a body-directed life.

If one explanation of Plato's apparently contradictory remarks about women is linked to the sharp distinction he makes between soul and body and the ranks he assigns them, a second explanation, paradoxically, is connected to the fact that sometimes the distinction is not so sharp.

Earlier we focused on Plato's insistence that we can't infer anything about a person's soul from the kind of body she or he has. This insistence has to be qualified when we notice that Plato elsewhere treats the soul as having a much closer, indeed an essential, relation to the body, inasmuch as certain states of the soul can only be expressed, or can best be expressed, in particular kinds of bodies. For example, Plato sometimes speaks as if he thought it easily imaginable for a soul of a man to come to inhabit the body of a woman. However, this kind of transformation is regarded as the appropriate turn of events only for the coward or for the man who has not led a righteous life.[21]

Plato seems to be saying—at least in these comments about reincarnation—that there is a fittingness of one kind of soul to one kind of body: the kind of soul you have shows in the kind of body you have, and can't be shown in another kind of body.[22] Or perhaps he is saying that the kind of soul you have *ought* to show in the kind of body you have—souls in the bodies of male soldiers ought to be brave souls—and if there isn't a good fit in this life there will be in the next. What we must notice here is that being stuck in a woman's body can be described as appropriate for a cowardly soul only if Plato believes that courage cannot be expressed in a body of the female form. The bodily medium is crucial to the message about the soul.[23]

I think we are observing here the conjunction of the two criteria said to reveal one's nature, that is, the kind of body one has and the kind of behavior one displays. Plato is implying that if a body is male, we expect certain kinds of behavior from it, for example, brave behavior. Given his general view, this means that if the body is male we expect the soul connected to it to be able to control it in a particular way. If the behavior of a male body is not what we'd expect from a male body, then the soul is not appropriate to that body; it ought really to live in a female body. So while we can't simply deduce from the presence of a male body what kind of soul it has, we can deduce what kind of soul it ought to have, that is, how the body ought to be conducted. This means that at least in these passages from the *Laws* and *Timaeus,* even if not always so clearly elsewhere, Plato is treating souls as if they are gendered—that is, he argues that some kinds of souls are manly, some are womanly; manly souls belong in males, womanly ones in females.

In the *Republic,* Plato makes sure that the expression of courage in women will not be different from the expression of courage in men: he insists that men and women have to *behave* in the same way to show that they are relevantly the same. Every act you perform counts. Your bodily activity is not simply correlated with activity and states of your soul; your bodily activity is the necessary expression of the state of your soul.[24] Doing what a cobbler does cannot be the expression of a soul contemplating the eternal Forms; thus the soul of a philosopher cannot be expressed in the life of a male cobbler. And though it can be expressed in the life of a woman, this is only so long as she acts in particular ways and engages in particular pursuits.

31

VI

We have been trying to account for Plato's apparently contradictory remarks about women—that they can be counted among the philosopher-rulers; that they lead just the kinds of lives the philosopher-rulers ought to avoid. But there is an alternative hypothesis to the idea that Plato contradicts himself: he uses "woman" ambiguously.

Plato's thinking of people as made up of body and soul allows for at least three different configurations of "woman." The female philosopher-ruler has a female body, but she doesn't have a typically feminine soul—that is, the kind of soul found in the typical Athenian female, a soul unable to resist the temptations of the body, a soul that doesn't know and doesn't care about the difference between appearance and reality. The female philosopher-ruler has a manly soul: the kind of soul that true philosophers have. Similarly, cowardly male soldiers have feminine souls: that is why in their next life they will come back in female bodies. In the examples below, the soul/body configurations described in b, c, and d all represent "woman" in some sense:

a. manly soul/male body: brave soldier; male philosopher-ruler
b. manly soul/female body: female philosopher-ruler
c. womanly soul/male body: cowardly male soldier
d. womanly soul/female body: typical Athenian woman

We might be tempted to use configuration b to represent the reincarnation of the cowardly soldier: for isn't such a person someone who used to be a man but now is in a woman's body? But d is really the better way to represent the reembodied cowardly soldier: if the soul always really belonged in a female body, it is a feminine or womanly soul. Example c represents a bad fit. We might have hoped that since there was a male body there would be a manly soul, as in a; but if someone with a male body behaves in a cowardly way, this shows that "he" really has a womanly soul. The configuration in b should be reserved for the philosopher-queens, who have a manly soul in a female body.

Part of what is confusing in the idea that there has to be the right "fit" between soul and body is this: if we can tell that there is not a fit between body and soul, then presumably there doesn't have to be a fit in order for us to know what kind of soul a person has. If we can tell that the soldier has a woman's cowardly soul without his having a female body, why is a "fit" necessary? For Plato, we see that the right fit in these cases represents the appropriate punishment for the soldier's cowardice. But we are still left in an epistemological and metaphysical quandary: Despite the demand for a right "fit," there doesn't have to be a male body in order for a manly soul to be recognized, nor does there have to be a female body for a womanly soul to be recognized.

This quandary appears in modern dress in Jan Morris's description of the complicated phenomenon of transsexualism. In *Conundrum* (New York: Signet, 1974), Morris insists that "she" had always had a woman's soul housed in a man's body. That she could think about herself in this way suggests that she thought her bodily identity to be neither indicative of nor necessary for her having a particular kind of soul: she "knew," even though she had a male body, that she had a womanly soul. On the other hand, she felt compelled to change her body in order to reveal the gender of her soul.

Morris seems to be saying that while gender identity is more important than sexual identity, a person's sex is the clue others take to his or her gender. Gender systems teach us to expect certain kinds of behavior from persons who have male bodies and other kinds from persons who have female bodies. If our expectations are met, the fit is supposed to be right; if they are not met, the fit is wrong. Though Morris can't be said to be a whole lot like Plato, her example may help us understand what makes Plato's ambiguous use of "woman" possible by reminding us that the existence of gender identities represents the likelihood that not all males will be masculine nor all females feminine.

Plato is indeed revolutionary in his imagining and his valuing the possibility that there are women who are not typically feminine. In contrast, his contempt for the feminine in both its male and female embodiments indicates the extent to which he accepted the sexist stereotypes of the time. The problem with the mass of women, according to Plato, is that they can't become the people male philosopher-rulers are; the problem with the mass of men is that they are too much like most women.

In criticizing men for being feminine, Plato opens up the logical space to think of women as masculine and to praise them for it. However, it is not clear that people must be either masculine or feminine. We have heard nothing about the third class of people in Plato's world, the artisans, farmers, and other producers, who may not be masculine in the way philosopher-rulers are but are not feminine in the way typical Athenian women or cowardly guardians are. (We shall return to the question of whether "masculine" and "feminine" exhaust the terrain of gender in the next chapter.)

What, then, can we conclude from this about what Plato might have meant when talking about "women"? What he means by "woman" in the fifth book of the *Republic* is quite different from what he means by "woman" elsewhere. Though both kinds of women are females, one kind is a female with a manly soul, the other kind a female with a womanly soul. That is, the one is what could become of a female person if she has a certain nature and is trained in the way of the philosophers; the other is what happens to a female person who hasn't such a nature and does not receive such training.

VII

Plato's claim to being a feminist surely has to do with his holding (1) that a woman's biology ought not to settle the question of her destiny, and (2) that women's intelligence and reason ought to be called upon in the running of the state. He refuses to assume that since women have different bodies than men they must have capacities significantly different from, and inferior to, those of men. According to Plato, not all women are inferior to all men; some women are equal to the best of men, and in fact superior to other men. In the best and most wisely governed state, we can expect to find women as well as men among the ruling class.

As has often been pointed out, Plato is not here relying upon or defending the notion of women's "rights." While the positions to which women will have access along with men are ones that involve great power and authority, every aspect of their lives is shaped to enable them to see and carry out their duties. They are not "free" in a sense very common to modern ears—free to do what they want, free not to have their lives interfered with by the needs and demands of others. As Ernest Barker puts it: "Plato is not a teacher of woman's rights so much as of woman's duties."[25] Or as Julia Annas has remarked: Plato "sees women merely as a huge untapped pool of resources: here are half the citizens sitting at home wasting effort doing identical trivial jobs! . . . Benefit to the state is the sole, frequently repeated ground" for the proposals about women's role in the ideal state.[26] Guardians have a single function: to run the state. From infancy they are to be trained to make sure that they develop the self-control and knowledge necessary for such heavy responsibility. If they are educated as Plato imagines, then in a sense they will be free to do what they want, but only because their desires will be constructed in such a way that they'll want to do exactly what they are supposed to do.

Moreover, part of the shaping of desire among the guardians and auxiliaries is their not wanting to have or own something by themselves: they will have no private property, which means among other things that men will not have their own wives or their own children (*Republic* 464a–b). However, this does not mean that women—even guardian women— cease to be property, or are to be in a position to decide whether or not they wish to be with men or to have children.[27] Women are now common property. Indeed, "more frequent intercourse with the women" will be the honor and prize for young men "who excel in war and other pursuits" (*Republic* 460b).

Nevertheless, Plato's claims are useful for feminists to turn back to, especially when what is claimed to be the wisdom of the ages is thrown against feminist proposals for creating a world in which it would not be assumed that women are the political, social, moral, and intellectual inferiors of men. But we must keep in mind that Plato's argument for the equality of some women to some men was inextricably intertwined with an argument for the superiority of that group of men and women to all other people. He may have refused to assume that biology is destiny, but that does not mean that all ways of ranking people disappear. The equality Plato talks about is only between men and women who would be guardians and philosopher-rulers. He is not talking about equality between slave men and philosopher women, or between slave women and philosopher women. Surely, then, we ought to ask: what kind of feminism is it that would gladly argue for a kind of equality between men and women of a certain class and at the same time for radical inequality between some women and some men, some women and some other women, some men and some other men?

When we emphasize that according to Plato bodily features don't provide grounds for distinguishing between people, we may thereby obscure the fact that he hardly thought that all people were the same "underneath"—indeed, that he didn't think all women were the same "underneath." Plato arrogates to philosopher-rulers the capacity and authority to decide what differences between people matter and why. Anybody can know whether a person is male or female; only philosopher-kings and -queens can tell what a person's soul is really like. This is a very important authority to have—as we saw, some take the exercise of it to be the most crucial task of philosopher-rulers.

Is the kind of power and authority Plato ascribes to philosopher-rulers a kind of power and authority that feminists ought to embrace? Should feminists support the notion that some women ought to be in the business of deciding what kinds of "natures" different kinds of people have and therefore what their best interests are? In order to find out the extent to which some versions of feminism may have more of Plato in them than they might ever have imagined, we need to ask still more questions: Is the authority about the significance of differences among people something that feminists have assumed in analyses of differences among women? How do we know which differences among us are significant and which aren't? Are some women in a better position than others to answer this?

If so, how does that authority come to inhere in them? Through some kind of special metaphysical insight such as Plato thought philosopher-rulers had? Through the political contests waged and adjudicated in all the usual places, including academic conferences, publishing houses, and the pages of book reviews?

We shall return to these questions in later chapters. For now, let us see what Aristotle thought to be important differences among women and what he took those differences to mean.

When you read about Black women being lynched, they aren't thinking of us as females. The horrors that we have experienced have absolutely everything to do with them not even viewing us as women.[1]

BARBARA SMITH

Who's Who in the Polis

How shall we go about investigating a philosopher's views about women? The most logical and straightforward approach would seem to be to focus on whatever the philosopher says about women, in particular on the differences he draws between women and men, and then to see what social and political implications he takes such differences to have.

Hence in recent years we have been directed to Aristotle's descriptions of the biological differences between males and females—in particular, their roles in reproduction—and to his description of the different rational capacities of males and females.[1] Aristotle believes that both kinds of difference bespeak the natural superiority of men to women: biologically, women provide simply the matter in which the seed, bearer of the purer and more important element of form provided by the male, can grow; and while women are not without reason, their reason hasn't the power or authority of that found in men.

In what follows I take a different tack in trying to get at Aristotle's views about women. Instead of focusing simply on his discussions of the differences between men and women, I begin by asking about another and very closely related distinction he makes: the distinction between women and slaves. This distinction cuts across that between male and female, since slaves can be either male or female.[2] The importance Aristotle attaches to the difference between "women" and "slaves" raises serious difficulties for any reading of his views about "woman's nature" based only on the distinction he draws between "men" and "women." For in

Aristotle, the significance of the distinction between men and women varies according to whether the men and women we are talking about are free or slave. There is no simple distinction in Aristotle between men and women. Although he almost always thinks of people as gendered, he does not think of them only in terms of gender. And if we don't see that, we can't fully capture what he says about gender differences: that is, we have to refer to what appears to be something other than gender to describe his account of gender.

What Aristotle says about the nature of free women is quite different from what he says about the nature of slave women. An account of "Aristotle's views about women" that doesn't inquire seriously into what he says about slave women not only announces that the position of slave women is theoretically insignificant, it also gives a radically incomplete picture of what he says about women who are not slaves.

I

It is mainly in the *Politics* that Aristotle talks about the political significance of the distinction in kind between male and female, between master and slave, and also between woman and slave. People come together, Aristotle says, out of the mutual need they have of each other for human life to be reproduced and maintained. But what makes a life a characteristically human one, and what makes that form of human community called the city-state or polis something different from cattle grazing together, is the end for the sake of which the polis exists: the possibility of a good life, a life lived in accordance with the highest human virtue.[3] The household, consisting of husband, wife, children, and slaves, is the place where basic life-sustaining activities take place. The polis, consisting of citizens deliberating about and executing public affairs, is the forum in which men can engage in the noblest activities of which humans are capable.[4]

In a well-ordered city-state, women and slaves are not parts of the polis, but they are the conditions of it. Without their work, the polis could not exist, but they do not participate in the activities of the polis.[5] They are not capable of living lives that exhibit the highest form of human excellence, though it would not be possible for others to live such lives without them. In a "well-ordered state the citizens should have leisure and not have to provide for their daily wants" (*Politics* 1269a34–35).[6] The work that women, slaves, and other laborers do is not the kind of work the good man or good citizen should perform, for "no man can practice human excellence who is living the life of a mechanic or laborer" (*Politics* 1278a22; see also 1328b38–1329a2). It is not simply that one needs leisure to develop such excellence (*Politics* 1329a1) and that performing menial duties would be degrading and disgraceful for good men and good citizens (*Politics* 1273a32 ff.); there is a danger of masters becoming too much like slaves or other laborers, or in any event ceasing to be able to do their proper work well, if these good citizens "learn the crafts of inferiors" (*Politics* 1277b6).[7] It also would be dangerous for statesmen to do women's work—for example, carding wool—for the contempt their subjects would then have for them is just the kind of trifle that can cause revolution (*Politics* 1312a1ff.).

According to Aristotle the relation between a man and a woman—in the *Politics,* as we shall see in more detail below, this means the relation between husband and wife, or more specifically, between a man who is a citizen and his wife—is quite different from the relation between master and slave, even though both are relations of those who are by nature fit to rule and those who are by nature fit to be ruled. This difference respects the different functions, virtues, and natures of women and slaves.

All things, including human beings, are defined by their special function—that which nature intended them and their kind alone to do well—and people are capable of performing their different functions well to the extent that they have the appropriate virtues (see e.g., *Politics* 1253a23, 1252b3). Both women and slaves are fit by nature to carry on activities and provide services within the household that make it possible for the man who is their natural ruler to do the work he is fit to do outside the household in the polis. Again, their function in the household is to make life possible, his function in the polis is to make a good life. Women are suited by their nature to bear children and be companions to their husbands, and to "preserve" what their husbands "acquire" (*Politics* 1277b25–26). Slaves are suited by their nature to "minister to the wants of individuals" (1278a12); "with their bodies [they] minister to the needs of life" (1254b25) and do menial labor under the direction of others.

These differences in function, virtue, and nature between women and slaves are reflected in the kind of relationships and kind of rule masters have over women on the one hand and slaves on the other. The relation between master and slave, Aristotle sometimes says, is very much like that between soul and body: the slave is the bodily instrument of the master and is the possession of the master. As the soul rules the body despotically, so masters rule slaves (*Politics* 1254b5). Insofar as both friendship and justice require a kind of common moral and legal status, neither is really possible between masters and slaves (see *Nicomachean Ethics* 1161b4–5), though sometimes Aristotle speaks of a kind of friendship (see *Politics* 1255b14) and a kind of justice (see *Nicomachean Ethics* 1134b8 ff.) that is possible between them.

The relationship between the ruler and his wife is between two free people (*Politics* 1256b1), not one free and one slave, and the rule here is more like that between intellect and appetite than between soul and body (*Politics* 1254b5).[8] Intellect and appetite are both parts of the soul, so are closer than soul and body, but still intellect is superior to appetite.[9] While both men and women in this instance are free, that is, neither is a natural slave (a reminder that "woman" or "wife" in this context of Aristotle's thought does not include slave women), nevertheless the man is superior to the woman and so ought to rule her. Their relationship, Aristotle seems to be saying, is more equal than that of master and slave, but it is still far from being one between equals. Thus while there is a kind of friendship appropriate for husband and wife, it is different from both a friendship between equals and from that between master and slave (*Nicomachean Ethics* 1158b12 ff.). Similarly, there is a kind of justice obtaining between husband and wife different from that between political equals but nonetheless "more fully realized" than the justice between master and slave (*Nicomachean Ethics* 1134b15–17). At one point in the *Poetics*, Aristotle describes the difference between a woman and a slave in this way: while a woman is "inferior," the slave is a "wholly worthless being" (1454a20).

This attempt to describe a relationship somewhere between radical inequality and full equality is reiterated in Aristotle's desire to call the rule of husband over wife constitutional as opposed to despotical. The rule of men over women can't really be constitutional, since the women don't get a turn to rule, but it is less one-sided than that of masters over slaves. For example, the man may hand over some of his affairs to his wife (*Nicomachean Ethics* 1160b35) but presumably not to his slaves. Similarly, Aristotle insists that the rule of husband over wife is for the sake of the wife, while that of master over slave is finally for the sake of the master (*Politics* 1278b31 ff.); but rule among those who are equal is for the common interest (*Politics* 1279a18 ff.).[10]

In sum, women and slaves have certain things in common: both do the work that makes the life of the polis possible and both have natures that exclude them from the ranks of those who are fit to rule. But the function, virtue, and nature of women differ from those of slaves; nature, Aristotle says, intended that.

II

Not all the women Aristotle knew about were free women, and not all the slaves he knew were men. What about female slaves? Does he even note their existence? He does indeed, right at the beginning of the *Politics*:

nature

Now nature has distinguished between the female and the slave. For she is not niggardly, like the smith who fashions the Delphian knife for many uses; she makes each thing for a single use, and every instrument is best made when intended for one and not for many uses. But among barbarians no distinction is made between women and slaves, because there is no natural ruler among them: they are a community of slaves, male and female. (*Politics* 1252b1–7)

While the passage begins by distinguishing between female and slave, it ends with a reference to female slaves.[11] What is Aristotle getting at here?

First of all we need to remember that in book 1 of the *Politics* Aristotle distinguished between those people who were slaves by convention and those who were slaves by nature. It is one thing, he said, to be enslaved by others in consequence of being defeated by them in war; it is another thing altogether to be fit by nature to be the slave of someone who is by nature your superior (we shall return to Aristotle's grounds for this distinction below). Now we only see what nature really intends for things or individuals or communities when such things are in their most perfect state.[12] In a community of natural slaves, we cannot see human excellence in its full flowering: excellence is found only in those who are natural rulers, and only when they are living in communities in which they can function as rulers. While nature distinguishes between the woman and the slave, we see the distinction at work only in the well-ordered state, not in a community of natural slaves.

Aristotle's point seems to be this: If you *are* a slave—a slave by nature and not by convention—then you can't also *have* slaves, people who are naturally subject to your rule. To put the point a slightly different way: if the entire population is a slave population, then in one sense there are slaves, in another there are not. According to Aristotle, a population is slave because by nature it is fit to be ruled by others; but the same population cannot contain slaves within it because it has no natural rulers among its members.[13] Where everyone is a slave (and hence where no one can be anyone else's slave), there is no distinction between slave and anyone else.

But even if all are slaves, some are women and some are men, as Aristotle himself says. So there is still a conceptual distinction between woman and slave, even though in a population of natural slaves, all the women are slaves. In the context of the *Politics*, it is clear that by "woman" Aristotle means the female companion of a natural ruler, that is, a free woman, not a slave woman. The function performed by a free woman who is a wife of a citizen is different from that performed by the citizen's

41

slaves, male or female. The wife's function, again, is to be a companion of sorts and to reproduce, not just any children, but children who will be citizens.[14] Indeed, as is argued in the *Generation of Animals* (767b), best of all she produces males just like the father. The slaves' function is to otherwise minister to his needs and presumably to a certain extent to the needs of his wife and children. A "woman" is the female who will have the citizen's legitimate children; a "slave" is a person, male or female, who does the menial work in the household.[15]

Thus Aristotle does not allow for the possibility of slaves who are women, but only for slaves who are female—for he draws a distinction between woman and slave in such a way that "woman" can only mean free woman, not slave woman. When Aristotle talks about women, he doesn't mean us to be thinking about slave women.[16]

In sum, then, there is only a category of "woman" distinct from that of "slave" under the following conditions: There is a community that exists for the sake of the good life, not just for life itself, in which the ruling men lead lives exhibiting the ends for which such communities exist. The free woman and the slave make the best life possible, even though neither participates in it. Without women, new citizens could not be born; without slaves, "everyday wants" could not be provided for: "Those who are in a position which places them above toil have stewards who attend to their households while they occupy themselves with philosophy or with politics" (*Politics* 1255b35–37). This division of labor also exempts the woman of the house from some tasks:

A man's [i.e., a citizen's] constitution should be inured to labor, but not to labor which is excessive or of one sort only, such as is practised by athletes; he should be capable of all the action of a freeman. These remarks apply equally to both parents. (*Politics* 1335b10–11)[17]

For the purposes of a well-ordered state, the distinction between male and female is important only for citizens; for slaves it is irrelevant. That is, when a people are a slave people, it doesn't matter—for the purposes of their function in a well-ordered political community—whether they are male or female.

Hence biology—in the sense of one's reproductive capacities—only makes a political difference, according to Aristotle, in concert with the difference between citizen and slave.[18] Though a slave may be female, what defines her function in the state is the fact of her being a slave, not the fact of her being female. Some females are meant by nature to be "slaves," others to be "women," free women. Moreover, since there are no natural rulers among slaves, a man who is a slave is not the natural ruler of a woman who is a slave (and surely not of a free woman). Thus a male slave isn't really a "man" insofar as Aristotle uses the term in the *Politics* to refer to natural rulers: maleness signals the superiority a man has over a woman only if the male in question is a natural ruler. This means that one of the marks of inferiority of a male slave is that he is not a better specimen of humanity than his wife.

What are said by Aristotle to be the prerogatives and functions and natures of "men" and "women" don't apply to males and females who are natural slaves. This is hardly an unfamiliar state of affairs. For example, notions of man as citizen, provider, and head of household, of woman as delicate and in need of protection, were supposed to be applicable to the men and women of the white slave-holding class in the United States, but not to the black men and women who were their slaves—a point to which we shall return in more detail in chapter 5.

III

It is clear from Aristotle's argument that something other than simple reproductive role decides one's role in the state, no matter what he says elsewhere about the natural biological superiority of male to female.[19] He never argues (and we wouldn't expect him to) that there is a difference in reproductive biology between a male who is a citizen and one who is a slave. Nor does he argue that there is any other bodily fact that reliably differentiates the two. The bodies of men who are citizens and men who are slaves are the same—reproductively they are the same, and they quite often look the same in stature and strength, to Aristotle's dismay:

Nature would like to distinguish between the bodies of freemen and slaves, making the one strong for servile labor, the other upright, and although useless for such services, useful for political life in the arts both of war and peace. But the opposite often happens—that some have the souls and others have the bodies of freemen. And doubtless if men differed from one another in the mere forms of their bodies as much as the statues of the Gods do from men, all would acknowledge that the inferior class should be slaves of the superior. And if this is true of the body, how much more just that a similar distinction should exist in the soul? But the beauty of the body is seen, whereas the beauty of the soul is not seen. It is clear, then, that some men are by nature free, and others slaves, and that for these latter slavery is both expedient and right. (*Politics* 1254b34–1255a2)[20]

In this way, whatever biological superiority male slaves have to female slaves, they are inferior to the wives of male citizens. And as we saw above, there are crucial differences, in Aristotle's view, between slave

43

women and free women, even though presumably both have the same re-productive biology.[21]

While we might expect to find Aristotle making a strong connection between the kind of soul one has (of which the mind is a part) and the kind of body one has, we have already begun to see why there cannot be a simple and reliable correlation between them: one can't tell from the fact that there is a female body whether one is in the presence of a "woman" or a female slave, nor can one tell from the fact that there is a male body whether one is in the presence of a "man" or a male slave.[22] Even strength or bulk of body isn't a sure guide, as we have seen. What, then, does differentiate among all these kinds of persons?

Aristotle sometimes speaks as if the inferiority of women to men, slaves to masters, were due to the fact that women and slaves are essentially bodies without souls and are hence in need of the direction and command of the souls of natural male rulers. For example, in *Generation of Animals* (732a, 738b), Aristotle describes the relative worth of the contributions of male and female as determined by the relative worth of soul to body, or of form to matter: the male provides the more divine element of soul, or form, while the female only provides the body, or the matter. As we saw earlier, Aristotle also sometimes speaks of the relation of master and slave as being just like the relation of soul and body; the rule of master over slave is a despotical one, just as is the rule of soul over body.

But in the *Politics,* Aristotle is thinking of women and slaves as members—in however attenuated a fashion—of the human community. Females of the human species are different from other females, and slaves are different from mere brutes, insofar as they have not merely a soul (all living things have a soul in some sense, according to Aristotle) but a human soul. While Aristotle is untroubled by the idea that humans are to rule animals, because he believes that animals' lack of reason establishes their inferiority to humans and disqualifies them from eligibility to rule, he seems to believe that all humans *qua* humans have reason and "share in the rational principle" (*Politics* 1259b27). On what grounds, then, can he argue for the inferior and subordinate status of women vis-à-vis men, slaves vis-à-vis masters?[23]

Fortunately, according to Aristotle, "the very constitution of the soul has shown us the way" (*Politics* 1260a5). The soul has two main parts or elements, the rational and the irrational, and it is "natural and expedient" for the rational to rule over the irrational (*Politics* 1254b4 ff.).[24] Just so, men are to rule women, for in women the deliberative capacity of the rational element is without authority—it is easily overruled by the irrational element.[25] Masters are to rule slaves, for while slaves, in virtue of the rational element in their souls, can hear and obey orders, they really don't have the capacity to deliberate. Indeed, all that distinguishes slaves from nonhuman beasts of burden is that they, unlike beasts, have just enough reason to understand the results of masters' deliberations.[26]

To twist a phrase from Nietzsche, Aristotle holds that women and slaves are human, but not too human. As humans they have at least a minimal level of reason—just enough to enable them to perform well their functions in the state. Because their work in the state is conditional for the expression of human excellence in the lives of the natural rulers, they must perform their functions well, that is, in accordance with the kind of excellence appropriate to those functions. Hence women need training (see *Politics* 1260b15), slaves need looking after (see *Politics* 1260b8). Women and slaves need at least some power of reasoning, but only that appropriate for the kind of activities they would be engaged in in the well-ordered state. Nature tossed them a dash of reason—enough to make them members of the same species as male citizens—but clearly not the kind of reason found in the souls of their natural rulers.[27]

IV

According to Aristotle, a well-ordered state respects, indeed expresses, what nature intended in the creation of different kinds of human natures. Some people are intended to rule, others to be ruled. We have been asking how, according to Aristotle, we can tell the kind of nature people have. Two criteria come to mind: (1) whether a person is male or female and (2) whether a person has the body of a freeman or the body of a slave.

We have seen that for Aristotle neither criterion alone, nor both together, is a sufficient indicator of the kind of nature people have: Point 1 will not hold because both male citizens and male slaves have male bodies, but their natures are not the same; both free women and slave women have female bodies, but their natures are not the same; and male and female slaves have different bodies but their natures are the same. Point 2 won't work, since as Aristotle ruefully admits, you can't always tell what kind of soul or nature someone has from the size or shape or appearance of his body.[28] We do know that a necessary condition of belonging by nature to the ruling element is being male.[29] But there is a further condition that obtains: (3) whether one is the kind of person in whom the rational part of the soul rules (indeed is meant to rule) the irrational part.[30]

Again, there is no simple correlation between having a male or female body and having a particular kind of psychic capacity or nature.[31] The kind of person you are, the kind of human nature you possess, is determined by the combination of biological and psychological characteristics you have:[32]

Biological/Psychological Description	Nature
female body/deliberative capacity without authority	"woman" (free female)
female body/no deliberative capacity	"slave" (female)
male body/deliberative capacity with authority	"man" (male citizen)
male body/no deliberative capacity	"slave" (male)

In Aristotle the distinction between men and women crosses the distinction between master and slave.[33] Even though typically his language (and, as we shall see below, that of his commentators and critics) suggests that women constitute one natural class, slaves another, we've seen that this obscures the fact that some females are slaves. Similarly, even though his language typically suggests that men constitute one natural class, women another, this obscures the fact that some males and some females are slaves. In Aristotle's scheme of things, then, one is never simply male or female, simply master or slave. We thus can't talk simply about the relationship between men and women or between masters and slaves. For what is true of the relationship between the male citizen and his wife (i.e., that he is her natural ruler) is not true of that between the male slave and female slave. What is true of the relationship between the male citizen and his wife (i.e., that he governs her in accordance with a "constitutional rule") is not true either of the relationship between the male citizen and the female slave or of that between the male slave and the free woman. At the same time, the difference between the male citizen and male slave does not exactly mirror that between the free woman and the female slave: the first is a difference between those with the full power of reason and those with scarcely any at all; the second is a difference between those with only an unauthoritative power of reason and those with scarcely any at all.

Whenever Aristotle speaks of the differences between "men and women," he is in fact distinguishing between men and women of a particular social class, the citizen class. Being female is not a necessary condition of belonging to the part of humanity meant to be ruled: males who are by nature slaves belong to that part also. Being female is a sufficient condition of belonging to the part of humanity meant to be ruled, but in importantly different ways for different females. It would be highly misleading to present Aristotle's views as if the similarity of being male outweighed the dissimilarity between being master or slave; and it is only slightly less misleading to present his views as if the similarity of being female outweighed the dissimilarity between being a free woman (or wife) or a female slave.[34]

Moreover, we've seen that it is differences in rationality to which Aristotle turns to ground his claims about relations of superiority and inferiority among all categories of persons. Hence it would be misleading to describe Aristotle simply as holding that rationality is male. For while it is true that Aristotle says that *only* men are fully rational, he clearly does not say that *all* men are fully rational, nor does he hold that all females lack rationality in the same way. Indeed, the difference is enough in Aristotle's mind to make him exclude female slaves from his discussion of the difference between "men" and "women." In order to understand what Aristotle believes about the nature and place of "women," then, we have to ask not only about the nature and function of citizen-class women vis-à-vis their men, but also about the nature and function of citizen-class women vis-à-vis slave men and slave women.

V

One of the methodological devices feminists have introduced into the study of human societies and of political and social theory has been to keep at the forefront questions such as: What about the women? What are women's lives like in such a society? How is their work assessed and valued? What are the prevailing attitudes about women? What notions are there of "women's nature"? Those of us who are feminists have quite rightly been annoyed by accounts of Aristotle's view of human nature that ignore or fail to appreciate the fact that what he says about "man's nature" isn't meant to describe "woman's nature" and that Aristotle's political views clearly incorporate a distinction between the sexes. But we have not been equally attentive to the fact that when Aristotle talks about "woman's nature" versus "man's nature" he isn't talking about all women, nor have we thought about how our own analyses of Aristotle's views of "women" might have to be revised if we investigate what he had to say about slave women as well as citizen-class women.

For the most part Aristotle's terminology, like that of much contemporary feminist inquiry, employs the concepts of "woman" and "slave" in a way that simply dismisses the existence of female slaves. If we don't explicitly ask what he has to say about female slaves, then like him we take the class of woman to include only free women. In my own earlier work on Aristotle and in that of many other feminist investigators, the status of female slaves has been either ignored or taken to be of no real significance for the understanding of the place of "women." For example, in an earlier essay I examined in some detail Aristotle's attempts to argue that "women are naturally subordinate to men."[35] But while the language I use replicates Aristotle's, I ignore the fact that according to his catalog of persons, functions, virtues, and natures some men are naturally subordinate to some women (or in any event not naturally superior to those women); some women are not naturally subordinate to some men; and some women are naturally subordinate to some other women.

We find in Susan Moller Okin's very important work the claim that "Aristotle's assumption that woman is defined by her reproductive function and her other duties within the household permeates everything he has to say about her."[36] But as we've seen, the reproductive function of a female slave does not determine what Aristotle has to say about her. Okin refers to slaves and even alludes to the fact that not all women belong to the same class, but she does not talk about where the female slave fits in, simply reiterating Aristotle's view that "women" and "slaves" have different functions.[37] Moreover, she complains when Aristotle retracts the distinction between the kind of justice between men and women and that between master and slave: "We are left with the impression that, so far as justice is concerned, Aristotle has relegated woman to an altogether sub-human position."[38] This almost sounds like the complaint found quite commonly in feminist thought that women have been treated like slaves—a complaint that challenges the position of "women," but not the position of "slaves," a group that includes females. When we attend to the fact that by "women" Aristotle means free women, then Okin's concern amounts to saying that one of the objectionable aspects of Aristotle's treatment of citizen-class women was that he didn't always respect the distinction he drew between them and those men and women who were slaves.

Sarah Pomeroy's very useful work describes in some detail the actual differences between classes of women in Athens around the time of Socrates, Plato, and Aristotle. Athenians of the Classical period, she says, "applied different standards to different economic and social classes of women and men, according to the categories of citizens, resident foreigners (metics), and slaves. Behavior appropriate to one group of women detracted from the status of another group.[39] These class differences were not unrelated: Solon's regulations enabled women of the citizen class to enjoy advantages "predicated on the status loss of lower-class women: the slaves who staffed the brothels."[40] But Pomeroy's own language works against these reminders that all women did not have the same status. For example, she talks of scholars "who considered the life of an Athenian woman little better than that of a harem slave" without noting that the "harem slave" is also presumably a woman; she speaks of how protective Athenians were of "their women," even though in the context of her chapter she makes it quite clear that "their women" could not possibly include slave women, of whom they were not protective.[41]

Jean Grimshaw's recent exciting contribution to the literature on feminism and the history of philosophical thought implicitly recognizes that the contrast in Aristotle between those who are fully rational and those who aren't can't be described simply as a contrast between men and women. It is rather between "free males," on the one hand, and "women and slaves," on the other.[42] But she does not argue as a consequence that if the distinction between master and slave in Aristotle means that we must indicate what category of male we are referring to, then it also means we must indicate what category of female we are referring to, or that we must explain why distinctions among women aren't significant.

In short, feminist scholars have not taken the place Aristotle assigns female slaves to be theoretically interesting—at best, female slaves are mentioned in small addenda standing in unclear relationship to what is taken to be the heart of the analysis of women's position. So let us ask instead what would happen if we began an investigation of the relevant parts of Aristotle's work by asking what he said or implied about slave women.

We've learned that there are a number of things we can't say about female slaves: (1) We can't say that their social and political position are determined by their biological or psychological difference from men. (2) Nor can we say their position is similar to that of slaves.

The first statement is misleading because female slaves' status as slaves complicates Aristotle's account of why any particular female ought to be excluded from full participation in the polis. For Aristotle, a female slave's biological difference from a male slave makes no difference to her function vis-à-vis the polis; and she is psychologically different, not from slave men, but from citizen men. The second statement is outrageous, since the women in question *are* slaves.

There is nothing problematic for many feminists about the fact that roughly half of the population Aristotle defined as "slaves" were women. Perhaps we assume that we can generate an account of the nature of slave women by adding together what Aristotle says about free women and what he says about slaves. But if it is possible to generate an account of Aristotle's views about female slaves by extrapolating from what he says about "women" and about "slaves," then it ought also to be possible to generate an account of his views about "women" by extrapolating from what he says about free men and slave women. What does it tell us about

49

feminist methodology that while the former seems perfectly logical, the latter seems terribly confused?[43]

We can begin answering this question with the reminder that because Aristotle insists on the distinction in function and nature between "women" and "slaves," the only way to construct what he says about the place of female slaves is to see into which of the two mutually exclusive categories he puts them. It should be clear by now that he takes their function to be that of a "slave," not a "woman." But is there any particular reason why feminists should be more concerned about females who are "women" than about those who are "slaves"? Is there any reason why we should take what a philosopher says about one group of women as what he said about all women?

VI

The following response might at first seem reasonable: that Aristotle didn't think of slave women as "women" is simply a reminder that slave women were oppressed as slaves, not as women, and if we want to understand the sexism present in a philosopher's work as distinct from, for example, the classism or racism to be found there, we have to look at what he says about those women whose main identifying feature in his eyes is their womanhood.[44]

Janet Radcliffe Richards has explicitly endorsed just this methodological principle. A feminist *qua* feminist, Richards insists, cannot be interested in any and all harm that is done to a woman, but only in the harm that is done to her as a woman; a feminist by definition must focus on sexism, not on racism or classism or any other form of oppression:

If, for instance, there are men and women in slavery, it is not the business of feminism to start freeing the women. Feminism is not concerned with a group of people it wants to benefit, but with a type of injustice it wants to eliminate.[45]

Richards might therefore argue that however disturbing slavery is, it has nothing to do with gender; indeed, she might try to use Aristotle on behalf of her position, since he took a female slave's status as a slave, not as a woman, to be the definitive fact about her.

A similar view appears in the recent work of Eva Cantarella on the place of women in the Greek polis: "The exclusion of the female slave [from the polis] was not linked specifically to her sex so much as to her servile status. She was 'different' from both free men and free women and equal to slaves of the male sex."[46] Cantarella thinks it therefore "more useful to concentrate on free women and the [legal] codification of their difference" in order to "follow the course that led to the exclusion of women" from the polis.[47] Cantarella's decision to concentrate on free and not slave women may seem perfectly appropriate, for the reasons Richards gives: If we want to understand how women are treated on account of being women, then let's look at women who were excluded on account of being women and not on account of being slaves. If it is their gender that explains their exclusion rather than their servile status, and we want to understand the role of gender in how women are treated, then surely it makes sense to focus on their case.

But we ought to examine this apparently straightforward methodological decision: if it is sound, it tells us that the proper, or anyway the prime, focus of feminist inquiry is how a particular group of women are treated. The idea is that however unjust and disturbing "racism" is, it is different from sexism.[48] Feminists, on this view, don't have to hold that sexism is in some sense more "fundamental" than any form of oppression, only that the analysis of sexism is what feminism is centrally about. Both Richards and Cantarella are saying that it is sexism—discrimination, exploitation, oppression on the basis of sex or gender—not classism or racism or any other form of oppression, that feminism wants to unearth and undermine. The clearest examples of sexism are found in the lives of women who are subject to no other form of discrimination, abuse, oppression, or exploitation. So no wonder, when we are reading Aristotle, we look at what he says about free women, not slave women. No wonder, if we are examining contemporary life in the United States, we look at the lives of white middle-class women. For if we want to understand how sexism functions in the treatment of women, then first we examine the lives of women whose class or racial or religious or other identity doesn't complicate their situation: if they are mistreated, it must be because of sexism, not anything else. And then we will have begun the account of other women's lives, too, insofar as they are subject to sexism, whatever other forms of oppression they might endure.

According to Richards and Cantarella, then, feminists interested in Aristotle should be first and foremost concerned with his treatment of free women. The study of how Aristotle regarded free women leads to an account of how he thought of any woman *as a woman*, even though knowing this does not yet give us his account of every woman's nature. That is, there is a difference in Aristotle (and most anyone else) between his account of "woman's nature" and that of "women's natures." His account of "woman's nature" is his account of woman as woman, while his account of "women's natures" is whatever account he gives of various kinds of women. This implies that slave women have a different nature as slaves

51

than they do as women; that the total picture of their nature is a combination of them as women and as slaves.

VII

We have asked whether there is any particular reason why feminists should be more concerned about what Aristotle said about free women than what he said about slave women or why we should take what he says about free women to be his account of "woman's nature." The answer we have found in Richards and Cantarella goes something like this:

1. Feminists as feminists are centrally concerned with sexism, the oppression women face as women.
2. The most paradigmatic examples of sexism are to be found in the lives of women who are subject only to sexism and not to other forms of oppression, for the treatment of these women has to do only with their gender and nothing to do with their class, race, nationality, servile status, etc.
3. Hence feminists as feminists are centrally concerned with the lives of women who are subject to sexism but not to other forms of oppression.

Now it is important to see that proposition 2 is flawed: women who are not oppressed on account of their "race" are nevertheless not without a "racial" identity, and this identity has as much to do with their position as their gender—indeed, it is part of what shapes their gender identity. For if their "racial" identity were different, they would be called "slave" instead of "woman," despite their femaleness. A female has the status of "woman" in Aristotle only if she is not a slave. We cannot ignore her status as a free woman simply because she is not a slave and hence not oppressed on account of it—anymore than we could ignore the sex of a natural ruler because he is not a woman and hence not oppressed on account of it.

Point 2 fails to ask what it is about this group of women that makes it true that they are subject to just one form of oppression. In general we have no trouble asking and answering the question of why some women are subject to many forms of oppression—because of their race, we say, because of their class, as well as their gender. The same answer applies to the question of why some women are subject to just one form of oppression—because of their class, because of their race. That is, no woman is subject to any form of oppression simply because she is a woman; which forms of oppression she is subject to depend on what "kind" of woman she is. In a world in which a woman might be subject to racism, classism, homophobia, anti-Semitism, if she is not so subject it is because of her race, class, religion, sexual orientation. So it can never be the case that the treatment of a woman has only to do with her gender and nothing to do with her class or race. That she is subject only to sexism tells us a lot about her race and class identity, her being free or slave, and so on. For her, being subject only to sexism is made possible by these other facts about her identity. So rather than saying she is oppressed "as a woman," we might more accurately say she is oppressed as a citizen-class woman is oppressed.

What would be the Richards/Cantarella account of why slave women are excluded from the polis? We might pose their view as follows and add it to our list above:

4. The treatment of some women has to do only with their "race," with their being slaves; sexism is not a factor here, because it is not as women that slave women are excluded.[49]

They thus provide what appears to be a very sound reason for attending only to what Aristotle says about free women if we want to know what role gender plays in his political views: If we want to know how a woman's gender identity affects her position vis-à-vis the polis, there's no point to examining how her "racial" identity affects her position. In Aristotle, slave women are excluded from the polis not because they are women but because they are slaves. Slave women's exclusion might well be disturbing, but analyzing it can't tell us about the role of gender as an obstacle to citizenship. An inquiry into the position of slave women does tell a different story than one into the position of free women—but that is what we'd expect, if slave women and free women are excluded from the polis on different grounds: the former because of their "race," the latter because of their gender.

But what appears to be a principled methodological reason for focusing on free rather than slave women obscures the essential role of "race" in the determination of the free woman's position. Her "racial" identity is as crucial in making possible her exclusion simply on the basis of gender as is the slave woman's "racial" identity in making her gender identity irrelevant to her exclusion (and remember that Richards and Cantarella insist that the slave woman's gender identity is irrelevant here). The free woman is not excluded on account of her "racial" identity, but she couldn't be excluded on the basis of her gender unless she had the "racial" identity she does, that is, unless she were a free woman. The situation of slave women makes us see that if not all women are excluded from the polis on account of sexism, then it is not your gender identity alone that subjects you to sexism. If it is true, as Richards and Cantarella propose, that some women are not subject to sexism, we have to look to factors other than sexism to explain the case of those who are.

VIII

Our examination of the distinction Aristotle draws between "women" and "slaves" leads to the recognition that for him one's gender identity is inseparable from one's "racial" identity: only certain males and females count as "men" and "women." But we can set out the following argument about an important way in which we can and should talk about gender independently of race or class.

The crucial distinction in Aristotle and others is not exactly male versus female. Although male slaves certainly are not without maleness, this does not mean for Aristotle that therefore they are the natural rulers of any woman at all. But what is crucial is an explicit or implicit concept of masculinity: what slaves and women lack are characteristically masculine traits. Rationality is not male—but it is masculine. And masculinity is a gender concept. What finally separates those meant to rule and those meant to be ruled, in both Plato and Aristotle, is being characterized as masculine.

For example, one of the things that separates philosopher-rulers from everybody else is whether their souls are masculine. The traits philosopher-rulers must have are traits of masculinity. In Aristotle, what characterizes natural rulers is a form of rationality that is masculine. Plato and Aristotle are alike in presenting an ideal of humanity that is above all else a masculine ideal. They only differ with respect to who could exemplify such an ideal: while Plato apparently can imagine females with masculine souls, Aristotle says that is impossible: there is no imaginable way for male excellence to be expressed in a female body.

This is to argue that both Plato and Aristotle have a normative notion of humanness that is inseparable from a notion of masculinity (which is of course normative). Aristotle arrogates both the notion of real manliness and of real humanness to male citizens. But to say simply this ignores the fact that the concept of masculinity is at once a gender and a "race" concept—for as is clear, even if only males can be masculine, not all males can be masculine. One must not only be male but be of a particular "race" to be masculine. Moreover, it is not as if the only possible way not to be masculine is to be feminine. In Aristotle, male slaves are not masculine, but they certainly are not feminine either; that is part of Aristotle's insistence on the difference between "women" and "slaves." Female slaves fail to be masculine in quite different ways than free women do. So "masculine" and "feminine" are not exhaustive political categories: that is, being masculine or feminine won't necessarily indicate where you belong within the polis.

It's true that for Aristotle being male is not a sufficient condition of being human, while being masculine is; but this just tells us what we knew before—that only certain kinds of men are really human. Interestingly enough, there are more alternatives to being masculine than to being male: if you are not male you are female,[50] while if you are not masculine that doesn't mean you are feminine. Gender possibilities are more numerous than sexual ones, as we have seen in the various configurations possible for soul and body. In Aristotle, while citizen men who are not masculine are probably considered effeminate (which is not the same as being feminine), male slaves are not effeminate, because they can't fall from the grace of masculinity. And while women can fail to be feminine, that doesn't mean they are masculine, even though being masculine is one way to fail at being feminine. Female slaves, as we've said, aren't feminine in Aristotle's scheme, but they clearly aren't masculine either. Attention to the treatment of female slaves in Aristotle leads us to see that "masculinity" and "femininity" are not simply gender concepts since gender is in part a function of "race" and "class."

IX

Whatever else feminism includes, central to it are investigations into how a person's sex and gender affect his or her place in the world. It would seem, then, to be an unexceptionable principle of any inquiry into someone's views about gender to focus on how he or she distinguishes between men and women. And yet we've seen in the case of Aristotle that this produces a very skewed account of his views about gender. To capture the distinction in Aristotle between sex and gender, it is not enough to observe that the gender "woman" is what females, the gender "man" what males, are expected to become. For this leaves out two startling conclusions we draw from Aristotle's account: (1) To have a gender identity is itself a "race" privilege.[51] (2) It is thus misleading to say that we have to look at both gender identity and "race" identity—free or slave—in order to see one's function vis-à-vis the polis.

In Aristotle a person's gender identity is determined by sexual and "race" identity and hence is not something added to "race" identity. Slaves are without gender because, for Aristotle's purposes, their sex doesn't matter. In any world in which for some people sex is made to matter—positively for males, negatively for females—then it also matters a lot if your sex doesn't matter. This suggests another reason why feminists like Richards and Cantarella might think it out of our jurisdiction as feminists to con-cern ourselves with female slaves: if the sex of female slaves doesn't matter—for the purposes, anyway, of someone with a lot of power and authority to determine where slaves "belong"—how can a theory prem-ised on the argument that sex does matter find room for them?

The assumption that gender is isolatable from "race" will blind us to some very important elements of Aristotle's views about gender: though no one can have a gender identity without having a sexual identity, hav-ing a particular "racial" identity is a necessary condition of having any gender identity at all. We can't understand Aristotle's views about gender without looking at those males and females he took to be neither "men" nor "women."

The critics often repeat in new contexts versions of the old assumptions they set out to contest.

MARTHA MINOW

Simone de Beauvoir and Women: Just Who Does She Think "We" Is?

We have seen the variety of ways in which Plato and Aristotle reveal their reluctance to welcome women into the community of fully formed human beings. Sometimes their point seems to be that women are just incapable of leading the kind of lives philosopher-rulers or citizens of the polis must live. Other times their concern is expressed more strongly: women constitute a threat to well-ordered lives and to harmonious communities, insofar as they give in to the demands of their bodies or the irrational element of their souls. At the same time, however, women's work is taken to constitute in part the conditions under which citizens of the polis can exercise exemplary human capacities. Women thus simultaneously make possible and undermine worthy forms of human living. In both Plato and Aristotle, women are characterized as being ruled by their bodies and easily overwhelmed by passion and desire. Without such traits humans would not be human; but in the struggle against or proper control over the body, the emotions, only the best kind of humans can succeed.

In *The Second Sex*, Simone de Beauvoir explores the many ways in which men have depicted women as ruled by forces in human nature that men can neither fully accept nor fully deny.[1] Although she does not examine in any detail the works of Plato and Aristotle, de Beauvoir is a crucial figure in any discussion about the response of feminists to the legacy of Plato and Aristotle preserved in attitudes toward women in the Western world. *The Second Sex* is a landmark work in contemporary feminist thought (even though for many years de Beauvoir apparently resisted being identified as a feminist).[2] She attempted to give an account of the situation of women in general and to include proposals for the conditions that would have to change if women were to become free. Although not all feminists subsequent to de Beauvoir referred to her work, or even necessarily knew about it, there is hardly any issue that feminists have come to deal with that she did not address. Indeed, she touched on issues such as attitudes toward lesbianism that some later feminists didn't dare to think about.[3]

De Beauvoir explicitly recognized that we live in a world in which there are a number of forms of oppression, and she tried to locate sexism in that context. I have suggested that a troubling characteristic of much contemporary feminist theory is its failure to take seriously the intertwining of sexism with other forms of oppression; and I have tried to indicate the ways in which the attempt to treat gender in isolation from factors such as race and class has both reflected and perpetuated a choice to focus on the lives of some women rather than others. I think that in de Beauvoir's work, we have all the essential ingredients of a feminist account of "women's lives" that would not conflate "woman" with a small group of women—namely, white middle-class heterosexual Christian women in Western countries. Yet de Beauvoir ends up producing an account which does just that. In this chapter, I shall explore how both de Beauvoir's theoretical perspective and her empirical observations lend themselves to a far richer account of "women's nature" than she herself ends up giving. (I am not going to argue about the strengths or weaknesses of her theory or the accuracy of her observations, but rather raise some questions about why she took them to lead in one direction rather than another.) Then I want to suggest reasons for the serious discrepancy between the potential broad scope of her views and the actual narrow focus of her position. De Beauvoir is a thinker of great perspicacity, so to explain the discrepancy simply in terms of a kind of race and class privilege that makes it easy for her to think of her own experience as representative of the experience of others is not enough. We need to ask what it might be in the language or methodology or theory employed by de Beauvoir that enables her to disguise from herself the assertion of privilege she so keenly saw in women of her own position.

I

Human beings aren't satisfied merely to live, de Beauvoir insists: we aspire to a meaningful existence.[4] But much about our constitution conspires against the possibility of such an existence: our being creatures of the flesh entails the ever-present possibility that our grand projects will be mocked. It is not only the facts of our birth and death that give the lie to our being pure, unembodied, immortal spirit. Our bodies need tending to each day, and there is nothing meaningful in the many activities involved in this tending. The feeding and cleaning of bodies, the maintenance of shelter against the powerful vagaries of the natural world, are necessary if we are to live. But if that is all we did, or all we thought we could do, we wouldn't find anything valuable about human life. As de Beauvoir says, unless we can engage in activities that "transcend [our] animal nature," we might as well be brute animals:

On the biological level a species is maintained only by creating itself anew; but this creation results only in repeating the same Life in more individuals. But man assures the repetition of Life while transcending Life through Existence; by this transcendence he creates values that deprive pure repetition of all value. (58, 59)

"Existing," as opposed to merely "living," is best expressed in those aspects of life that are the function of "the loftiest human attitudes: heroism, revolt, disinterestedness, imagination, creation" (588). Only "existing" gives any reason for life; mere living "does not carry within itself its reasons for being, reasons that are more important than life itself" (59).[5] To exist is to be a creative subject, not a passive object of the forces of nature; it is to be molding a new future through the power of one's intelligence, rather than being at the play of the repetitive rhythms of one's animal nature. Existing is as different from living as consciousness is from matter, will from passivity, transcendence from immanence, spirit from flesh (134).

But life is necessary for existence, and we must preserve life even while we struggle against its demands. Descent into life is possible because of the never fully eradicated allure of dumbness and unfreedom, the ever-present possibility of forgoing (or seeming to forgo) the responsibilities, uncertainties, and risks of intelligence and freedom. Men, de Beauvoir says, make women the repository of the multiform threats to a life of transcendence, agency, freedom, spirit; woman remains "in bondage to life's mysterious processes" (72), "doomed to immanence" (68). Her life "is not directed towards ends: she is absorbed in producing or caring for things that are never more than means, such as food, clothing, and shelter. These things are inessential intermediaries between animal life and free existence" (569). Though woman is no less capable of real "existence" than man, it is in her corporeality rather than his own that man sees palpable and undeniable reminders of his own animal nature, of his own deeply regrettable and undignified contingency. Desirous of seeing no part of himself in her, he regards her as thoroughly Other, or as thoroughly Other as he can, given that he nevertheless needs her as a companion who is neither merely an animal nor merely a thing: "Man knows that to satisfy his desires, to perpetuate his race, woman is indispensable" (74).

Although women are constitutionally no less desirous or capable than men of "existing" rather than merely "living," historically most women have not resisted men's definition of them as embodying mysterious, dumb forces of nature. They have done little to try to undermine the economic, social, and political institutions that reinforce and are reinforced by such attitudes. In this, de Beauvoir says, women are unlike other oppressed groups—for example, Blacks, Jews, workers.

There are two reasons for this. First, women are spread throughout the population, across racial, class, ethnic, national, and religious lines, and this presents huge obstacles to their working together politically. They don't share the same economic and social position, nor do they have a shared consciousness. Moreover, "the division of the sexes is a biological fact, not an event in human history" (xix). In all other cases of oppression, she claims, both the oppressors and the oppressed have taken their relative positions to be the result of historical events or social change and hence in principle capable of alteration: "A condition brought about at a certain time can be abolished at some other time, as the Negroes of Haiti and others have proved." Similarly "proletarians have not always existed, whereas there have always been women" (xviii).

De Beauvoir's point here presumably is not that whites never have taken racial differences to be biological; rather she seems to be pointing out that the idea that biological differences entitle whites to dominate Blacks has been undermined in theory (to the extent that differences between Black and white are held to be less significant than their similarities as human beings) and nullified in political struggles (through which Blacks make clear their capacity to regard themselves as "subjects" and whites as "others") (xviii). De Beauvoir seems to be saying here that owing to a deep and apparently unbridgeable biological divide, women constitute for men the Other, whereas Blacks or the proletariat, for example, have not always constituted an Other for those by whom they may be dominated.

At the same time, despite these differences among women and between women and other oppressed groups, women do share something in common—but what they share paradoxically works against any possible solidarity. They "identify with each other" (513) but do not communicate, as men do, "through ideas and projects of personal interest," and are only "bound together by a kind of immanent complicity" (511). By this de Beauvoir means that women are aware of inhabiting a special domain separate from men—in which they discuss recipes, frigidity, children, clothing—but nevertheless they regard each other as rivals for the attention of the masculine world. They are capable of ceasing to be Other. Despite what men find it convenient to believe, the difference between men and women is no more a biological given and historical necessity than the difference between bourgeoisie and proletariat. There is, however, a difference between the biological condition of being female and the social condition of being woman. So despite the differences among women, their different social and political locations, they could join in resisting the domination of men. But they haven't.[6]

And why haven't they? Sometimes de Beauvoir suggests that it is because being a "true woman" is inseparable from being the Other, so that it is logically impossible both to be a real woman and to be a subject, while there is no definitional problem, whatever other problems there are, in being a Black, or a worker, or a Jew, and also a subject. But this does not explain why women don't refuse to be "true women." And indeed sometimes de Beauvoir suggests that women simply choose to take the less arduous path: "No doubt it is more comfortable to submit to a blind enslavement than to work for liberation" (246); to "decline to be the Other, to refuse to be a party to the deal—this would be for women to renounce all the advantages conferred upon them by their alliance with the superior caste" (xx).[7]

Hence sometimes when she says that economic independence is the necessary condition of women's liberation, there is the suggestion that only if women are forced by circumstance to provide for themselves will they embrace their transcendence rather than fall into their immanence, see themselves as subjects rather than objects, as Self rather than Other. Women recognize the importance and value of transcendence, but only enough to search for men whose creative and productive flights will rub off on them, metaphysically speaking. Women want what men have, but only in wanting the men who have it. What we need, de Beauvoir is saying, is a world in which if women are to get it at all, they must do it on their own.

In short, de Beauvoir argues that there are at least three things that help to explain the fact of women's domination by men: (1) Men's having the attitudes they do toward women; (2) the existence of economic, social, and political institutions through which such attitudes are expressed, enforced, and perpetuated; (3) women's failure to resist such attitudes and institutions.

II

Our earlier discussions should have made us suspicious of any attempt to give a general account of the treatment and experiences of women. This is not to say that some such account is impossible, only that it surely can't be given if only one group of women is the basis for it. Claims made about "women" may be true about one group of women in one time and place but are very misleading if taken to be about all women in all times and places. There is also much in de Beauvoir's account to warn us against such overgeneralization.

Both her observations of differences among women and her more general theoretical perspective provide de Beauvoir with the ingredients of a very rich account of what it has meant to be "woman" and how women have been treated—in fact, they suggest a much richer account than she actually gives us. In each of the three subsections below, we begin with a description of the riches her account sometimes offers and then go on to look at how the analysis proceeds otherwise to deplete itself. Later we shall examine some possible reasons for her failure to embrace some of the implications of her own views.

Differences among Women

As noted above, de Beauvoir more than once remarks upon class, racial, and national differences among women and how such differences bear on the economic, social, and political positions of women thus variously situated. Her comments on the lack of a sense of shared concerns among women are quite arresting: "If [women] belong to the bourgeoisie, they feel solidarity with men of that class, not with proletarian women; if they are white, their allegiance is to white men, not to Negro women" (xix; cf. 103, 566, 590). The housewife is hostile toward her "servant [and toward] the teachers, governesses, nurses and nursemaids who attend to her children" (513).

Freed from the male, [the middle-class woman] would have to work for a living; she felt no solidarity with workingwomen, and she believed that the emancipation of bourgeois women would mean the ruin of her class. (103)

De Beauvoir, then, is saying that the women least prepared to have their status changed have been white middle-class women, who are willing to keep the sexual status quo in return for the privileges of their class and race.

In all such examples, she cites the unwillingness of women with race or class privileges to give them up as the main obstacle to women's all doing something together to resist the domination of men. That is, what prevents a white middle-class woman from attacking sexism is her awareness that if she undermines sexism she will thereby undermine her race and class privilege. This ties in with de Beauvoir's point about the difference class makes to privilege based on sex. She argues that the less class privilege men and women enjoy, the less sexual privilege men of that class have; the more extreme class oppression is, the less extreme sex oppression is. So according to de Beauvoir sexism and classism are deeply intertwined. An important way in which class distinctions can be made is in terms of male-female relationships: we can't describe the sexism women are subject to without specifying their class; nor can we understand how sexism works without looking at its relation to class privilege.[8] What makes middle-class women dependent on men of their class is the same as what distinguishes them from working-class women.[9]

But de Beauvoir does not heed her own insights here. On the contrary, she almost always describes relations between men and women as if the class or race or ethnic identity of the men and women made no difference to the truth of statements about "men and women." This poses some very serious difficulties for her attempt to give a general account of "woman." On her own terms it ought to be misleading to say, as she does, that we live "in a world that belongs to men" (xx, 512, 563), as if all differences between princes and paupers, masters and slaves, can be canceled out by the fact that they are all male.[10] In describing the psychological development of girls, she remarks upon the ways in which everything in a girl's life "confirms her in her belief in masculine superiority" (38). And yet she later makes clear that a white girl growing up in the United States hardly believes that Black men are superior to her: "During the War of Secession no Southerners were more passionate in upholding slavery than the women" (566). She describes ways in which girls of the upper classes are taught to believe in their superiority to working-class men: "In the upper classes women are eager accomplices of their masters because they stand to profit from the benefits provided. . . . The women of the upper middle classes and the aristocracy have always defended their class interests even more obstinately than have their husbands" (590). Whether or not de Beauvoir is entirely accurate in her descriptions of some women's passionate insistence on preserving privilege—were they really more fierce about it than the men of their race and class?[11]—the point is that these

63

descriptions undermine her claims elsewhere about the common position of women.

De Beauvoir's perceptiveness about class and race inequality should make us wonder about her account of the "man" as "citizen" and "producer" with "economic independence" and all "the advantages attached to masculinity" in contrast to the "woman," who is "before all, and often exclusively, a wife," "shut up in the home," enjoying "vast leisure," and entertaining at tables "laden with fine food and precious wines" (430, 443, 497, 508, 663).

> Since the husband is the productive worker, he is the one who goes beyond family interest to that of society, opening up a future for himself through co-operation in the building of the future: he incarnates transcendence. Woman is doomed to the continuation of the species and the care of the home—that is, to immanence. (404)

Here de Beauvoir, despite evidence she provides to the contrary, makes it look as if racism, for example, had never existed and never affected the conditions under which a man can "incarnate transcendence." Here and elsewhere when she points to the role women play in reproducing family and species—"the oppression of woman has its cause in the will to perpetuate the family and to keep the patrimony intact" (82)—she chooses to ignore questions about legitimacy even while alluding to them elsewhere. She quotes Demosthenes: "We have hetairas for the pleasures of the spirit, concubines for sensual pleasure, and wives to give us sons" (81); and her argument implies among other things that human beings typically do not "continue the species" randomly or without regard to what kinds of beings will populate the future. We saw concern in both Plato and Aristotle about joining the right kind of men with the right kind of women to produce philosopher-rulers and citizens of the polis. De Beauvoir surely was aware of the extent to which racial, class, and religious conventions dictate what comprises appropriate sexual behavior and "legitimate" reproduction. Indeed, as we shall see below, she explicitly points out but does not consider the implications of the fact that everything she says about sexual privilege only works when the man and woman belong to the same race and class (605).

De Beauvoir sabotages her insights about the political consequences of the multiple locations of women in another way: she frequently compares women to other groups—in her language, "Jews, the Black, the Yellow, the proletariat, slaves, servants, the common people." For example, she asks us to think about the differences between the situation of women, on the one hand, and, on the other, "the scattering of the Jews, the introduction of slavery into America, the conquests of imperialism" (xviii). She discusses with considerable appreciation Bebel's comparison of "women and the proletariat" (49). She remarks that some of what Hegel says about "master and slave" better applies to "man and woman" (59). In reflecting on slavery in the United States, she says that there was a "great difference" between the case of American Blacks and that of women: "the Negroes submit with a feeling of revolt, no privileges compensating for their hard lot, whereas woman is offered inducements to complicity" (278). She speaks of the role of religion in offering "women" and "the common people" the hope of moving out of immanence: "When a sex or a class is condemned to immanence, it is necessary to offer it the mirage of some form of transcendence" (585). She compares the talk of women about their husbands to conversations "of domestics talking about their employers critically in the servants' quarters" (579).

I bring up these comparisons not in order to assess their historical accuracy but to note that in making them de Beauvoir obscures the fact that half of the populations to whom she compares women consist of women. This is particularly puzzling in light of her recognition of the ways in which women are distributed across race, class, religious, and ethnic lines. She sometimes contrasts "women" to "slaves," sometimes describes women as "slaves" (e.g., 454, 569), but she never really talks about those women who according to her own categories belonged to slave populations—for example, Black female slaves in the United States. She does say at one point that "there were women among the slaves, to be sure, but there have always been free women" (131); and then she proceeds to make clear that it is free women whom she will examine. She also says that in "classes in which women enjoyed some economic independence and took part in production . . . women workers were enslaved even more than the male workers" (119–20). But in contrasting "women" to a number of other groups, and in choosing not to pay attention to the women in those other groups, she expresses her determination to use "woman" only in reference to those females not subject to racism, anti-Semitism, classism, imperialism.

Perhaps she is aware at some level that this is the price she must pay for consistency: for where she does describe briefly the situation of females who belong to the groups she contrasts to "women," what she says does not follow from her account of "women." For example, she claims that in the Middle Ages peasant men and women lived on a "footing of equality" (94), and that "in the working classes economic oppression nullified the inequality of the sexes" (96). If she believes this, then of course she has to restrict her use of the word "woman" to those females not subject to the other forms of oppression she refers to; otherwise her large claims about the subordination of women to men would be undermined by her own account. And yet at the same time, she subjects them to question, which we see as we turn to a third way in which de Beauvoir fails to pay attention to her own significant insights.

As noted earlier, toward the end of *The Second Sex*, de Beauvoir acknowledges that the differences in privilege and power between men and women she has been referring to are "in play" only when men and women are of the same class and race (605). This is a logical conclusion for someone who holds, as we've seen she does, that the wives of white slaveowners in the United States fought even harder than their husbands to preserve the privileges of race; since she thought of "slaves" as male, she could hardly maintain that men who were slaves dominated women who were not. But there is a problem even in the way she signals here that claims about privilege based on sex apply only within the same class or race. For that suggests that sexism within one class or race is just like that within any other class or race. If so, her claims do have a kind of generality after all—for example, while what characterizes relations between white men and white women does not characterize those between white men and Black women, or between Black men and white women, it does nevertheless characterize those between Black men and Black women. But we've seen that de Beauvoir also holds that sexual oppression is essentially nullified when men and women are subject to other forms of oppression. In that case, her claim is not really that the sexism she describes operates only when class and race are constant, but rather that she is talking about the sexism in effect only when the men and women involved are not subject to class or racial oppression. She herself leads us to the conclusion that the sexism she is concerned with in *The Second Sex* is that experienced by white middle-class women in Western countries.

The Creation of Women

"One is not born, but rather becomes, a woman" (249). This opening sentence from book 2 of *The Second Sex* has come to be the most often cited and perhaps most powerful of de Beauvoir's insights. Among other things it offers a starting point for the distinction between sex and gender. It is one thing to be biologically female, quite another to be shaped by one's culture into a "woman"—a female with feminine qualities, someone who does the kinds of things "women," not "men," do, someone who has the kind of thoughts and feelings that make doing these things seem an easy expression of one's feminine nature.

If being a woman is something one can become, then it also is something one can fail to become. De Beauvoir insists that while being or not being female is a biological matter, becoming or not becoming a woman is not. "Civilization as a whole" produces women (249). In the absence of other humans, no female would become a woman; particular human "intervention in her destiny is fundamental" to who and what she becomes:

Woman is determined not by her hormones or by mysterious instincts, but by the manner in which her body and her relation to the world are modified through the action of others than herself. (682)

In particular,

in men's eyes—and for the legion of women who see through men's eyes—it is not enough to have a woman's body nor to assume the female function as mistress or mother in order to be "true woman." (245)

What she has to do to become a "true woman" is to be seen and to see herself as Other in contrast to the Self of the male, as inessential in contrast to the essential, as object in contrast to the subject. Females of the species don't come created in this way; they are made this way by the concerted efforts of men and women.

Moreover, de Beauvoir insists that humans create whatever significance is attached to having a body and more particularly to having a male or female body. She directs us to thinking about "the body as lived in by the subject" as opposed to the body as described by the biologist (33). The consciousness one has of one's body in this way is acquired "under circumstances dependent upon the society of which [one] is a member" or indeed even upon the class one belongs to (44). De Beauvoir suggests, for example, that the physical event of having an abortion is experienced differently by conventional middle-class women and by those "schooled by poverty and misery to disdain bourgeois morality" (461). Along similar lines, she claims that the biological changes that take place during menopause are experienced differently by those "true women" who have "staked everything on their femininity" and by "the peasant woman, the work man's wife," who, "constantly under the threat of new pregnancies, are happy when, at long last, they no longer run this risk" (542).

Biology is not destiny in at least two senses, according to de Beauvoir. First, being female is not the same thing as being a "woman"; nor does it determine whether and how one will become a "woman." Second, different women experience biological events associated with being female differently, depending on how their bodies are otherwise employed and their beliefs about what are the proper things to do with or to their bodies. But de Beauvoir doesn't take this insight as far as she might in the directions to which her own comments lead. She seems to be saying that there is no particular significance that must be given to biological facts about our bodies, that whether or how a female becomes a "woman" depends upon human consciousness and human action. But she is well aware of the fact that in many ways human consciousness and human action take quite different forms in different societies. We get a hint of this in her comment quoted above about how a woman's consciousness of femininity is dependent upon the society in which she lives, as well as in her reminder that the intervention of others is so crucial a factor in the creation of a "woman" out of a female that "if this action took a different direction, it would produce a quite different result" (682).

This surely points to the variability in the creation of "women" across and within cultures. Here is where de Beauvoir's lack of attention to females belonging to the populations she contrasts to "women" is particularly disappointing. She doesn't reflect on what her own theoretical perspective strongly suggests and what her own language mirrors: namely, that different females are constructed into different kinds of "women"; that under some conditions certain females count as "women," others don't. This is where her inattention to certain historical facts—for example, that Plato allowed only a very small group of females among the philosopher-rulers—takes its toll.

Whether or not she was a close reader of the philosophers, de Beauvoir's own descriptions of differences among women point to precisely the kind of variability in the construction of "women" that one would expect if, as she claims, women are not born but made and if at the same time differences of class, race, and ethnicity are in force. Indeed, her off-hand reminder that claims about sexual privilege apply only when race and class are kept constant underscores the point: If all males were constructed into "men" in the same way, and all females made into "women" in the same way, one wouldn't have to be cautious about making generalizations about men and women across class and race lines. For example, whatever characterized relations between white men and white women would also characterize relations between white men and Black women.

Moreover, de Beauvoir's analysis of racial oppression, cursory as it is, tells us that she believes people have attached different significance to racial differences at different times. She counts as successful social change those economic and political reversals in which a people once regarded as Other no longer are regarded as such by those who formerly dominated them. When she comments, early in the book, on the change of status of Blacks in Haiti after the revolution (xviii—xix), and much later on how Black suffrage helped to lead to the perception of Blacks as worthy of having the vote (686), she is alluding to changes in the significance attached by whites to what they take to be biological differences between whites and Blacks. If we follow up her insistence that we pay attention to "the body as lived in by the subject" (33), we might begin to ask not only about living in a male or female body in the context of sexism but also about living in a black or white or brown or yellow or red body in the context of racism. Though de Beauvoir refers to the variability in ideals of feminine beauty (146) and, as we've seen, is certainly aware of racial oppression, she does not speak at length about women subject to racism and so does not talk about the ways in which notions of beauty are racially coded. While she certainly is aware of the significance attached to skin color, she does not join that to her point about the distinction between other physical differences among human bodies (i.e., sexual differences) and what humans make of those differences.

The Real and the Ideal Woman

A third promising ingredient of de Beauvoir's analysis is her attack on the discrepancy between the reality of actual women and a static ideal of "woman." The latter is not an empirical generalization based on observations of specific women but a male myth about the nature of femininity:

As against the dispersed, contingent, and multiple existences of actual women, mythical thought opposes the Eternal Feminine, unique and changeless. If the definition provided for this concept is contradicted by the behavior of flesh-and-blood women, it is the latter who are wrong; we are told not that Femininity is a false entity, but that the women concerned are not feminine. (237)

De Beauvoir believes that this mythical ideal reaches deep into the idea of woman as Other, and as we've seen, she sometimes speaks as if men's treatment of women as Other is inevitable. But on the other hand, it is clear that she thinks that if political and economic conditions change in the right direction, women will be seen in their historical specificity—that is, women might come to be truly known by men rather than being the occasion for men's projection of a mythic ideal of femininity.

It is noteworthy that the feminine comrade, colleague, and associate are without mystery [being "mysterious" is one version of the mythic ideal]; on the other hand, if the vassal is male, if, in the eyes of a man or a woman who is older, or richer, a young fellow, for example, plays the role of the inessential object, then he too becomes shrouded in mystery. And this uncovers for us a substructure under the feminine mystery which is economic in nature. (241–42)

The more relationships are concretely lived, the less they are idealized. The fellah of ancient Egypt, the Bedouin peasant, the artisan of the Middle Ages, the worker of today has in the requirements of work and poverty relations with his particular woman companion which are too definite for her to be embellished with an aura either auspicious or inauspicious. (244)

De Beauvoir seems to be making a brief here for establishing a set of conditions under which people can see each other as they actually are. The liberation of women depends upon establishing economic and political conditions under which men won't simply project their notion of "woman" onto women but will look at who women in fact are, observing "the behavior of flesh-and-blood women." De Beauvoir has high regard for what she refers to as "knowledge," "empirical law" (237), "laws of nature," "scientific explanation" (580). Though she does not explain exactly what she means by these terms, it is clear that she accuses men of not being very scientific in their claims about women.[12] Men are right to look for universally true statements about women, but they don't realize that the only solid grounds for such claims are empirical observations. Clear thinking about women would lead to universally true statements about them.

De Beauvoir has not of course laid out a full-blown epistemology here, but the hints of one point to the potential richness of her account of women. As we have noted on several occasions, de Beauvoir at one level is quite aware of the diverse historical, economic, and political situations of women, of the differences class and race make to women's relationships with men and to their relationships with other women. She likens the notion of the "Eternal Feminine" to a Platonic "Idea, timeless, unchangeable" (237). As an existentialist, she has no truck with the idea of an "essence" of anything—of humanity, of man, of woman. We are not who or what we are by virtue of being particular instances of some transcendental entity; rather, "an existent *is* nothing other than what he does . . . he is to be measured by his acts" (241).

De Beauvoir suggests that a search for some essence of "woman" is deeply misplaced: we would look in vain for some metaphysical nugget of pure womanhood that defines all women as women. We have to look at what women do to find out who they are. This means that we cannot decide prior to actual investigation of women's lives what they do or do not have in common; and this means that we cannot assume that what we find to be true about the lives of women of one class or race or nationality or historical period will be true about the lives of other women.[13] De Beauvoir warns us against any inclination to assume that the lives of women of one race or class are representative of the lives of all other women. Both existentialism and "scientific thinking" tell us we have to look and see what women are really like.

But at the same time, de Beauvoir also warns, neither existentialism nor "scientific reasoning" will lead us to the viewpoint of "woman," who "lacks the sense of the universal" and takes the world to be "a confused conglomeration of special cases" (580). So while we can't assume, ahead of time, that any particular universal truth about "humanity" or "men" or "women" will be true, we can assume that investigation of women's lives will lead to such a truth or truths about women. Women's isolation from one another—the very isolation that de Beauvoir cites as one reason for their not constituting a likely political class—accounts in large part for their lacking "the sense of the universal": "She feels she is a special case because she is isolated in her home and hence does not come into active contact with other women" (580). If she had the opportunity to know about other women's lives, she might come to see the grounds for universal truths in the similarities in cases she earlier had taken to be special, unique, *sui generis*.

De Beauvoir has a lively concern that views about women be based neither on the assumption that women necessarily share some metaphysical essence nor on the assumption that women share nothing at all. Yet the universal truths she claims to be noting about "women" do not follow from the observations she makes about differences among women.

III

In *The Second Sex*, de Beauvoir gives us directions for thinking about women that she refuses to follow—or more accurately, that she only sometimes follows. Moreover, when she does come down the paths she has pointed to, she misdescribes what is found there. As we have seen, on the one hand she refers to what she herself takes to be significant differences among women; but on the other, she dismisses those differences as irrelevant to understanding the condition of "woman," insofar as she takes the story of "woman" to be that provided by examination of the lives of women not subject to racism, classism, anti-Semitism, imperialism, and so forth. According to her, the situation of "woman" must be contrasted to that of Blacks, Jews, the working class.

De Beauvoir notes how important it is to remember that claims about the difference between men's and women's social and economic position can only hold when we keep race and class constant; yet she also typically speaks of "men" and "women" as if their class and race identity didn't matter.

She points to the ways in which biological females are made into "women" through the concerted efforts of the societies into which they are born; still she forgets about the fact that by her own reckoning different females are made into "women" in so many different ways that they see themselves as particular kinds of women and may have a deep investment in not becoming any other kind of women. This happens whenever white women have wished to preserve the privileges based on their being white women rather than Black women; whenever rich women have wished to preserve the privileges based on their being wealthy women rather than poor women; and, she might have added, whenever heterosexual women have wished to preserve the privileges based on their not being lesbians.

She insists on the importance of recognizing the role of social institutions in shaping what it means to us to live in our bodies; yet she ignores the effect of the history of racism in constructing what it means to have white or black or brown or yellow or red skin.

She insists on the importance of attention to the actual facts of women's lives as opposed to relying on what she describes as male fantasy and female gossip; but at the same time she presents as conclusions from a study of "woman" what even on her own reckoning has to be seen as a study of a particular and not necessarily representative group of women. She chastises women who have clung to the privileges of race and class even though her appropriation of "woman" to describe the situation of women of her own race and class expresses just such privilege.

Does de Beauvoir simply not notice the directions in which her work points? Is she simply not aware that on the basis of evidence she herself presents, she has misrepresented the situation of one group of women as the situation of "woman," of women in general? Or is there some reason she may think it both possible and important to lay out general truths about "woman"—about how "woman" has been perceived by "man," about the ways in which the condition of "woman" is and is not like the condition of Blacks, Jews, the poor—despite the variety of social, economic, and political circumstances of different groups of women?

Let us look at two possible explanations of these contradictory strands in de Beauvoir's thought. The first comes from Judith Okely.[14] She suggests that one important reason de Beauvoir doesn't talk much about the effects of race and class oppression on women is that as an existentialist she takes individual will to be a much more significant determinant of one's position in life than factors such as race and class. But this won't work: on those grounds, de Beauvoir would also have to discount sex or gender as a significant, even if not wholly sufficient, determinant; and moreover, Okely's comment ignores the considerable amount of material in de Beauvoir on the effects of race and class oppression.

A second promising explanation links de Beauvoir's ultimate silence about race and class to white middle-class privilege in the following way: there is something in de Beauvoir's work that suggests that the viewpoint such privilege expresses is ineradicable; that de Beauvoir is bound to take the case of women like herself to be the case of "women," and that it is inevitable that she would take women different from herself to be Other. This explanation is less easily dismissed than Okely's, but it too proves finally unconvincing, as we shall see.

Let us recall briefly what de Beauvoir described as the attitudes men have taken toward women: while thinking of themselves as destined for activities of transcendent spirit, men think of women as doomed to leading lives of fleshly immanence; men take themselves to be active Self, women to be passive Other. But it is not clear what role de Beauvoir takes these attitudes to play in men's domination of women. First of all, she doesn't really discuss in detail the relation between such attitudes and the economic, social, and political institutions that underwrite male domination. There is the suggestion that the attitudes she describes complement the institutions and that they will no longer be sustained in the absence of such institutions—that where there is not economic and political inequality between men and women of a certain class, the men of that class don't regard the women as Other.

But on the other hand, she suggests that the desire for transcendence is part of the constitution of human beings, that it is a transhistorical and transcultural characteristic of humans and hence will exist no matter what the political and economic institutions of a society. Indeed, while the liberation of women will be marked by their no longer being seen by men (or by themselves) as creatures of immanence, it will also inaugurate the moment at which women think of themselves as "transcendent." So it is not as if de Beauvoir thinks the dichotomous attitudes she describes will or should disappear (even if she implicitly suggests a redescription of them). The question is whether she thinks anyone aspiring to a "meaningful existence" will inevitably believe there to be constant threats to such an existence located either in people or in things that will as a consequence be treated as Other. De Beauvoir certainly leans toward an affirmative answer to this: "At the moment when man asserts himself as subject and free being, the idea of the Other arises" (73), and "Man never thinks of himself without thinking of the Other; he views the world under the sign of duality" (63).

Hence we must ask whether the liberation of women would mark the moment at which humans no longer think in terms of some people as transcendent, spirit, subject, Self, and others as immanent, flesh, object, Other; or whether it simply would mark the moment at which men and women stop thinking of men as transcendent and women as immanent, start thinking of both men and women as transcendent, and continue to think of someone (who else is left?) or something else as immanent. Indeed, in the introduction to *The Second Sex* de Beauvoir insists: "Otherness is a fundamental category of human thought. . . . No group ever sets itself up as the One without at once setting up the Other over against itself" (xvii). A bit later she refers to "the imperialism of the human consciousness, seeking always to exercise its sovereignty." It includes "the original category of the Other and an original aspiration to dominate the Other" (52). She has already told us that even when regarded as Other by men, women with race and class privilege will insist in turn on seeing members of the races and classes they dominate as Other. Their ceasing to be regarded by men as Other won't necessarily mean that these women will cease regarding other men and women as Other. The very attitude they must take up about themselves (the one that men have had about themselves) inevitably involves taking up quite a different attitude about some Others.

Earlier we saw de Beauvoir arguing that the fear of losing race and class privilege has been strong enough in some women to prevent them from resisting sexism; now it looks as if she is also implying that those who end up resisting sexism will do so in a way that is geared toward not losing race and class privilege. Perhaps she believes that if this group of women engage in battles to end their own subordination, they will ipso facto be undermining the conditions of their own race and class privilege and that any economic and political gains they make for themselves will also accrue to all other women. But we must have doubts about where she stands here, especially given her silence about the possible connections between being a transcendent Self and being a sexist or racist or imperialist. There is nothing in her account that tells us that real "transcendence" is incompatible with taking it to be one's right, or even one's obligation, to subordinate others' wills, resources, and lives to one's own. At the same time, there is much in de Beauvoir to suggest that despite her early references to the "imperialism of the human consciousness," she is not about to treat her own or any one else's decisions or behavior as the inexorable working out of the need for human transcendence. Indeed, for her to do so would be at odds with her own emphasis on the responsibility of any woman at any time for her own position. First of all, as an existentialist, de Beauvoir is not in the business of trying to show how a particular behavior is the inevitable outcome of a given human propensity or need. Moreover, as we have seen, she thinks women share the responsibility for being treated as Other, insofar as she takes them to be in many ways complicit in their domination by men. Finally, we have also seen that she implicitly has criticized women who have refused to give up their race or class privilege. We thus have no good reason to think de Beauvoir would regard the race and class privilege expressed in her focus on women of her own kind as the inevitable price of thinking about her own liberation.[15]

IV

But what then will explain the contradictory pulls in de Beauvoir's account of women? The point of asking this is not to exonerate her from the charge of inconsistency or of misrepresenting the situation of white middle-class women as that of "women in general." The point, rather, is to see where white middle-class privilege has to lodge in order to make itself resistant to observations and theoretical perspectives that tell against it.

Certain strands of de Beauvoir's thought lead inexorably in the direction of a central focus on white middle-class women to illuminate the condition of "woman." As we've seen, at least some of the time she holds the following conditions to be true:

1. If one is not a "man," one is either a woman or a Black, a woman or Jewish, a woman or a poor person, etc.
2. Sexism is different from racism and other forms of oppression: sexism is the oppression women suffer as women, racism the oppression Blacks, for example, suffer as Blacks.
3. Sexism is most obvious in the case of women not otherwise subject to oppression (i.e., not subject to racism, classism, anti-Semitism, etc.).

Now insofar as de Beauvoir takes these conditions to be true, it is quite logical for her to take the examination of white middle-class women to be the examination of all women. Indeed, anyone who assumes the truth of these three conditions will take it to be the most logical thing in the world for feminists to focus on white middle-class women. De Beauvoir certainly is not alone on this position.[16] To the degree that conditions 1, 2, and 3 seem logical, we ought to think of the white middle-class privilege her work expresses, not as a personal quirk in de Beauvoir, but as part of the intellectual and political air she and many of us breathe.

There are two important features of what we might call the 1-2-3 punch. First, it has the status of near truism: Points 1 and 2 may appear to be true by definition (de Beauvoir, as we saw, at times took them utterly for granted), and 3 may seem just to be a matter of common sense, something not even needing the confirmation of historical inquiry (aren't the effects of sexism on women more distinct and hence easier to investigate when other forms of oppression don't affect the women in question?). Second, it leads to the focus on white middle-class women *without mentioning white middle-class women.*

These two features are crucial to the way in which white middle-class privilege works in feminist theory and hence crucial to understanding why we would miss a golden opportunity if we simply dismissed de Beauvoir's focus as an individual expression of her privilege and leave it at that. (Indeed, it would also be an expression of that privilege to mention its presence but not bother to explore and expose its depth and pervasiveness.) Privilege cannot work if it has to be noted and argued for. For someone to have privilege is precisely *not* to have to beg for attention to one's case. For feminist theory to express white middle-class privilege is for it to ensure that white middle-class women will automatically receive attention. How can it ensure this without making explicit what it is doing? Conditions 1–3 do the trick, by making the default position of feminist inquiry an examination of white middle-class women: unless otherwise noted, that's who we are going to be talking about.

De Beauvoir was very attuned to the expression of privilege in women's behavior: as we saw, she took note of the desire of white slaveowners' wives to preserve the racial status quo; she talked about the hostile treatment of female domestic workers by their middle- and upper-class female employers. But privilege, we well know, can lodge almost anywhere, and since it works best when it is least obvious, it is not surprising that we should find it reflected in what appear to be axioms of her inquiry into the condition of "women."

Insofar as any of us agree to points 1–3 (and the agreement is likely to be implicit, not explicit), we are not likely to give much weight to those strands in de Beauvoir's thought that might give us reason to question their status. For example, we aren't likely to be struck by the fact that if, as de Beauvoir claims, one of the reasons women don't seem to form a natural political class is that we are found in every population, then, contra 1, it is very odd to contrast women with Blacks, Jews, the poor. Nor are we likely to notice the force of de Beauvoir's saying that we ought always to ask about the race and class of any men and women we are talking about, since claims about sexual hierarchy hold only when race and class are kept constant: if this is so, the sexism women are subject to will vary in accordance with their race and class privilege. But in that case, contra 2, there is no simple form of sexism the same for all women as women. Thus even if, as condition 3 claims, sexism is easier to track in the case of women not otherwise subject to oppression, it doesn't mean the sexism one finds is just like the sexism one would find in the case of women who are subject to other forms of oppression. We have to be very careful: the oppression white middle-class women are subject to is not the oppression women face "as women" but the oppression white middle-class women face. Their race and class are not irrelevant to the oppression they face even though they are not oppressed on account of their race and class.

V

We have been trying to see what might explain the discrepancy between the implicit complexity of de Beauvoir's assessment of the lives of women and the oversimplification in her explicit rendering of "woman's situation" and of gender relations. We've suggested that while it is true that such oversimplification expresses the privileged tunnel vision of someone of de Beauvoir's own race and class, we must also take the task of unmasking privilege seriously by trying to locate the places it finds a home, rather than simply noting that it must be at work. Since de Beauvoir herself was highly attuned to and bothered by the presence of such privilege, we honor her work by asking how such privilege functions in her own thinking.

What we've begun to see is that taking the lives of white middle-class women to be paradigmatic for the situation of "woman" is a logical conclusion from several apparently straightforward facts that de Beauvoir seems to accept about how to investigate gender and how to examine sexism. Because they have the status of truisms, they are unlikely to be shaken by other parts of her account, parts that might lead to doubts about the soundness of these truisms but themselves without axiomatic strength. In short, de Beauvoir ends up giving more weight to those parts of her account that draw attention to the condition of "women in general" than to those that allude to differences among women. As we've seen, she attaches great importance to being able to give an account of the condition of "women in general" and so perhaps regards attention to differences among women to be an unnecessary distraction. Her analysis itself reminds us that what she calls the condition of "women in general" isn't that at all, but it is worth looking again briefly at why she was so eager to provide a general account.

There's no doubt that the case de Beauvoir makes about "woman" would be less compelling, at least to many of her readers, if she were to wonder aloud whether there is any difficulty posed for her account by the fact that there are women among the populations she contrasts to "woman"; if she were to say, "Notice, by the way, that the account I give of relations between middle-class men and women is not the same one I give of relations between working-class men and women"; if she did not hide away on page 605 of a 689-page book the reminder that any time we speak of male-female relations we must make sure that the men and women are of the same race and class.[17]

Such explicit musings would produce a less forceful argument for anyone who thinks that if we cannot talk about "woman" or about "women in general," then no case can be made about the injustice done to women, no strategy devised for the liberation of women. According to this line of thinking, a coherent feminist political analysis and agenda requires that we be able to talk about the history of the treatment of all women, as women. In order to be taken seriously, feminists have to make a case that they are speaking about more than a small group of people and that those referred to have been mistreated. So, for example, a group of white middle-class women would not claim that harm has come to them for being white or middle-class, but for being women. And they might well believe that not only would it be irrelevant to refer to being white and middle-class, but it would suggest that the group is not as representative as it otherwise would appear. So were de Beauvoir to make more explicit than she does who "woman" refers to in her analysis, she would defuse its potential impact: the case would not be that of "woman" but of particular women.

Furthermore, as we've seen, de Beauvoir thinks women lack a "sense of the universal" (580). This has been a crucial part of their failure to resist the domination of men: not caring to notice the similarities in their experiences, each one given to "overestimat[ing] the value of her smile" because "no one has told her that all women smile." They fail to "sum . . . up in a valid conclusion" the many instances that ground claims about the conditions of "woman's" existence. Until women see beyond their own individual cases, they will not "succeed in building up a solid counteruniverse whence they can challenge the males" (581). De Beauvoir may well regard it as a kind of weakness on her part were she to resist generalizing from the case of a woman like herself.

But it is one thing to urge women to look beyond their own cases; it is quite another to assume that if one does one will find a common condition or a common hope shared by all women. Perhaps there is a common condition or hope,[18] but de Beauvoir's own work speaks against it. Given her insistence on the different social and economic positions occupied by women, she suggests, not that similarities among women's various conditions are there to be found, but rather that they need to be created. Indeed de Beauvoir implies, as we've seen, that class and race privileges are perceived by some women to be so important that they will be extremely reluctant to work for economic and political changes that would dissolve the difference between the conditions of their own lives and the conditions of the lives of those women without such privileges. Since de Beauvoir cites the diversity of women across race and class lines as a large part of the reason for their not having a shared consciousness or joint political projects, she could not assume that what women would find if they looked at each other would be something that was true about all of them.

Examining the tensions in de Beauvoir's work ought to make us wonder whether the same tensions aren't going to be present in any version of feminism: Is there any way of taking differences among women seriously without at the same time undermining the kind of case about women as women that feminism seems to require? Is there any way to make a case about "women in general" that doesn't in fact represent the situation of one group of women only?

These aren't new kinds of questions for feminism. We've asked ones similar to them again and again about theories of "human nature": Can we take seriously differences among men and women and still come up with a tidy theory about humans "as humans"? Is there any account of "human nature" that, in the guise of a universal account, doesn't end up conflating the situation of one group of humans with the situation of all?

In chapter 7 we will consider the implications of the existence of differences among women for the idea that we can talk about "women in general." For the moment we might note that "the 1-2-3 punch" represents a version of the idea that we can, indeed that feminism must, talk about gender in isolation from race and class. Certainly on the face of it, it seems impossible to make any case about the significance of gender for women unless we can talk about gender in isolation from race and class, that is, unless we can talk about the effect of gender on a woman, not the effect of some other fact about her. Is it possible to do that? We now turn to a prominent example from the feminist literature that promises both to focus on gender and gender relations in isolation from other aspects of identity and other forms of oppression and to suggest the ways in which sexism and those other forms of oppression are connected.

*see plurality stressed in the very structure of a theory, I know
to do lots of acrobatics—of the contortionist and the walk-on-
d—to have this theory speak to me without allowing the
....ory to distort me in my complexity.*

MARÍA LUGONES

Gender in the Context of Race and Class: Notes on Chodorow's "Reproduction of Mothering"

In the past three chapters we've explored ways in which it can be misleading to talk about gender as if it exists in isolation from other variables of
human identity such as race and class. Simultaneously, we have examined
ways in which gender issues are not simply parallel to but intertwined
with race and class issues. For example, we have seen that we can't adequately describe Plato's proposal for a kind of "equality" between men
and women without noting that he is referring to a very small group of
men and women and that he thinks of females who would be philosopher-
rulers as different in kind from other females. Aristotle doesn't even think
of female slaves as "women," and his claims about the superiority of
"men" to "women" don't apply to relations between male and female
slaves. In many parts of her work, Simone de Beauvoir treats both the
meaning and the consequences of being a "woman" as being dependent
upon one's race, class, and nationality.

It is theoretically significant for any feminist analysis of gender and of
sexism if statements that appear to be true about "men and women"
clearly aren't true when we specify that we are talking about men and
women of different classes or races. What Plato says about the relation
between male philosopher-rulers and female philosopher-rulers doesn't
apply to the relation between male philosopher-rulers and females who
are part of the "masses." What Aristotle says about the natural superiority of free men to free women doesn't apply to slave men and free
women. De Beauvoir cautions (and then forgets) that the kind of sexual

80

privilege she is talking about only applies when the race and class of the men and women in question is the same.[1] If all women had the same gender—if what it meant to be a "woman" was the same for all of them no matter what their race or class or nationality—and if all women were subject to sexism in the same way, this wouldn't happen. If gender identity were isolatable from class and race identity, if sexism were isolatable from classism and racism, we could talk about relations between men and women and never have to worry about whether their race or class were the same or different. We could make believe that we could get an accurate account of what Plato and Aristotle and de Beauvoir said about relations between men and women without making any reference to whether the men and women in question were philosopher-rulers, guardians, artisans, or slaves, poor, Black, or Jewish. If gender were isolatable from other aspects of identity, if sexism were isolatable from other forms of oppression, then what would be true about the relation between any man and woman would be true about the relation between any other man and any other woman.

Much of feminist theory has proceeded on the assumption that gender is indeed a variable of human identity independent of other variables such as race and class, that whether one is a woman is unaffected by what class or race one is.[2] Feminists have also assumed that sexism is distinctly different from racism and classism, that whether and how one is subject to sexism is unaffected by whether and how one is subject to racism or classism.

The work of Nancy Chodorow has seemed to provide feminist theory with a strong foundation for these arguments. It has explicitly and implicitly been used to justify the assumption that there is nothing problematic about trying to examine gender independently of other variables such as race, class, and ethnicity. Though Chodorow's writings have received sometimes scathing criticism from feminists, more often they have been seen by feminist scholars in many different disciplines as providing a particularly rich understanding of gender.[3] Indeed, Chodorow offers what appears to be a very promising account of the relations between gender identity and other important aspects of identity such as race and class. For while she treats gender as separable from race and class, she goes on to suggest ways in which the sexist oppression intimately connected to gender differences is related to racism and classism.

I hope to show that while Chodorow's work is very compelling, it ought to be highly problematic for any version of feminism that demands more than lip service to the significance of race and class, racism and classism, in the lives of the women on whom Chodorow focuses. The problem, as I see it, is not that feminists have taken Chodorow seriously, but that we have not taken her seriously enough. Her account points to a more complicated understanding of gender and the process of becoming gendered than she herself develops. She tells us to look at the social context of mothering in order to understand the effect of mothering on the acquisition of gender identity in children; but if we follow her advice, rather than her own practice, we are led to see that gender identity is not neatly separable from other aspects of identity such as race and class. They couldn't be if, as Chodorow insists, the acquisition of gender occurs in and helps perpetuate the "hierarchical and differentiated social worlds" we inhabit.

I

According to *The Reproduction of Mothering*, there are systematic differences between girls and boys, between women and men, that are biological; but there also are systematic differences in behavior and in what some psychologists refer to as "intrapsychic structures."[4] The latter differences cannot be accounted for by the biological differences. But neither can they be explained by reference to learning to behave in certain ways, whether by exposure to role models, ideological messages, or coercion. Neither account enables us to understand the psychological investment girls and boys come to have in becoming women and men and the psychological investment women and men have in reproducing girls and boys. In particular, we have to understand the different "relational capacities" and "senses of self" in girls and boys, women and men. These differences are produced by the sexual division of labor in which women, and not men, mother; and that division of labor is in turn reproduced by these differences. The sexual division of labor can reproduce itself because through it are produced women and men who "develop personalities which tend to guarantee that they will get gratification or satisfaction from those activities which are necessary to the reproduction" of the sexual division of labor (173).

In short, we can't adequately describe gender differences without focusing on the different senses of self women and men have that are linked to their thinking or not thinking of themselves in ways that prepare them for mothering; at the same time, neither can we explain how these gender differences come about without focusing on the fact that it is women and not men who mother. For it is the mothering of girls and boys that women do that explains why girls and boys develop different relational capacities and different senses of self—why girls in turn go on to mother and boys not only do not mother but demean mothers and mothering.

Our becoming girl-gendered or boy-gendered, then, is a process mediated by our mothers:

An account of the early mother-infant relationship in contemporary Western society reveals the overwhelming importance of the mother in everyone's psychological development, in their sense of self, and in their basic relational stance. It reveals that becoming a person [girl or boy] is the same thing as becoming a person in relationship and in social context. (76)

But mothering itself is a mediated activity. "Women's mothering does not exist in isolation" (32). It is an intricate part of the sexual division of labor; it is part of a "social organization" that "includes male dominance, a particular family system, and women's dependence on men's income" (21). It is "informed by [the woman's] relationship to her husband, her experience of financial dependence, her expectations of marital inequality, and her expectations about gender roles" (86).

Chodorow believes that "all societies are constituted around a structural split . . . between the private, domestic world of women and the public, social world of men" (174). There is a division of labor between the public, "nonrelational" sphere (179), where men have their primary location, and a private, "relational" sphere, where women have their "primary social and economic location" (11, 13). Mothering in such a context is a process geared to producing girls who will be fit denizens of the private sphere and boys who will participate in the public world—the "capitalist world of work" in Western society (180–81). How does this happen?

In answering this, Chodorow is trying to carry out the promise contained in the subtitle of the book: "psychoanalysis and the sociology of gender." Her focus on the social context of gender and mothering makes use of Freud and object-relation theorists. Briefly, mothers see their daughters as "more like and continuous with" themselves than their sons are (166). Girls are not called upon to individuate themselves, to see themselves as distinct from their mothers, as early, as firmly, or as finally as boys are. A girl's sense of self is not as threatened by her ties to her mother as a boy's is; the resolution of his oedipal stage means he must give up his mother in a way his sister does not have to. At the same time, because a girl learns what it is to be a woman by identifying with her mother (175), and because the asymmetrical organization of parenting means the mother is present, this process of identification takes place in the context of a personal relationship. However, part of the asymmetrical organization of parenting is that the boy's father is not present in the way the mother is; learning what it is to be masculine hence happens, not in the context of a personal relationship, but "through identification with cultural images of masculinity and men chosen as masculine models" (176). Because of the context in which mothering takes place, mothers have different kinds of relationships with their daughters than they do with their sons. And these different kinds of relationships produce different psychic configurations in girls and boys—configurations that prepare the growing girls and boys to come to find satisfaction in the very same division of labor in the context of which mothering occurs.

According to Chodorow, then, the most significant difference between girls and boys, women and men, is in terms of the degree to which they see themselves as related to and connected with others. "The basic feminine sense of self is connected to the world, the basic masculine sense of self is separate" (169). This is the psychological counterpart of the roles women and men are expected to play: "Women in our society are primarily defined as wives and mothers, thus in particularistic relation to someone else, whereas men are defined primarily in universalistic occupational terms" (178). As long as it is only women who mother, in the social context in which they do, these differences in women and men will continue to exist. If we want to change or to put an end to such differences, the institution of mothering has to change.

Chodorow says in a later article in the feminist journal *Signs* that any feminist ought to want to eliminate those kinds of differences between men and women, because "a treating of women as others, or objects, rather than subjects, or selves" not only adversely affects women but "extends to our culture as a whole."

The boy comes to define his self more in opposition than through a sense of his wholeness or continuity. He becomes the self and experiences his mother as the other. The process also extends to his trying to dominate the other in order to ensure his sense of self. Such domination begins with mother as the object, extends to women, and is then generalized to include the experience of all others as objects rather than subjects. This stance, in which people are treated and experienced as things, becomes basic to male Western culture.[5]

Here Chodorow elaborates on a quotation from Lévi-Strauss she placed at the beginning of her 1979 article, "Gender, Relation, and Difference in Psychoanalytic Perspective":

I would go so far as to say that even before slavery or class domination existed, men built an approach to women that would serve one day to introduce differences among us all.[6]

Though Chodorow does not take it upon herself to explain or defend these points in any more detail, it seems fairly clear that she takes sexism to be independent of racism and classism but at the same time to be both the model for them (the domination of male over female is adapted for the purposes of other forms of domination) and the cause of them (if men weren't so insecure about their sense of self vis-à-vis their mothers, they wouldn't need to define anyone else as Other).

II

As mentioned earlier, Chodorow's feminist critics have not been shy about pointing to what they take to be particularly vulnerable aspects of her account of gender acquisition: her reliance on some of the more troubling aspects of Freud, her uncritical use of the distinction between "public" and "private" spheres, her assumption of women's heterosexuality.[7] Though I share her critics' concerns, I want to focus on aspects of her work that have not received sufficient attention. But first I shall describe what I take to be some of the initially more helpful directions of Chodorow's work and some of the questions she leaves unanswered.

Perhaps the most politically significant part of Chodorow's account is her reminder that mothering occurs in a particular social context. It is informed, she notes, by the mother's relation to her husband, her economic dependence on him, her experience of male dominance. But why does Chodorow focus on only these elements of the larger social context? After all, most societies—including that of contemporary North America, about which she is most concerned—are also characterized by other forms of dominance, other sorts of hierarchies. Women mother in societies that may be racist and classist as well as sexist and heterosexist. Are we to believe that a woman's mothering is informed only by her relation to a husband or male lover and her experience of living in a male-dominated society, but not by her relation to people of other classes and races and her experience of living in a society in which there are race and class hierarchies? Chodorow wants us to think about the "specific implications of the actual social context in which the child learns" (47). But if I do that, then it does not seem accurate to describe what my mother nurtured in me, and what I learned, as being simply a "girl." I was learning to be a white, middle-class Christian and "American" girl. Chodorow rails against the view that "feminine biology shapes psychic life without mediation of culture" (149). But does only one part of the culture mediate mothering?

"Families," Chodorow says, "create children gendered, heterosexual, and ready to marry" (199)—or anyway they are supposed to. But do families have no racial or class or ethnic identity? Do they create children prepared to marry anyone, no matter the person's race, class, ethnicity, religion? Is the creation of children in the ways Chodorow lists the only thing families are supposed to do? As Chodorow herself so usefully points out, the socialization that must take place in order for the society to continue to reproduce itself "must lead to the assimilation and internal organization of generalized capacities for participation in a hierarchical and differentiated social world" (32). Families are organized so as to produce new beings who will "get gratification or satisfaction from those activities which are necessary to the reproduction of the larger social structure" (36–37). But is this true for only certain elements of that larger social structure? If children are said to be prepared to participate in a sexually unequal society (173), why aren't they also said to be prepared to participate in a society where there are racial, class, and other forms of inequality? [8]

As we've seen, Chodorow certainly is not unaware of forms of domination other than sexism, and undoubtedly she would acknowledge that the raising of children contributes in some ways (and presumably in different ways in different families) to the perpetuation of racism, classism, and other forms of oppression. She probably would respond to the questions above by saying that the production of gender identity in families is separate from, even if at some point in tandem with, the production of other aspects of identity such as race or ethnicity or class. But let us look in more detail at what she means by "gender" and see whether what she tells us about gender indeed means that it can or must be specified independently of elements of identity such as race and class.

Chodorow refers to a "core gender identity" that, along with a sense of self, is established in the first two years. This core gender identity is a "cognitive sense" of oneself as male or female.[9] As we saw above, according to Chodorow the distinction between a "basic feminine sense of self" and a "basic masculine sense of self" involves seeing oneself as connected to or seeing oneself as separate from the world (169). But she also describes gender in more specific terms:

I am using *gender* here to stand for the mother's particular psychic structure and relational sense, for her (probable) heterosexuality, and for her conscious and unconscious acceptance of the ideology, meanings, and expectations that go into being a gendered member of our society and understanding what gender means. (98)

Part of gender ideology is that men are superior to women, for male superiority is built "into the definition of masculinity itself" (185). Gendered senses of self have to be politically loaded, since they prepare girls and boys to enter a world in which there is a sexual division of labor that is itself politically loaded: male domination couldn't continue, Chodorow reasons, unless gender differentiation included gender hierarchy. Whether or not Chodorow thinks that the engendering of baby humans *causes* sexual domination, she clearly thinks that coming to be and think of oneself as masculine or feminine involves assuming one's place (and having a sense of one's place) in a world in which masculine beings dominate feminine ones.[10] Mothering in a sexist context reproduces sexism insofar as it creates young humans well adapted psychologically to take their place in a sexist world.

Chodorow begins her book with the claim that "women's mothering is one of the few universal and enduring elements of the sexual division of labor" (3). She means by this that no matter how else cultures and subcultures differ with respect to the division of labor along sexual lines, the work of mothering is always done by women. At the same time Chodorow says that mothering "is not an unchanging transcultural universal" (32). By this she seems to mean that as the world into which children enter changes over time, so the responsibilities of women preparing children for entry into the world change. For example, "the development of industrial capitalism in the West entailed that women's role in the family become increasingly concerned with personal relations and psychological stability" (32). Together these two claims suggest that while it is women who everywhere mother—that is, who not only feed and clean infants but provide them with "affective bonds and a diffuse, multifaceted, ongoing personal relationship" (33)—the kind of development they unconsciously and consciously encourage in their children will depend on the particular requirements of the world in which they live and for which they must prepare the children. To learn one's gender identity is among other things to learn what work one is supposed to do and also to want to do that work (or at least not *not* want to because it isn't the kind of work one is supposed to do).

There are, then, according to Chodorow two universals: a sexual division of labor and, within that division, the assignment of mothering to women. Two things are not universal: the particular tasks (other than mothering) that are assigned along sexual lines and the content of mothering. Indeed, Chodorow says that class differences within a society—below she is speaking of modern capitalist societies—are reflected in "parental child-rearing values":

Working-class parents are more likely to value obedience, conformity to external authority, neatness, and other "behavioral" characteristics in their children; middle-class parents emphasize more "internal" and interpersonal characteristics like responsibility, curiosity, self-motivation, self-control, and consideration. (176)

87

Whether or not Chodorow's descriptions of class differences are accurate, it is important to note that she does think class may make an important difference to mothering. "We know almost nothing" about effects of class differences on mothering, she cautions, and admits that "all claims about gender differences gloss over important differences within genders and similarities between genders" (215). Moreover, in a later response to critics, she says that among the things she would stress more than she did in her book is

how women's mothering and early infantile development is tied to the treatment of people as things and rigid self-other distinctions that characterize our culture and thought. That is, I would examine the link between what seems exclusively gender related and the construction of other aspects of society, politics and culture [and also would encourage study of] class and ethnic differences, differences in family and household structure, differences in sexual orientation of parents, and historical and cross-cultural variations in these relationships.[11]

From this further foray into Chodorow's account of gender, several things emerge: that according to her analysis, sexual hierarchy is built into definitions of masculine and feminine, and that we know little about the effect of class differences on the mothering practices that reproduce gender identities. But if she says these things about gender, it makes it harder rather than easier to show that gender is isolatable from other elements of identity.

First of all, what kind of difference could the study of class and ethnic differences make to the study of gender identity and the role of mothering in its production and reproduction? Unless Chodorow thinks they might make a significant difference, she presumably will not think it important to investigate any further. Her own theory reveals something of her answer to this question. One of the major functions of families, she told us, is to produce beings who will "get gratification or satisfaction from those activities which are necessary to the reproduction of the larger social structure" (36–37). But investigation of ethnicity and class and race within that social structure might make us consider the possibility that what one learns when one learns one's gender identity is the gender identity appropriate to one's ethnic, class, national, and racial identity. Understanding gender, Chodorow told us, includes understanding "the ideology, meanings, and expectations that go into being a gendered member of our society" (98). But if, for example, masculine identity is rich enough to include the notion of male superiority, as Chodorow says it is (185), then we are not barred from asking whether it doesn't also include notions of class or race superiority. In a racist society such as the United

States, is the ideological content of masculinity the idea that any man is superior to any woman?

At this point we may usefully recall the scope of Aristotle's claim about the natural superiority of men to women: he clearly did not think this applied in the case of slave men and slave women nor in the case of slave men and free women. The ideology of masculinity in the United States hardly includes the idea that Black men are superior to white women. So if gender is supposed to include ideology, and if learning one's gender identity prepares one for what is expected of a person gendered in the way one is, then we can't describe masculinity as including simply the notion that men are superior to women. If a poor Black boy in the United States thinks that being "masculine" entitles him to dominate white women, since he's male and they are female, he's not been prepared well for the society into which he's been born (and as we shall discuss below, it is highly unlikely that his mother would be unaware of this). This is not to say that he may not wish to dominate white women (along with Black women), but rather to remind us that if Emmet Till had been white, he wouldn't have been murdered by white men for talking to a white woman, nor would his murderers have been acquitted.[12]

III

An especially interesting feature of Chodorow's account is that on the one hand, she seems to want to insist that gender is isolatable from race and class, and sexism from racism and classism; but on the other, she thinks there are significant connections between sexism and other forms of domination. Indeed, as we have seen, on more than one occasion she expresses the conviction that other forms of domination are in some sense rooted in the sexism that mothering reproduces.[13]

Sandra Harding has tried to spell out in more detail the connection sketched out in Chodorow's work between men's psychological investment in dominating women and the existence of racism and classism:

Personality differences created by the material conditions of infant care . . . create patterns of dominating social relations which are more general than class oppression and gender oppression, as well as adult men's pyschological investments in not giving up their controlling positions in *either* patriarchy or capitalism (not to mention their dominating roles in race relations and the selective institutionalization of heterosexism).

. . . .

The vast panorama of the history of race relations becomes one more male drama in which the more powerful group of men works out its infantile project of dominating the other. Race relations are fundamentally social relations between men, where women find themselves supporting characters or, occasionally, thrust forward to leading roles in a script they have not written and can not direct.[14]

The argument about the relation between sexism and other forms of oppression would thus seem to go something like this: In all invidious hierarchies, those in the more powerful position regard those in the less powerful position as Other, as object, as thing. The sexist way men regard women as Other is the model for the racist or the classist way these men regard other people. That is, the gender distinctions are translated into invidious race and class distinctions—not just logically, but developmentally as well: sexist parenting relations reproduce sexist gender distinctions between men and women that in turn lead to racist and classist distinctions between groups of people.

This is a powerful account of the relation between sexism and other forms of oppression. But it is riddled with difficulties. I want first to point out some of those difficulties and then to mark the possible significance of our readiness to accept such a problematic account of the relations among forms of oppression.

First of all, there is enormous ambiguity about just what is meant by gender, class, and race oppression—quite crudely, about who is oppressing whom. Feminists like Chodorow and Harding argue in the following way:

1. Men come to take themselves to be superior to women.[15]
2. Thus men come to take themselves to be superior to everyone else.

But because we are talking in the second of these statements about superiority on racial grounds (for example), we can express it more accurately thus:

3. Men of one race take themselves to be superior to men (and presumably to women) of another race.

But if that's the case, then 1 and 3 are really about two different groups of people: statement 1 applies to all men, statement 3 only to some men—presumably a subset of the first group. Neither Chodorow nor Harding, I think, would want to say that statement 1 is true only about a subset of all men.[16] And if racism and classism are said to grow out of sexism, then statement 2 can't be true of all men, since we can't portray the same group of people as both perpetrators and victims of either racism or classism any more than we can portray the same group of people as both perpetrators and victims of sexism. Men are the perpetrators, women the victims, of sexism. Even if Chodorow or those following her would modify this to indicate that men are harmed by sexism and that women in some way collaborate in it, they nevertheless would insist that sexism is an asymmetrical relation insofar as it involves the domination of women by men. Similarly (and so with similar qualifications) one group of men are the perpetrators, another the victims, of classism or racism (we shall return to the question of women's roles below). Thus statement 1 is about one group of men, all men, and 3 is about another, a subset of all men. But is the kind of superiority the same in both cases? That is, is the inferiority of women to men just like the inferiority of some men to others?

The grounds of superiority in the two cases must be different, for no one can hold that some men are inferior to other men in just the same way and for just the same reason that women are inferior to men. Such a position would be self-contradictory, for this amounts to maintaining both that some men are inferior to other men in the way women are inferior to men and that all men are superior to women.

So more accurately put, the relation between sexism and other oppressions must go something like this:

4. All men take themselves to be superior, as men, to all women, as women.
5. Men of one race (e.g., whites) take themselves to be superior to men (and women) of another race (e.g., Blacks); in short, whites as whites take themselves to be superior to Blacks as Blacks.

That is, the superiority learned in the acquisition of gender identity is that of male to female, but this is somehow generalized to the superiority of one race to another. This avoids the problem of incoherence, since it certainly seems logically possible to hold both that all men are superior as men to all women and that some men are superior to other men (and women), not as men, but as members of a particular race. But this account has its own insurmountable problems.

For one thing, it doesn't explain how hierarchy based on one element of human identity is translated into hierarchy based on another: how are sexual differences translated into racial ones? The answer to this is further complicated by the fact that the racial differences cited as the grounds for the superiority of one group of men over another group of men are at the same time grounds on which some women are more like some men than the two groups of men are alike. The racial grounds on which some men make certain men Other simultaneously make some women not so Other after all. How can the sexual discrimination be translated into the racial oppression when sexual differences crucially separate men and women while racial differences don't? Rather than being supported by sexism,

racism seems to work against it—for if sexism insists on differences between men and women, racism requires that the similarity between men
and women of the same race be emphasized.

Moreover, the proposed account can't possibly cover all actual cases of
the relation between sexism and racism. For example, it was part of the
racist ideology of slavery in the United States that the blackness of the
Black man cancelled any idea that he as a man was superior to any woman
as a woman. It is part of racist ideology that Black men are superior neither to white women nor to Black women. How, then, could this be a
generalization from the idea that all men are superior to all women? (It
might be useful to note at this point that Aristotle's normative notion of
"man" enabled him to hold that all "men" are superior to all "women"
even though not all males are superior to all females.)

The second difficulty with Chodorow's account of the relation between
sexism and other forms of oppression is its use to explain how the engendering of infants leads to adult psychological investment in maintaining
domination on the basis of race and class. If the account is supposed to
explain the "relational stance" of those who become the perpetrators of
racism and classism, then it doesn't describe the psychological development of all men, for it ignores the development of the victims of those
oppressions. The quote from Harding suggests that both victims and perpetrators of racism (and by implication classism) are equally desirous of
dominating and that the only difference between them is that one manages to dominate; it implies that the psychological stance from which one
desires to dominate the other is just the same as the psychological stance
from which one desires to resist domination. This then becomes an account of racism that makes the particular race of any group irrelevant—it
doesn't really matter who dominates whom—and implicitly asserts that if
the victims of racism had their way they would be the perpetrators.[17]

Perhaps the idea is that what everybody—male, female, Black, white,
rich, poor—acquires through asymmetrical parenting arrangements is a
readiness to treat everyone else as subordinate Other; this prepares them
to live as adults in a world in which everyone treats everyone else as a
subordinate Other, or would if they could. What everybody learns is a
general pattern of dominant/subordinate relations, which enables them to
plug into specific patterns of such relations as articulated, for example, in
racist white/Black relations in the United States.

But there are several problems with this elaboration upon Chodorow's
account. What she actually says is that little boys take up "a treating of
women as others, or objects" and that this is then generalized to other
people.[18] She doesn't say that everybody does this—in particular, since

she is distinguishing little boys from little girls, she surely isn't attributing such attitudes to little girls. There is no doubt that girls can come to have such attitudes, but Chodorow doesn't explain how they do. And if she were to say that women are like men in this way, then just as Harding's argument suggests that Blacks might just as well have come to dominate whites, so it would also have to be said that women might just as well have come to dominate men. That is, if on the elaboration of Chodorow's views it doesn't really matter who has actually come to dominate whom racially, then it can't really matter who has in fact come to dominate whom sexually. Everybody is psychologically prepared to treat everybody else as an Other, and it is simply a historical accident that men happen to dominate women, whites happen to dominate Blacks.

A third difficulty with the account: it very neatly leaves out of serious consideration the racism and classism of women. If it is the sexism that little boys learn that explains the existence of racism and classism, then there is no room at all to talk about the racism and classism of some women, for they were never little boys. That is, Chodorow makes it look as if it is only the racism and classism of men (certain men) that needs accounting for. If it is only the perpetrators of sexism who develop into racists, then the victims of sexism can't develop into racists—not even of the sideline variety Harding describes.

But this we know to be false. The idea that race relations are really men's business and that women are only supporting characters ignores huge chunks of history and makes it look as if no women ever really think of the men and women of a class or race that is "beneath" theirs as Other. The relation proposed by Chodorow ignores the difference in status between women that it itself implies (i.e., it is not simply men who are subject to racism and classism). This is not to say that women have had just the same role in racism and classism that men have; the extent of women's responsibility, not to mention examination of the criteria for responsibility, need exploration by feminists.[19] But it seems to me that we ought to be not only puzzled but alarmed by any feminist account of racism and classism that takes the racism and classism of women to be of no particular theoretical concern. Any theory that posits sexism as the foundation for other forms of oppression thereby makes it highly unlikely that women will be seen as significant contributors to those other forms of oppression. For if women aren't responsible for sexism, how can any of us be responsible in any sense for the forms of oppression that are said to be rooted in sexism? If only masculine gender identity includes coming to regard other people as Other or "thing," women by definition aren't prepared psychologically to become racists or classists. How handy: I couldn't possibly be a racist or classist, since my psyche just didn't develop that way!

IV

Chodorow invites us to consider the difference class makes to parenting and suggests that the sexism built into the context of early psychological development has some role to play in the maintenance, perhaps even in the creation, of racial and class hierarchies. Her account thus raises some very crucial methodological questions for anyone who thinks that a complete feminist analysis of sexism ought to include at least some examination of the relation between sexism and other forms of oppression. The methodological questions have to do with where and how issues about race and racism, class and classism, enter into the analysis. As we have seen, Chodorow herself suggests at least two places they might intersect. Starting with her suggestions and thinking of other points of entry, we can generate a fairly long list of the ways we might begin to examine connections between issues of race and class and those of gender: [20]

1. Does race or class identity affect gender identity? For example, are there elements of race and class in notions of masculinity and femininity?

Isn't the idea of superiority built, as Chodorow affirms, into the notion of "masculinity" understood to apply only under certain conditions? Does the ideology packed into the notion of masculinity include the notion that any man is superior to any woman? Does the ideology packed into the notion of femininity include the notion that any woman is inferior to any man, that all women are inferior in just the same way to all men?

2. Does a child's sense of self include a conscious or unconscious sense of race or class? (This is closely connected to question 1.)

If we are looking for an account of psycho-social development that explains how children come to be psychologically and socially prepared for the positions set for them in a hierarchically ordered political and social and economic world, we might do well to ask whether children learn what it means to be men or women by learning what it is to be men or women of their race, class, ethnicity.

3. What are the hierarchies in the world into which children are born and socialized? Is sexual privilege or domination affected by the race and class of the men and women in question?

The world into which the children enter is one in which race and class identity cuts across gender identity (men can be Anglo- or Afro-American, women can be upper class or working class, and so on), and racism and classism cut across sexism (there are significant differences in the situations of highly educated well-to-do women with tenured jobs and poor women on welfare). It would be much easier to account for how children are prepared for entry into such a complex world if what they learned when they learned their gender identity was not simply that they were boys or girls but something more complicated—for example, that they were white male or female, Black male or female, and so forth.

4. What are the ways in which sexism might be related to other forms of oppression? For example, is sexism a support for or cause of racism or classism? Or is it in some sense more closely intertwined with them?

Perhaps we can begin to account for the reproduction of racism by taking our task to be not simply to explain how men have come to think of themselves as superior to women, but rather to explain how children learn that the superiority built into "masculine" is meant to be the prerogative of a certain group of men; and to explain how it is possible for a group of women thinking of themselves as inferior to "men" to also think of themselves as superior to some men and some women.

V

Chodorow's work (and the work she draws on) suggests some obstacles to the kind of inquiry I am proposing, for it seems to be a fairly universal phenomenon that people do not become conscious of their racial, class, ethnic, religious, or national identity until long after they have a sense of their gender identity. How can their gender identity be intertwined with other aspects of their identity if they can be conscious of the former but not of the latter?

This question echoes Descartes's famous argument about the separation of self (that is, he says, of mind) from body. In the *Meditations*, Descartes insisted that while he had grounds for doubting whether he had a body (since he had reasons for doubting the evidence of his senses), he knew for certain that he existed. The "I" that I know to exist cannot be a body, for how could the "I" that I know to exist be a body if I can doubt that there is a body but not doubt that this "I" exists?

How can gender identity have anything to do with racial or class identity, if a person can have a clear sense of their gender identity while simultaneously having no particular awareness of their racial or class identity?

The response that has often been made to Descartes goes something like this: It doesn't necessarily follow that because you can doubt whether x exists, while being certain that y exists, x is not the same as y. I can doubt or feel that it is impossible to know whether Marian Evans existed, while feeling certain that George Eliot existed, but this hardly shows that Marian Evans cannot be George Eliot.[21]

Similarly, it can hardly follow from the fact that I describe my gender identity as "woman" that there are neither racial nor class dimensions to my understanding of "woman"—anymore than if I described what I learned in college and graduate school simply as "philosophy" it would follow that there are no Western cultural dimensions to my understanding of philosophy. Just because some people don't think of themselves as having any class identity, it doesn't mean that they have none. Indeed, under certain circumstances, the very lack of awareness of elements of one's identity is a significant reflection of that identity. For example, my being and having a sense of myself as white in this society can be said to be reflected in the fact that it does *not* occur to me to note it, nor am I required by convention to note it: the conventions about self-description allow me to refer to myself simply as "woman." But if I were a Black woman, people would think I was withholding important information if I did not qualify "woman" with "Black." One therefore cannot argue, from the fact that someone is conscious of her gender identity but not conscious of her racial identity, that her gender identity has nothing to do with her racial identity.

But perhaps Chodorow's point is that gender identity is so basic that it is not really conscious; that the most significant effects of girls' and boys' relationships to their mothers (and fathers) occur long before children are conscious of either their gender identity or their race or class identity. What we develop at such an early stage is a general relational stance: girls see themselves in relation to their mothers and as connected to the world; boys see themselves as separate from and in opposition to their mothers and as separate from the world. And this supposedly is true no matter the race or class of the mother and children.

However, there are at least two major problems with this representation of Chodorow's views about gender identity. First of all, as noted several times above, Chodorow describes masculine gender identity as including the belief in male superiority (185). That is a fairly sophisticated notion to be packed into a preconscious sense of oneself. Second, Chodorow needs a fairly rich picture of gender identity in order for her claims about the relation between gender identity and the readiness to occupy one's appropriate place in the world to make sense. We live in a world in which gender differentiation is thoroughly intertwined with gender hierarchy, and one can't learn the one without learning the other (even if there might be some society, in the past or in the future or even right now, in which differences between genders did not have built into them the notion that one gender is better than the other).[22] Learning gender identity would not be the important thing Chodorow believes it to be unless learning it explained why men and women are so well prepared for living in and reproducing a hierarchical social world. Chodorow can't have it both ways. She can't have a notion of gender identity that is devoid of significant conscious content and also use that notion to explain what she thinks it explains: hence her insistence that the sense of masculinity that boys acquire includes not simply the general notion of being separate from women but the notion of being superior to them. But—to repeat a point made several times above—if what children learn in acquiring gender identity is rich enough to explain how they are so psychically ready to assume their place in a hierarchical world, how can it not include an understanding of gender identity appropriate for one's race, class, ethnic group? For I learn that my place in the established hierarchies of the social world is not determined simply by whether I am male or female but also by whether I am white or Black, rich or poor. In the society in which my mother and then I grew up, the differences between white and Black, middle and working class, Christian and Jew, were no less differences than the one between girl and boy.

VI

If we take seriously Chodorow's insistence on the social context in which mothering and the acquisition of gender takes place, we might then take note of concrete examples of "senses of self" in specific social contexts. Because mothering may be informed by a woman's knowledge of more than one form of dominance, the development of gender occurs in a context in which one learns to be a very particular girl or boy, and not just simply a girl or boy. If we look at biographical and autobiographical literature by and about women of various races and classes, we get a much more complicated picture than Chodorow's account gives us of the world in which mothers mother. It is indeed a "hierarchical and differentiated social world"—as Chodorow says—but differentiated and ranked not only along gender lines. For example, Mary Burgher has described how,

in her autobiography or in her daughter's, the Black mother's knowledge and endurance of America's racial hostility and violence are envisioned as strengthening and motivating tools with which she prepares others of her race for self-sufficient and productive lives.[23]

How do some women of color in the United States take to the suggestion that awareness of race and racism was absent from, or anyway not an important consideration in, their mothers' or their own minds as children, or that the learning of gender identity was separable from the learning of race identity? Here's Nikki Giovanni:

It's great when you near your quarter-century mark and someone says, "I want an experience on how you came to grips with being colored." The most logical answer is, "I came to grips with Blackdom when I grabbed my mama"—but I'm told on [TV] that we don't necessarily know our mothers are colored, and you can win a great big medal if you say it loud.[24]

And Barbara Cameron:

One of the very first words I learned in my Lakota language was *wasicu* which designates white people. . . . During my childhood . . . my mother . . . explained the realities of being an Indian in South Dakota.[25]

None of this is to say that mothers are never ambivalent about the racial or ethnic identity of their children, only that they are keenly aware of it. Cherríe Moraga has described the role of her mother in her learning what it meant to be a "fair-skinned" Chicana:

Everything about my upbringing . . . attempted to bleach me of what color I did have. . . . To [my mother], on a basic economic level, being Chicana meant being "less." It was through my mother's desire to protect her children from poverty and illiteracy that we became "anglocized"; the more effectively we could pass in the white world, the better guaranteed our future.[26]

Work done in the social sciences also reveals how Black women's or Chicanas' raising of their children is informed by a kind of awareness of and wariness about the world that goes beyond an awareness of "male dominance" or "gender role expectations." As Gloria Joseph has pointed out, a theory about relationships between mothers and children could hardly be complete "without a consideration of racial relations and racism."[27] In concrete terms, such considerations remind us that

the Black mother has a more ominous message for her child and feels more urgently the need to get the message across. The child must know that the white world is dangerous and that if he does not understand its rules it may kill him.[28]

Insofar as a Black mother's mothering is informed by and takes place in a social context in which there is racism, it cannot be said that she is preparing her male child to assume his appointed superior place among the "men," as Chodorow argues. In fact she is preparing him "for his subordinate place in the world"[29]—or are we to assume that his maleness will be recognized by his mother, his father, his sister, himself, and everyone else, as something separable from his Blackness?

Dorcas Bowles has addressed head on the question of the conditions under which a Black female's sense of self (and indirectly a Black male's sense of self) develops.[30] Her work makes us think about the ways in which Black mothering is different from white mothering in terms of the knowledge mothers have about how their children will be greeted by a racist society. This knowledge of difference, and this difference in knowledge, may be connected with differences in what a mother's love or nurturing means. Chodorow tends to write as if the kind of care mothers provide is everywhere the same—despite her acknowledgment of the likelihood of cultural differences on this score. There is indeed no reason to presuppose that what counts as "mother's love" will not vary from culture to culture, from subgroup to subgroup.[31] Daryl Dance recounts a story by John Williams about the confusion two Black children feel about their mother's treatment of them. On the one hand, they remember that treatment with considerable hostility; on the other, they begin to wonder about how love might be expressed by a Black woman in a racist society:

Love? What is that? Giving love to children was a luxury she couldn't afford and when she could, she had got out of the habit. I don't mean that she didn't have the feeling. Love? You know, that's whipping the crap out of your children so that they don't crack their heads against the walls that make up the labyrinth, and if they don't they might live and make out somehow. That's a kind of love, isn't it?[32]

But it is not just the mothering of Black women or other women of color that is informed by knowledge of racial distinctions and racial hierarchies. In *Killers of the Dream*, Lillian Smith describes the childhood lessons she learned from her Southern white parents, especially her mother:

I do not think our mothers were aware that they were teaching us lessons. It was as if they were revolving mirrors reflecting life outside the home, inside their memory, outside the home. . . . We learned from this preview of the world we were born into, what was expected of us as human creatures.

We were taught in this way to love God, to love our white skin, and to believe in the sanctity of both.[33]

Smith goes on to explain ways in which lessons about whiteness were intertwined with lessons about sex and one's body: They were told, she says,

Parts of your body are segregated areas which you must stay away from and keep others away from. These areas you touch only when necessary. In other words, you cannot associate freely with them any more than you can associate freely with colored children.[34]

At the same time, they were also taught that

though your body is a thing of shame and mystery, and curiosity about it is not good, your skin is your glory and the source of your strength and pride. It is white, [which] proves that you are better than all other people on this earth.[35]

Smith also explores the different kinds of relationships white male infants had with their own mothers and their Black nurses, and the likely effects of those relationships on their adolescent and adult sense of themselves as well as on their sense of white women and Black women. In light of these reflections, it seems positively bizarre for Chodorow to suggest that the only part of the social context that informs a woman's mothering is her sense of gender differences and gender inequalities. Chodorow does point—in a footnote—to the phenomenon of Black slave women's mothering of white slaveowners' children, but only to say that it seems to support her view that good mothering (such as the Black women were said to have provided for their owners' children) cannot be explained merely by reference to their coercion (33). She does not seize the opportunity to reflect on what this phenomenon might tell us about the social context of mothering.

Is the situation Smith describes too peculiar, too unusual, too atypical, to be used to challenge Chodorow's views? My mother was white, and a Christian, but she didn't tell me not to play with Black children or with Jewish children; indeed, both my parents stuck to what they perceived to be Christian principles of all people being one in the sight of God, even when other members of their church refused to. However, that doesn't mean my mother's mothering was not informed by awareness of her family as white and other families as Black, or her family as Christian (nay, Episcopalian) and others Jewish. My brothers and sisters and I may have learned different lessons about the difference between being white and being Black than Lillian Smith and her siblings did, but we surely did learn such lessons and they were inextricably tied to what we learned about being girls and boys—or if they weren't so tied, we have not learned from Chodorow's account on what grounds they can be excluded.

VII

Once we begin to look at the social context of mothering, and hence at the social context of gender, we have to think about what it means to say that women possess the same gender. For if it is true that gender identity is not separable from other aspects of identity, then, as the examples discussed above suggest, one's sense of oneself as a "woman" is not separable from one's sense of oneself as, say, Chicana, Black, or white; one is known as and knows oneself as Chicana, Black woman, or white woman. Or are we in our entirety divisible into parts? Can I point to the "woman" part, then to the "white" part? Would it be desirable to be able to do so? No doubt we have linguistic habits that suggest we are so divisible: We ask and are asked "to think about ourselves as women," or "to think about our experiences as women," or "to identity with other Blacks." We say things like, "As a woman, I think that . . . , while as a Jew, I think that . . ." We say things like, "Daily, we feel the pull and tug of having to choose between which parts have served to cloak us from the knowledge of ourselves."[36] We sometimes ask ourselves where and with whom we feel most ourselves—with other women, with other lesbians, other Blacks, other Hispanas, other Jews? What do such habits and grammatical possibilities tell us?

One thing they tell us is that there are a lot of different ways of sorting human beings. If we look at that variety, we of course see that sorting along one dimension cuts across another. The dimension "women" cuts across race and class and nationality; the division "race" cuts across sex and class. Any given individual will be included in any number of divisions, and no individual will be included in only one. Why there are the sortings there are depends among other things on the goals of the sorters and the point of the sorting. Is there some sorting that is more fundamental in some sense than any other? Are some principles of sorting somehow built into the nature of things, while others are more conventional and hence, it would seem, more subject to change? Can a person change any of the ways in which she is sorted? Can she disguise any of those ways? Do answers to these two questions have implications for what is more "fundamental"? These are rather metaphysical concerns—with political consequences if not political presuppositions. We can't begin to go into these questions here (although we shall come back to them in chapter 6), but we can say that the experience and meaning of being sorted out along one dimension of human identity is very much influenced by the experience and the meaning of being sorted out along another dimension. This means that even if you are sorted out along one dimension with others, your experience is nevertheless likely to be different from those others insofar as you are not sorted together along another dimension. For example, socialist feminists have shown us why accounts of living under conditions of class oppression cannot be the same for men and for women because of the invidious sorting also done along the lines of sex and gender identity.[37] By the same token, accounts of living under conditions of sexual oppression cannot be the same for women of all classes. And this, I think, tells us that while in one sense women are all of the same gender, what it means to be a "woman" depends on what else is true about oneself and the world in which one lives. All women are women, but there is no being who is only a woman. For different reasons and on different occasions, being a woman may be, both in the eyes of others and in the eyes of a woman herself, the most important fact about her. But it is not the only fact about her, and the meaning of that fact about her—to herself and to others—will depend on other facts about her. Thus it has been suggested that great differences between the lives of affluent and working-class women in Victorian England, as well as great differences between the ideologies about their lives, meant that "it was as if there were two different human species of females." [38] How many different "species" there are depends on how crucial other variables are in giving shape and meaning to women's experiences at any particular time and place.

All this is perfectly compatible with the well-founded feminist desire to focus on the fact of a certain and a very large number of humans being women. It is very important and very useful to be able to do this. But there is great variety in what it means to be a woman—both to outsiders and to us ourselves—and it is precisely that variety which feminism explores (even when it claims to be doing something more "universal" about "women in general") and from which feminists act. It is the burden of Chodorow's work and the work of those influenced by her, to tell us about how gender identity is constructed and maintained by societal institutions, and how gender identity might be different if institutional arrangements, such as asymmetrical patterns of parenting, were different. But once we begin to think of gender identity, as opposed to sexual identity, as part of a society's conventions—even as part of every society's conventions—then we can't assume that what it is to be, and to be thought of as, a "woman" will always and everywhere be the same. [39] The process of becoming a girl, and then a woman, occurs, as Chodorow herself tells us, in a social context. But attention to that context seems to tell us how inextricably intertwined that process is with the acquisition and the meaning of other parts of our identity.

VIII

Despite my repeated insistence that gender exists and must be seen in the context of other factors of identity, it may seem as if we will never be able to say anything coherent about gender if it must be looked at in connection with race and class rather than in isolation from them. Indeed, the project of trying to see how such factors affect gender may seem methodologically unsound. The argument about its fundamental wrong-headedness would go something like this: precisely because these other factors affect gender, in order to examine gender differences carefully we have to remove these other factors from consideration. This is the point de Beauvoir makes when she says in passing that descriptions of sexual hierarchy only apply when race and class are kept constant. If we want to understand the difference gender makes to human social and psychological development and to relations between people, we will obtain the clearest picture if we eliminate other variables that might blur the focus. In most families, the race and class of the parents is the same, and the same as that of the children. This is what makes the family an especially appropriate locus for the investigation of gender differences. Race and class typically aren't variable factors in the relationship between the father and mother, or in the relationship between mother and the children. Where they are variables, we can't be sure that it is simply gender that makes the difference in the different relational stances of the boys and girls.

This reminder about the ways in which issues of race and class might influence gender issues points in two directions: on the one hand, it recognizes the important presence of race and class by saying we must make sure they are kept constant; but on the other hand, in keeping them constant, it may look as if we indeed are isolating gender from race and class. In that sense it suggests that while examination of gender differences must recognize the impact of race and class, it does so by keeping them from skewing the examination of gender.

The methodological point about the optimal conditions under which to examine gender difference seems to be an instance of a more general principle of investigation in the social (and natural) sciences: If you want to see what difference any particular difference makes to a situation, be sure to cancel out the effects of other possible differences in such a situation. For example, if we want to examine differences in the way men and women use language, presumably we won't compare how males use the Russian language with how females use the English language. If we want to examine differences in the way boys and girls are brought up, presumably we won't compare how little boys in northern India are brought up, with how little girls in northern Ireland are brought up. If you want to focus on what differentiates women from men, then compare them to men of the same class or race or nationality.

But does this mean that what people share is irrelevant to what differentiates them—so irrelevant, for example, that in discussing gender differences, as long as we stick to the principle and keep race and class constant, we can describe the differences we find simply as differences between men and women?

Suppose someone undertook to describe gender differences between white men and white women of the same class in the United States. Because race is a constant, can we say that it has no significance in their relationship? The very consideration that enables us to "cancel out" race makes it necessary to reintroduce it when describing the differences. If we can only get at gender differences in this case by canceling out racial differences, that means we cannot assume that the gender differences apply when speaking about other racial groups and surely not where there are racial differences between the men and women in question. That is, our description of how sexual difference influences relations between men and women of the same race does not automatically apply to men and women of a different race nor to men of one race and women of another.

This means that simply because race and class are kept constant doesn't mean they have no effect. To talk about gender differences where race and class are constants is to talk about gender differences in the context of class and race similarity; but far from freeing us from the context of race and class, keeping them constant means they are constantly there. The same point applies when we are talking about race or class differences where gender is the same. We can show this by noticing some important characteristics of four types of cases where people differ by sex or race but not both: for example, relations between white men and white women, Black men and Black women, white men and Black men, white women and Black women.

1. Two people are differentiated by sex, one is subject to sexism.
   a. Neither is subject to racism (e.g., white men and white women).
   b. Both are subject to racism (e.g., Black men and Black women).

2. Two people are differentiated by race, one is subject to racism.
   a. Neither is subject to sexism (e.g., white men and Black men).
   b. Both are subject to sexism (e.g., white women and Black women).

1a. In a society such as the United States, which is both sexist and racist, relations between white men and white women are affected not only by the sexism that interprets the sexual differences between them, but also by the racism that interprets the difference between their shared racial identity and the racial identity of (for example) Blacks. Think of white slaveowners and their wives: the meaning of the sexual difference between them was constructed in part by the alleged contrast between them as whites and other men and women who were Black; what was supposed to characterize their relationship was not supposed to characterize the relationship between white men and Black women or white women and Black men. (Indeed, we would expect that to the degree that definitions of sexual relations are an important part of a group's definition of itself, then the more it insists on the differences between itself and another group, the more intent it will be on distinguishing its version of male/female relationships from the version found in the other group).[40] So even though the white men and women were of the same race, and even though they were not the victims of racism, this does not mean that we can understand the relationship between them without reference to their race and to the racism that their lives enacted. The racial awareness of whites shows up not simply in what they think about Blacks but in what they think about themselves as whites. Did a white slaveowning man ever forget that his wife was white? Did she ever forget that he was white? Did they ever forget that the Black men and women around them were Black?

The point of this example is that racism can be a factor in relations between people even when they are of the same race and not subject to racism; and even more particularly that racism can play a large role in shaping the sexism that exists between such people.

1b. Nor can we say that the only oppression that can be operative in relationships between Black men and Black women of the same class will have to do simply with sexism and nothing to do with racism or classism because their race and their class is the same. For example, the racist conditions under which slaves lived did much to shape the possibilities for equality or inequality between them. As Jacqueline Jones has pointed out recently, it is not simply that slave men lacked the institutional means—private property and the legal and social institutions that support it—by which they might dominate women.[41] When people are rendered powerless politically, socially, economically, it doesn't make a lot of sense to refer to their shared state as one of "equality." Men and women being jointly subject to racism affects the possibility and the meaning of the sexual differences between them.

The point is not simply the well-documented fact that relationships between Black men and Black women under slavery were affected at every turning by the fact of whites' control of Black lives.[42] It is rather to ask whether their understanding of themselves and each other as men and women could possibly be independent of themselves as Black men and women.

So the fact that race is a constant in relationships between white men and white women hardly means that race and racism can have no effect on the sexism that operates in some degree or another on their relationship to each other. Nor does the fact that race is a constant in relationships between Black men and Black women mean that race and racism can have no effect on the possible shapes sexism takes in their relationship. Sexual relations within the races are affected by racial relations between them.

Now let us move on to the other set of cases, in which we can see how notions of appropriate racial roles and relations between people of the same sex are affected by notions of appropriate sexual roles and relations between people of opposite sexes.

2a. We can't rule out sexism as a factor in relationships between men of different races or classes simply because there is no sexual difference between them and because neither is the victim of sexism. For example, we can't understand the racism that fueled white men's lynching of Black men without understanding its connection to the sexism that shaped their protective and possessive attitudes toward white women. The ideology according to which whites are superior to and ought to dominate Blacks is nested with the ideology according to which white men must protect their wives from attack by Black men and keep their race pure from pollution by miscegenation (of course white men routinely gave the lie to this ideology in their failure to protect their wives from their own violence as well as in their enormous contribution to the mixed-race population). That men aren't subject to sexism doesn't mean sexism has no effect on their relationships to each other, especially when the men are from different races in a racist society.

2b. For similar reasons, it would be extraordinarily odd to say that in a relationship between two women of different races or classes, sexism can't be at work since there is no sexual difference between them (following the general principle under discussion, that if two people share a characteristic, that characteristic cannot be a factor in the difference between them). White women performed acts of violence against Black slave women with whom their husbands had sexual relations.[43] Often these racist acts were shaped by feelings of sexual jealousy rooted in and sustained by sexism: for such jealousy is a function of the sexism that makes the "proper" attention of her husband a condition of a woman's sense of self-worth.[44]

Let us review briefly where we are. The general point of the above examples is this: If it is crucial whether any two people or groups of people differ on some score, it will also be crucial whether they are the same on that score. If I am white and it is a significant factor in my relationship with someone that he or she is Black, then it surely is also a significant factor if he or she is white. If racial difference is significant, so is racial similarity, whether or not the persons in question are subject to racism. If sexual difference is significant, so is sexual similarity, whether or not the persons in question are subject to sexism.

We have, then, been asking whether the best way to acknowledge the influence of race and class differences on gender differences is to see that they are kept constant. Thus we've looked at the suggestion that the only way we can accurately describe gender is to isolate its effects from the influence of race and class. We don't need to talk about race and class, because they can't make a difference: we've ensured that, and must ensure it, in order to have a clear look at gender differences.

Our response to this line of thought has been to point out that even if the gender relations in question are those between men and women or boys and girls of the same race and class, it is inaccurate to report them simply as gender relations, since the description of them holds by hypothesis only for men and women or boys and girls of the same race and class. Moreover, we have seen a number of reasons why we can't say a factor of human identity has no effect on relations between people if they share that factor. On the contrary, if it would affect their relationship were they to differ in that way, it also affects their relationship if they do not. So even if the race and class of the men and women, boys and girls, is the same, we can't assume that therefore such factors have no effect on their gender relations.

Now someone might propose that race or class could drop out in another way after reporting carefully on differences between, for example, white men and white women, Black men and Black women. Suppose—contrary to the examples we've discussed above—it turned out that sexism were the same between white men and white women, Black men and Black women. It still wouldn't follow that we needn't look at race or class or culture in order to understand male/female relationships, for our exploration tells us nothing so far about relations between men and women across race and class. And if this is different—for example, if what characterizes the relationship between white men and white women does not characterize the relationship between Black men and white women, or between white men and Black women—then it is misleading to talk simply of relationships between "men and women," for whether what we say is true is going to depend on which men and women we are talking about.

IX

According to Chodorow, we recall, girls and boys, women and men, are distinguished from each other in terms of their "relational sense," that is,

107

the degree to which their sense of self incorporates an understanding of oneself as basically connected with others or as fundamentally distinct from others. This fits them either for women's work, which increasingly has involved affective ties with others, or for men's work, which increasingly has had no room for affect. This does not mean, and presumably Chodorow wouldn't say it means, that men have no relation to others or that men are free of affective states. Nevertheless, she sometimes tends to talk as if the "private sphere" women are said to occupy is one in which people are connected and see themselves that way, while people in the "public sphere" are separate, not only from those in the private sphere, but from each other.

Yet she also contrasts the spheres by saying that in the private sphere the "exercise of influence" is in "face-to-face, personal contexts," while the public sphere is a context "defined by authority" (180). "Male superiority," Chodorow says, "is built into the definition of masculinity itself" (185). But if the public, masculine sphere is in large part defined by authority, then it is a sphere involving people in relation to one another, for surely authority is a relation. Moreover, it is hard to imagine how male domination works—for those for whom it works—unless men see themselves as related to other men. Chodorow herself hints at this when she says early on that "public institutions, activities and forms of association . . . tie men to one another apart from their domestic relationships" (9). Capitalism as Chodorow describes it requires (though does not necessarily succeed in getting) workers to see themselves "in relation," even if it is not a relation that seems very positive (186 and passim).

Perhaps men deny their relation to others, but denial of connection is not the same as absence of connection. Indeed, on some views, denial of connection is not only compatible with but perhaps even evidence of the presence of connection. Chodorow attends to this to a certain extent, but she does not really note the discrepancy between the ideology of men as separate and highly individuated and the reality of their relationships. Such ideology discourages us from seeing that while not all relations may be the kind we think of when we think about mothers and children, that doesn't mean they aren't relations. Similarly, not all "affections" may be the kind we are encouraged to think of when we think about nurturing children, but that doesn't mean they aren't affections. Fear, pride, and anger are affects just as much as love and motherly caring (which itself of course is not free of fear, anger, pride, or jealousy). What Chodorow describes as the public world (or sphere) of work is teeming with affect—whether it be boredom, pride, anger, jealousy, hope, contempt, or fear.[45]

Chodorow really doesn't say very much in detail about what she means by the presence or absence of affect and affective ties, but she might insist that a highly organized, bureaucratized work world requires those who are in it to repress affect—thus a worker might be bored, or angry, but can't show it; a corporation vice-president might be proud but had better not strut. In the domestic sphere, however, women's mothering, even if it is merely adequate, requires the expression of certain feelings, such as a constant concern for the welfare of the child.

However, one might respond in reply that factory workers would not be able to perform routine and boring work day after day unless they had a fairly high level of fear or anxiety that without this work they would be without income. In a capitalist economy of the kind Chodorow describes, how much is the willingness to work in a low-level, low-paying job sustained by the hope of rising through the well-marked ranks? Chodorow herself indicates how important the creation of appropriate affect is among those who work in the "public sphere" as well as in the "private sphere," arguing that any adequate account of why women mother and why men do not has to describe and explain why women and men seek out and find satisfaction in the activities prescribed for them by the sexual division of labor. We need, she insists, to focus on the rather good fit between the psyches of women and men and the social roles they are expected to play. Just as there couldn't be such a fit if women were not affectively prepared for their work, so there wouldn't be if men were not affectively prepared for theirs. Men have pulled one over on us if we believe that they are without emotion; they have been able to describe their emotional states as the absence of emotion and women's as the presence, when in fact perhaps there are just different sets of emotions. This is parallel to white Anglo-Saxon Protestants believing that only Italians, Hispanos, Jews, Chinese, and others have "ethnic" identities. Of course men have emotions, and Chodorow's own theory points us to that very fact. Their work requires them to have certain emotions just as women's does. Paradoxically, it may require them to fear showing emotion, or to take pride in not showing it.

It is thus not the absence of affect that characterizes the public world, but perhaps it is an absence of affective ties. Men have feelings, but not the kind that reflect relations with other people—if they fear, it is for themselves; if they feel pride, it is in themselves. But Chodorow implicitly argues against this when, for example, she says that in highly placed jobs workers have to make the "goals and values of the organization for which they work . . . their own" (186). Men's "affective ties" with one another in such circumstances may be strictly contained, and may exclude the forms of affection thought proper only for the domestic realm, but that

109

does not mean there are no such ties. Again, are we to believe that male domination is a significant factor in our lives, and that men typically feel superior to women, without believing that this signals the presence of some important kinds of affective ties among men?

If Chodorow sometimes tends to ignore or underrate the strength of affect and affective ties in the public sphere, she also tends to exaggerate and misrepresent the strength of affect and affective ties in what she calls the private sphere. Late in the book, she remarks that "women tend to have closer personal ties with each other than men have, and to spend more time in the company of women than they do with men" (200). This is misleading because it fails to note that there are phenomena such as racism, classism, ethnocentrism, heterosexism, anti-Semitism, and so on, that shatter the cozy image of easy womanly alliance suggested by Chodorow's remark. Is it clear that women tend to have closer personal ties with women of different classes or races than they do with men of their own class and race? Once again we have to ask Chodorow to be more specific about women's senses of themselves as "women," of the nature of their "personal ties" with each other, of the real extent of their identification with each other.

Indeed, part of Chodorow's claim about the separability of gender from other aspects of identity comes out in her statement that girls, in learning to identify with their mothers, learn also to identify with "women in general" (77, 137, 175). What Chodorow seems to mean by this is that a girl learns to think, feel, and act like a woman, to have feelings about her mother and other women, and to have the kind of sense of self that women have through her relationship to her mother and other women in her immediate community. That is how she "learns what it is to be womanlike" (175).

But Chodorow's claim that a girl comes to identify with "women in general" goes against her own view that the development of girls' sense of self involves a very concrete relationship while that of boys involves a much more abstract one. As we asked earlier: Is a girl only aware of her mother's being a woman, and not of her mother's being Black or white? Does a girl learn who and what she is and is not only by reference to her difference from boys and men? Is she taught that her difference from the boys and men of her own race and class is the same as her difference from the boys and men of other races and classes?

Finally, is it really possible to learn about or identify with "women in general"? There are multitudes of persons all correctly referred to as "women," but it doesn't follow that there *must* be something we all have in common that explains what "women in general" means, nor does it follow that if we learn something essential about one woman we thereby learn it about all women. If there is something women have in common, it surely is not something we can come to know by extrapolation from our own case and the cases of those like us. It is not something a girl can come to know through interactions among members of her family constellation—no matter how she feels and no matter how she describes that feeling. And if it were true that in learning to become girls and women we really learned to "identify" with women in general, how do we explain the failure of women who have enjoyed race and class privilege to see as fellow women those to whom such privilege does not accrue? Seeing another as a woman no doubt is different from seeing another as "sister," but Chodorow tends to conflate the two when she talks about girls identifying with women and having a strong relational sense. She is right to point to the social context in which mothering, and the development and learning of gender, takes place. But in that context we know that it is an achievement for women of one class or race or nationality to "identify" with women of another class or race or nationality—it is hardly a given, and it is surely not something that comes automatically with the acquisition of gender identity.

What is the connection between Chodorow's implicit claim that gender is isolatable from other elements of identity and her claim that a central difference between feminine and masculine gender identity has to do with the degree to which one is, and sees oneself as being, in relation to and connected with others? The first claim, unlike the second, says nothing about the content or substance of gender identity, and someone could agree with Chodorow about the first but disagree about the second, placing some other quality or personality trait or disposition at the heart of gender identity. Hence a criticism of one of her claims does not entail a criticism of the other. I have reasons for questioning both claims. While I have been especially concerned about the first—that gender is an independent variable of human identity—I have also raised questions about the second, which involves Chodorow's concept of relatedness. For if the first claim gives us an unwarranted sense of the shared *identity* of women across lines of race, class, and ethnicity, the second promotes an unwarranted sense of a shared *community* of women across such lines. Our actual histories, rich with the differences and marked by painful divisions among us, tell us that such identity and community do not follow, when they do come about, merely from the fact of our having become women.

X

It is a general principle of feminist inquiry to be sceptical about any account of human relations that fails to mention gender or consider the pos-

111

sible effects of gender differences: for in a world in which there is sexism, obscuring the workings of gender is likely to involve—whether intentionally or not—obscuring the workings of sexism. We thus ought to be sceptical about any account of gender relations that fails to mention race and class or to consider the possible effects of race and class differences on gender: for in a world in which there is racism and classism, obscuring the workings of race and class is likely to involve—whether intentionally or not—obscuring the workings of racism and classism.

For this reason alone we may have a lot to learn from the following questions about any account of gender relations that presupposes or otherwise insists on the separability of gender, race, and class: Why does it seem possible or necessary to separate them? Whatever the motivations for doing so, does it serve the interests of some people and not others? Does methodology ever express race or class privilege—for example, do any of the methodological reasons that might be given for trying to investigate gender in isolation from race and class in fact serve certain race or class interests?

These questions are not rhetorical. For very good and very important reasons, feminists have insisted on asking how gender affects or is affected by every branch of human inquiry (even those such as the physical sciences, which seem to have no openings for such questions). And with very good reason we have been annoyed by the absence of reference to gender in inquires about race or class, racism and classism. Perhaps it seems the best response, to such a state of affairs, first to focus on gender and sexism and then to go on to think about how gender and sexism are related to race and racism, class and classism. Hence the appeal of the work of Nancy Chodorow and the variations on it by others. But however logically, methodologically, and politically sound such inquiry seems, it obscures the ways in which race and class identity may be intertwined with gender identity. Moreover, since in a racist and classist society the racial and class identity of those who are subject to racism and classism are not obscured, all it can really mask is the racial and class identity of white middle-class women. It is because white middle-class women have something at stake in not having their racial and class identity made and kept visible that we must question accepted feminist positions on gender identity.

If feminism is essentially about gender, and gender is taken to be neatly separable from race and class, then race and class don't need to be talked about except in some peripheral way. And if race and class are peripheral to women's identities as women, then racism and classism can't be of central concern to feminism. Hence the racism and classism some women

112

face and other women help perpetuate can't find a place in feminist theory unless we keep in mind the race and class of all women (not just the race and class of those who are the victims of racism and classism). I have suggested here that one way to keep them in mind is to ask about the extent to which gender identity exists in concert with these other aspects of identity. This is quite different from saying either (1) we need to talk about race and class instead of gender or (2) we need to talk about race and class in addition to gender. Some feminists may be concerned that focus on race and class will deflect attention away from gender and from what women have in common and thus from what gives feminist inquiry its distinctive cast. This presupposes not only that we ought not spend too much time on what we don't have in common but that we have gender in common. But do we have gender identity in common? In one sense, of course, yes: all women are women. But in another sense, no: not if gender is a social construction and females become not simply women but particular kinds of women. If I am justified in thinking that what it means for me to be a woman must be exactly the same as what it means for you to be a woman (since we both are women), I needn't bother to find out anything from you or about you in order to find out what it means for you to be a woman: I can simply deduce what it means from my own case. On the other hand, if the meaning of what we apparently have in common (being women) depends in some ways on the meaning of what we don't have in common (for example, our different racial or class identities), then far from distracting us from issues of gender, attention to race and class in fact helps us to understand gender. In this sense it is only if we pay attention to how we differ that we come to an understanding of what we have in common.[46]

113

> You don't really want Black folks, you are just looking for yourself with a little
> color to it.
>
> BERNICE JOHNSON REAGON

Gender & Race:
The Ampersand Problem in Feminist Thought

In earlier chapters we have examined how attempts to focus on gender in isolation from other aspects of identity such as race and class can work to obscure the effect race, class, and gender have on each other.[1] In particular, we've looked at how gender can be treated in a way that obscures the race and class identity of privileged women—for example, of contemporary white middle-class women or the free women of ancient Greece—and simultaneously makes it hard to conceive of women who are not of that particular class and race as "women." Precisely insofar as a discussion of gender and gender relations is really, even if obscurely, about a particular group of women and their relation to a particular group of men, it is unlikely to be applicable to any other group of women. At the same time, the particular race and class identity of those referred to simply as "women" becomes explicit when we see the inapplicability of statements about "women" to women who are not of that race or class.

As mentioned in the Introduction, some of these points are illustrated tellingly in an article in the *New York Times* about how "women and Blacks" have fared in the U.S. military.[2] The author of the article does not discuss women who are Black or Blacks who are women. Indeed, it is clear that the "women" referred to are white, the "Blacks" referred to are male, even though, in a chart comparing the numbers and the placement of "women" and "Blacks," a small note appears telling the reader that Black women are included in the category "Blacks."[3] There are several things to note about the sexual and racial ontology of the article. The racial identity of those identified as "women" does not become explicit until reference is made to Black women, at which point it also becomes clear that the category "women" excludes Black women. In the contrast between "women" and "Blacks" the usual contrast between "men" and "women" is dropped, even though the distinction is in effect between a group of men and a group of women. But the men in question are not called men. They are called "Blacks."

It is not easy to think about gender, race, and class in ways that don't obscure or underplay their effects on one another. The crucial question is how the links between them are conceived. So, for example, we see that de Beauvoir tends to talk about comparisons between sex and race, or between sex and class, or between sex and culture; she describes what she takes to be comparisons between sexism and racism, between sexism and classism, between sexism and anti-Semitism. In the work of Chodorow and others influenced by her, we observe a readiness to look for links between sexism and other forms of oppression depicted as distinct from sexism. In both examples, we find an additive analysis of the various elements of identity and of various forms of oppression: there's sex *and* race *and* class; there's sexism *and* racism *and* classism. In both examples, attempts to bring in elements of identity other than gender, to bring in kinds of oppression other than sexism, still have the effect of obscuring the racial and class identity of those described as "women," still make it hard to see how women not of a particular race and class can be included in the description.

In this chapter we shall examine in more detail how additive analyses of identity and of oppression can work against an understanding of the relations between gender and other elements of identity, between sexism and other forms of oppression. In particular we will see how some very interesting and important attempts to link sexism and racism themselves reflect and perpetuate racism. Ironically, the categories and methods we may find most natural and straightforward to use as we explore the connections between sex and race, sexism and racism, confuse those connections rather than clarify them.

As has often been pointed out, what have been called the first and second waves of the women's movement in the United States followed closely on the heels of women's involvement in the nineteenth-century abolitionist movement and the twentieth-century civil rights movement. In both centuries, challenges to North American racism served as an impetus to, and model for, the feminist attack on sexist institutions, practices, and ideology. But this is not to say that all antiracists were antisexists, or that all antisexists were antiracists. Indeed, many abolitionists of the nineteenth century and civil rights workers of the twentieth did not take sexism seriously, and we continue to learn about the sad, bitter, and confusing history of women who in fighting hard for feminist ends did not take racism seriously.[4]

Recent feminist theory has not totally ignored white racism, though white feminists have paid much less attention to it than have Black feminists. Much of feminist theory has reflected and contributed to what Adrienne Rich has called "white solipsism": the tendency "to think, imagine, and speak as if whiteness described the world."[5] While solipsism is "not the consciously held belief that one race is inherently superior to all others, but a tunnel-vision which simply does not see nonwhite experience or existence as precious or significant, unless in spasmodic, impotent guilt-reflexes, which have little or no long-term, continuing momentum or political usefulness."[6]

In this chapter I shall focus on what I take to be instances and sustaining sources of this tendency in recent theoretical works by, or of interest to, feminists. In particular, I examine certain ways of comparing sexism and racism in the United States, as well as habits of thought about the source of women's oppression and the possibility of our liberation. I hope that exposing some of the symptoms of white solipsism—especially in places where we might least expect to find them—will help to eliminate tunnel vision and to widen the descriptive and explanatory scope of feminist theory. Perhaps we might hasten the day when it will no longer be necessary for anyone to have to say, as Audre Lorde has, "How difficult and time-consuming it is to have to reinvent the pencil every time you want to send a message."[7]

I shall not explicitly be examining class and classism, though at a number of points I suggest ways in which considerations of class and classism affect the topic at hand. Many of the questions I raise about comparisons between sexism and racism could also be raised about comparison between sexism and classism or racism and classism.

I

It is perhaps inevitable that comparisons of sexism and racism include, and often culminate in, questions about which form of oppression is more "fundamental."[8] Whether or not one believes that this way of thinking will bear any strategic or theoretic fruit, such comparisons have come to inform analyses of the nature of sexism and the nature of racism. To begin, I will examine some recent claims that sexism is more fundamental than racism, a highly ambiguous argument. In many instances the evidence offered in support turns out to refute the claim; and this way of comparing sexism and racism often presupposes the nonexistence of Black women, insofar as neither the description of sexism nor that of racism seems to apply to them. This is a bitter irony indeed, since Black women are the victims of both sexism and racism.

We need to ask first what "more fundamental" means in a comparison of racism and sexism. It has meant or might mean several different though related things:[9]

It is harder to eradicate sexism than it is to eradicate racism.

There might be sexism without racism but not racism without sexism: any social and political changes that eradicate sexism will eradicate racism, but social and political changes that eradicate racism will not eradicate sexism.

Sexism is the first form of oppression learned by children.

Sexism predates racism.

Sexism is the cause of racism.

Sexism is used to justify racism.

Sexism is the model for racism.

We can trace these arguments in the work of two important feminist theorists: Kate Millett in *Sexual Politics* and Shulamith Firestone in *The Dialectic of Sex*. It is worth remembering that these authors did not ignore race and racism. But their treatments of the subjects enable us to see that as long as race is taken to be independent of sex, racism as independent of sexism, we are bound to give seriously misleading descriptions of gender and gender relations.

In *Sexual Politics*, Kate Millett seems to hold that sexism is more fundamental than racism in three senses: it is "sturdier" than racism and so presumably is harder to eradicate; it has a more "pervasive ideology" than racism, and so those who are not racists may nevertheless embrace sexist beliefs; and it provides our culture's "most fundamental concept of power."[10] But as Margaret Simons has pointed out, Millett ignores the fact that Black women and other women of color do not usually describe their own lives as ones in which they experience sexism as more fundamental than racism.[11] There is indeed something very peculiar about the evidence Millett offers in behalf of her view that sexism is the more endemic oppression.

On the one hand, she states that everywhere men have power over women. On the other hand, she notes with interest that some observers have described as an effect of racism that Black men do not have such

117

power over Black women, and that only when racism is eradicated will Black men assume their proper position of superiority. She goes on to argue that "the military, industry, technology, universities, science, political office, and finance—in short, every avenue of power within the society, including the coercive force of the police, is entirely in male hands." [12] But surely that is white male supremacy. Since when did Black males have such institutionally based power, in what Millett calls "our culture"? She thus correctly describes as sexist the hope that Black men could assume their "proper authority" over Black women, but her claim about the pervasiveness of sexism is belied by her reference to the lack of authority of Black males.

There is no doubt that Millett is right to view as sexist the hope that racial equity will be established when Black males have authority over Black females, but it also is correct to describe as racist the hope—not uncommonly found in feminist arguments—that sexual equity will be established when women can be presidents or heads of business. That is no guarantee that they will not be running racist countries and corporations. As Elizabeth F. Hood said: "Many white women define liberation as the access to those thrones traditionally occupied by white men—positions in the kingdoms which support racism." [13] Of course, one might insist that any truly antisexist vision also is an antiracist vision, for it requires the elimination of all forms of oppression against all women, white or Black. [14] But, similarly, it can be said that any truly antiracist vision would have to be antisexist, for it requires the elimination of all forms of oppression against all Blacks and other people of color, women or men.

In arguing for the position in *The Dialectic of Sex* that racism is "extended sexism," Shulamith Firestone provides another variation on the view that sexism is more fundamental:

Racism is sexism extended. . . . Let us look at race relations in America, a macrocosm of the hierarchical relations within the nuclear family: the white man is father, the white woman wife-and-mother, her status dependent on his; the blacks, like children, are his property, their physical differentiation branding them the subservient class, in the same way that children form so easily distinguishable a servile class vis-à-vis adults. The power hierarchy creates the psychology of racism, just as, in the nuclear family, it creates the psychology of sexism. [15]

It is clear that Firestone sees sexism as the model for racism; as the cause of racism, so that racism cannot disappear unless sexism does; and as the historical precursor of racism. Moreover, with this model she sees the goal of the Black man (male child) to be to usurp the power of the white man (father), which means that the restoration of the authority of the

Black man will involve his domination of women.[16] Hence sexism according to Firestone is more fundamental than racism, in the sense that the eradication of racism is portrayed as compatible with the continuation of sexism.

Here, as in the case of Millett, the evidence Firestone offers actually undermines her claim. First of all, she points out, and her analogy to the family requires, that the Black man is not really "the *real* man."[17] However much the Black man tries to act like the white man, and however much his treatment of Black women resembles the white man's treatment of white women and Black women, he isn't really The Man. Now if this is so, it seems odd to claim that sexism is more fundamental than racism, since according to Firestone's own account the Black man's identity as a man is obscured or erased by his identity as a Black. Thus according to her own account, the racial identity of being an inferior assigned him by racists is more fundamental than the sexual identity of being a superior assigned him by sexists.

Firestone also claims that "the All-American Family is predicated on the existence of the black ghetto whorehouse. The rape of the black community in America makes possible the existence of the family structure of the larger white community."[18] But to say in these ways that racism makes sexism possible is to say that in the absence of racism, sexism could not exist—surely just the opposite of the claim that sexism is more fundamental than racism, the claim Firestone wishes to establish.

II

If Millett's and Firestone's accounts tend to ignore facts about the status of Black men, other similar accounts ignore the existence of Black women. In the process of comparing racism and sexism, Richard Wasserstrom describes the ways in which women and Blacks have been stereotypically conceived of as less fully developed than white men: In the United States, "men and women are taught to see men as independent, capable, and powerful; men and women are taught to see women as dependent, limited in abilities, and passive."[19] But who is taught to see Black men as "independent, capable, and powerful," and by whom are they taught? Are Black men taught that? Black women? White men? White women? Similarly, who is taught to see Black women as "dependent, limited in abilities, and passive"? If this stereotype is so prevalent, why then have Black women had to defend themselves against the images of matriarch and whore?

Wasserstrom continues:

As is true for race, it is also a significant social fact that to be a female is to be an entity or creature viewed as different from the standard, fully developed person who is male as well as white. But to be female, as opposed to being black, is not to be conceived of as simply a creature of less worth. That is one important thing that differentiates sexism from racism: the ideology of sex, as opposed to the ideology of race, is a good deal more complex and confusing. Women are both put on a pedestal and deemed not fully developed persons.[20]

He leaves no room for the Black woman. For a Black woman cannot be "female, as opposed to being Black"; she is female *and* Black. Since Wasserstrom's argument proceeds from the assumption that one is either female or Black, it cannot be an argument that applies to Black women. Moreover, we cannot generate a composite image of the Black women from Wasserstrom's argument, since the description of women as being put on a pedestal, or being dependent, never generally applied to Black women in the United States and was never meant to apply to them.

Wasserstrom's argument about the priority of sexism over racism has an odd result, which stems from the erasure of Black women in his analysis. He wishes to claim that in this society sex is a more fundamental fact about people than race. Yet his description of women does not apply to the Black woman, which implies that being Black is a more fundamental fact about her than being a woman and hence that her sex is not a more fundamental fact about her than her race. I am not saying that Wasserstrom actually believes this is true, but that paradoxically the terms of his theory force him into that position. If the terms of one's theory require that a person is either female or Black, clearly there is no room to describe someone who is both.

A similar erasure of the Black woman, through failure to note how sexist stereotypes are influenced by racist ones, is found in Laurence Thomas's comparison of sexism and racism.[21] Like Wasserstrom, Thomas believes that sexism is more deeply ingrained in our culture. Racist attitudes, he says, are easier to give up than sexist ones for two reasons: First, "sexism, unlike racism, readily lends itself to a morally unobjectionable description," and second, "the positive self-concept of men has been more centrally tied to their being sexists than has been the positive self-concept of whites to their being racists."[22]

Thomas argues that it is not morally objectionable that "a natural outcome of a sexist conception of women" is the role of men as benefactors of women—part of men's role vis-à-vis women is to "protect women and to provide them with the comforts of life."[23] But at best, Thomas's claim about the man's role as benefactor of woman only applies to men and women of the same race (and probably of the same class). It is of course difficult to explain how claims about roles are established, but the history of race relations in the United States surely makes ludicrous the idea that the role of white men is to be the benefactors of Black women—to "protect" them and to "provide them with the comforts of life." This neither describes what white men have done, nor what they have been told they ought to have done, with respect to Black women.

Thomas's description of sexism in relations between women and men leaves out the reality of racism in relations between Blacks and whites. If he wishes to insist that his analysis was only meant to apply to same-race sexual relations, then he cannot continue to speak unqualifiedly about relations between men and women. My point is not that Black men cannot in any way be sexist to white or to Black women, for indeed they can, just as white women can be racist to Black men or to Black women. My point, rather, is that a theory of sexism that describes men's and women's roles can itself reflect the racist society in which it develops, insofar as it is based on an erasure of the realities of white racism.

Thomas also holds that sexism is more central to the positive self-concept of men than racism has been to the positive self-concept of whites. He claims that, although being benefactors of women is essential to men's self-esteem as "real" men, for whites it is not necessary to own slaves or to hate Blacks in order to be "really" white.[24] Once again, we have to see what happens to Thomas's claim when we put "Black" or "white" in front of "men" or "women" in his formula: "For white men, being benefactors of Black women is essential to their self-esteem as 'real' men." That is false. Indeed, in a racist society, white men's self-esteem requires the opposite position and attitude toward Black women.

Reflection on this leads to doubts about the second part of Thomas's claim—that whites don't have to be racists in order to be "really" white. Does he mean to say that in our society a white man feels no threat to his self-esteem if a Black man gets the job for which they both are candidates? That a white man feels no threat to his self-esteem if a Black man marries the white woman the white man is hoping to marry? That a white man feels no threat to his self-esteem if he lives in a neighborhood with Blacks? Certainly not all white men's self-esteem is so threatened. But this is a racist society, and generally, the self-esteem of white people is deeply influenced by their difference from and supposed superiority to Black people.[25] Those of us who are white may not think of ourselves as racists, because we do not own slaves or hate Blacks, but that does not mean that much of what props up our sense of self is not based on the racism that unfairly distributes benefits and burdens to whites and Blacks.

121

For example, think for a moment about a case of self-esteem that seems on the surface most unlikely to be supported by racism: the self-esteem that might be thought to attend sincere and serious philosophical reflection on the problems of racism. How could this be said to be based on racism, especially if the philosopher is trying to eliminate racism? As the editors of the *Philosophical Forum* in an issue on philosophy and the Black experience pointed out, "Black people have to a disproportionate extent supplied the labor which has made possible the cultivation of philosophical inquiry."[26] A disproportionate amount of the labor that makes it possible for some people to have philosophy as a profession has been done by Blacks and others under conditions that can only be described as racist. If the connection between philosophy and racism is not very visible, that invisibility itself is a product of racism. Any feminist would recognize a similar point about sexism: it is only in footnotes and prefaces that we see a visible connection made between a man's satisfaction in having finished an article or book and a woman's having made that completion possible.[27]

At several points early in his essay, Thomas says that he is going to consider the "way in which sexism and racism each conceives of its object: woman and Blacks, respectively."[28] But there are many difficulties in talking about sexism and racism in this way, some of which we have noted, and others to which we now turn.

III

First of all, sexism and racism do not have different "objects" in the case of Black women. It is highly misleading to say, without further explanation, that Black women experience "sexism and racism." For to say merely that suggests that Black women experience one form of oppression, as Blacks (the same thing Black men experience) and that they experience another form of oppression, as women (the same thing white women experience). While it is true that images and institutions that are described as sexist affect both Black and white women, they are affected in different ways, depending upon the extent to which they are affected by other forms of oppression. Thus, as noted earlier, it will not do to say that women are oppressed by the image of the "feminine" woman as fair, delicate, and in need of support and protection by men. As Linda Brent succinctly puts it, "That which commands admiration in the white woman only hastens the degradation of the female slave."[29] More specifically, as Angela Davis reminds us, "the alleged benefits of the ideology of femininity did not accrue" to the Black female slave—she was expected to toil in the fields for just as long and hard as the Black male was.[30]

Reflection on the experience of Black women also shows that it is not as if one form of oppression is merely piled upon another. As Barbara Smith has remarked, the effect of multiple oppression "is not merely arithmetic."[31] This additive method informs Gerda Lerner's analysis of the oppression of Black women under slavery: "Their work and duties were the same as that of the men, while childbearing and rearing fell upon them as an added burden."[32] But as Angela Davis has pointed out, the mother/housewife role (even the words seem inappropriate) doesn't have the same meaning for women who experience racism as it does for those who are not so oppressed:

In the infinite anguish of ministering to the needs of the men and children around her (who were not necessarily members of her immediate family), she was performing the only labor of the slave community which could not be directly and immediately claimed by the oppressor.[3]

The meaning and the oppressive nature of the "housewife" role has to be understood in relation to the roles against which it is contrasted. The work of mate/mother/nurturer has a different meaning depending on whether it is contrasted to work that has high social value and ensures economic independence or to labor that is forced, degrading, and unpaid. All of these factors are left out in a simple additive analysis. How one form of oppression is experienced is influenced by and influences how another form is experienced. An additive analysis treats the oppression of a Black woman in a society that is racist as well as sexist as if it were a further burden when, in fact, it is a different burden. As the work of Davis, among others, shows, to ignore the difference is to deny the particular reality of the Black woman's experience.

If sexism and racism must be seen as interlocking, and not as piled upon each other, serious problems arise for the claim that one of them is more fundamental than the other. As we saw, one meaning of the claim that sexism is more fundamental than racism is that sexism causes racism: racism would not exist if sexism did not, while sexism could and would continue to exist even in the absence of racism. In this connection, racism is sometimes seen as something that is both derivative from sexism and in the service of it: racism keeps women from uniting in alliance against sexism. This view has been articulated by Mary Daly in *Beyond God the Father*. According to Daly, sexism is the "root and paradigm" of other forms of oppression such as racism. Racism is a "deformity *within* patriarchy. . . . It is most unlikely that racism will be eradicated as long as sexism prevails."[34]

Daly's theory relies on an additive analysis, and we can see again why such an analysis fails to describe adequately Black women's experience.

Daly's analysis makes it look simply as if both Black women and white women experience sexism, while Black women also experience racism. Black women, Daly says, must come to see what they have in common with white women—shared sexist oppression—and see that they are all "pawns in the racial struggle, which is basically not the struggle that will set them free as women."[35] But insofar as she is oppressed by racism in a sexist context and sexism in a racist context, the Black woman's struggle cannot be compartmentalized into two struggles—one as a Black and one as a woman. Indeed, it is difficult to imagine why a Black woman would think of her struggles this way except in the face of demands by white women or by Black men that she do so. This way of speaking about her struggle is required by a theory that insists not only that sexism and racism are distinct but that one might be eradicated before the other. Daly rightly points out that the Black woman's struggle can easily be, and has usually been, subordinated to the Black man's struggle in antiracist organizations. But she does not point out that the Black woman's struggle can easily be, and usually has been, subordinated to the white woman's struggle in antisexist organizations.

Daly's line of thought also promotes the idea that, were it not for racism, there would be no important differences between Black and white women. Since, according to her view, sexism is the fundamental form of oppression and racism works in its service, the only significant differences between Black and white women are differences that men (Daly doesn't say whether she means white men or Black men or both) have created and that are the source of antagonism between women. What is really crucial about us is our sex; racial distinctions are one of the many products of sexism, of patriarchy's attempt to keep women from uniting. According to Daly, then, it is through our shared sexual identity that we are oppressed together; it is through our shared sexual identity that we shall be liberated together.

This view not only ignores the role women play in racism and classism, but it seems to deny the positive aspects of racial identities. It ignores the fact that being Black is a source of pride, as well as an occasion for being oppressed. It suggests that once racism is eliminated, Black women no longer need be concerned about or interested in their Blackness—as if the only reason for paying attention to one's Blackness is that it is the source of pain and sorrow and agony. The assumption that there is nothing positive about having a Black history and identity is racism pure and simple. Recall the lines of Nikki Giovanni:

> and I really hope no white person ever has cause
> to write about me
> because they never understand Black love is

Black wealth and they'll
    probably talk about my hard childhood
and never understand that
    all the while I was quite happy.[36]

Or recall the chagrin of the central character in Paule Marshall's story "Reena," when she discovered that her white boyfriend could only see her Blackness in terms of her suffering and not as something compatible with taking joy and pleasure in life.[37] I think it is helpful too in this connection to remember the opening lines of Pat Parker's "For the white person who wants to know how to be my friend":

The first thing you do is to forget that i'm Black.
Second, you must never forget that i'm Black.[38]

Perhaps it does not occur to feminists who are white that celebrating being white has anything to do with our celebrating being women. But that may be so because celebrating being white is already taken care of by the predominantly white culture in which we live in North America. Certainly feminist theory and activity on the whole have recognized that it is possible, if difficult, to celebrate being a woman without at the same time conceiving of woman in terms of the sexist imagery and lore of the centuries. (That celebrating womanhood is a tricky business we know from the insidiousness of the "two-sphere" ideology of the nineteenth century and of the image of the "total woman"—in Daly's wonderful phrase, the "totaled woman"—of the twentieth century: as if by celebrating what men tell us we are, the burden magically disappears because we embrace it.) But just as it is possible and desirable to identify oneself as a woman and yet think of and describe oneself in ways that are not sexist, so it is possible and desirable to identify oneself as a Black woman and yet think of oneself in ways that are not racist.

In sum, according to an additive analysis of sexism and racism, all women are oppressed by sexism; some women are further oppressed by racism. Such an analysis distorts Black women's experiences of oppression by failing to note important differences between the contexts in which Black women and white women experience sexism. The additive analysis also suggests that a woman's racial identity can be "subtracted" from her combined sexual and racial identity: "We are all women." But this does not leave room for the fact that different women may look to different forms of liberation just because they are white or Black women, rich or poor women, Catholic or Jewish women.

IV

As we saw in the Introduction, feminist leaders such as Elizabeth Cady Stanton used racist arguments in pleas to better the condition of "women." Though such blatant racism is not as likely to appear in contemporary feminism, that doesn't mean that visions of a nonsexist world will also be visions of a nonracist world. In the rest of the chapter I will explore how some ways of conceiving women's oppression and liberation contribute to the white solipsism of feminist theory.

As I have argued in detail elsewhere, feminist theorists as politically diverse as Simone de Beauvoir, Betty Friedan, and Shulamith Firestone have described the conditions of women's liberation in terms that suggest that the identification of woman with her body has been the source of our oppression, and hence that the source of our liberation lies in sundering that connection.[39] For example, de Beauvoir introduces *The Second Sex* with the comment that woman has been regarded as "womb"; and she later observes that woman is thought of as planted firmly in the world of "immanence," that is, the physical world of nature, her life defined by the dictates of her "biologic fate."[40] In contrast, men live in the world of "transcendence," actively using their minds to create "values, mores, religions."[41] Theirs is the world of culture as opposed to the world of nature. Among Friedan's central messages is that women should be allowed and encouraged to be "culturally" as well as "biologically" creative, because the former activities, in contrast to childbearing and rearing, are "mental" and are of "highest value to society"—"mastering the secrets of atoms, or the stars, composing symphonies, pioneering a new concept in government or society."[42]

This view comes out especially clearly in Firestone's work. According to her, the biological difference between women and men is at the root of women's oppression. It is woman's body—in particular, our body's capacity to bear children—that makes, or makes possible, the oppression of women by men. Hence we must disassociate ourselves from our bodies— most radically—by making it possible, or even necessary, to conceive and bear children outside the womb, and by otherwise generally disassociating our lives from the thankless tasks associated with the body.[43]

In predicating women's liberation on a disassociation from our bodies, Firestone oddly enough joins the chorus of male voices that has told us over the centuries about the disappointments entailed in being embodied creatures. What might be called "somatophobia" (fear of and disdain for the body) is part of a centuries-long tradition in Western culture. As de Beauvoir so thoroughly described in *The Second Sex*, the responsibility for being embodied creatures has been assigned to women: we have been associated, indeed virtually identified, with the body; men (or some men) have been associated and virtually identified with the mind. Women have been portrayed as possessing bodies in a way men have not. It is as if women essentially, men only accidentally, have bodies. It seems to me that Firestone's (as well as Friedan's and de Beauvoir's) prescription for women's liberation does not challenge the negative attitude toward the body; it only hopes to end the association between the body, so negatively characterized, and women.

I think the somatophobia we see in the work of Firestone and others is a force that contributes to white solipsism in feminist thought, in at least three related ways. First, insofar as feminists ignore, or indeed accept, negative views of the body in prescriptions for women's liberation, we will also ignore an important element in racist thinking. For the superiority of men to women (or, as we have seen, of some men to some women) is not the only hierarchical relationship that has been linked to the superiority of the mind to the body. Certain kinds, or "races," of people have been held to be more body-like than others, and this has meant that they are perceived as more animal-like and less god-like. For example, in *The White Man's Burden*, Winthrop Jordan describes ways in which white Englishmen portrayed black Africans as beastly, dirty, highly sexual beings.[44] Lillian Smith tells us in *Killers of the Dream* how closely run together were her lessons about the evil of the body and the evil of Blacks.[45]

We need to examine and understand somatophobia and look for it in our own thinking, for the idea that the work of the body and for the body has no part in real human dignity has been part of racist as well as sexist ideology. That is, oppressive stereotypes of "inferior races" and of women (notice that even in order to make the point in this way, we leave up in the air the question of how we shall refer to those who belong to both categories) have typically involved images of their lives as determined by basic bodily functions (sex, reproduction, appetite, secretions, and excretions) and as given over to attending to the bodily functions of others (feeding, washing, cleaning, doing the "dirty work"). Superior groups, we have been told from Plato on down, have better things to do with their lives. It certainly does not follow from the presence of somatophobia in a person's writings that she or he is a racist or a sexist. But disdain for the body historically has been symptomatic of sexist and racist (as well as classist) attitudes.

Human groups know that the work of the body and for the body is necessary for human existence, and they make provisions for that necessity. Thus even when a group views its liberation in terms of being free of association with, or responsibility for, bodily tasks, its own liberation is likely to be predicated on the oppression of other groups—those assigned to do the body's work. For example, if feminists decide that women are not going to be relegated to doing such work, who do we think is going to do it? Have we attended to the role that racism and classism historically have played in settling that question? We may recall why Plato and Aristotle thought philosophers and citizens needed leisure from this kind of work and who they thought ought to do it.

Finally, if one thinks—as de Beauvoir, Friedan, and Firestone do—that the liberation of women requires abstracting the notion of woman from the notion of woman's body, then one might logically think that the liberation of Blacks requires abstracting the notion of a Black person from the notion of a black body. Since the body, or at least certain of its aspects, may be thought to be the culprit, the solution may seem to be: Keep the person and leave the occasion for oppression behind. Keep the woman, somehow, but leave behind her woman's body; keep the Black person but leave the Blackness behind. Once one attempts to stop thinking about oneself in terms of having a body, then one not only will stop thinking in terms of characteristics such as womb and breast, but also will stop thinking in terms of skin and hair. We would expect to find that any feminist theory based in part on a disembodied view of human identity would regard blackness (or any other physical characteristic that may serve as a centering post for one's identity) as of temporary and negative importance.

Once the concept of woman is divorced from the concept of woman's body, conceptual room is made for the idea of a woman who is no particular historical woman—she has no color, no accent, no particular characteristics that require having a body. She is somehow all and only woman; that is her only identifying feature. And so it will seem inappropriate or beside the point to think of women in terms of any physical characteristics, especially if their oppression has been rationalized by reference to those characteristics.

None of this is to say that the historical and cultural identity of being Black or white is the same thing as, or is reducible to, the physical feature of having black or white skin. Historical and cultural identity is not constituted by having a body with particular identifying features, but it cannot be comprehended without such features and the significance attached to them.

V

Adrienne Rich was perhaps the first well-known contemporary white feminist to have noted "white solipsism" in feminist theorizing and activity. I think it is no coincidence that she also noticed and attended to the strong strain of somatophobia in feminist theory. *Of Woman Born* updates the connection between somatophobia and misogyny/gynephobia that Simone de Beauvoir described at length in *The Second Sex*.[46] But unlike de Beauvoir or Firestone, Rich refuses to throw out the baby with the bathwater: she sees that the historical negative connection between woman and body (in particular, between woman and womb) can be broken in more than one way. Both de Beauvoir and Firestone wanted to break it by insisting that women need be no more connected—in thought or deed—with the body than men have been. In their view of embodiment as a liability, de Beauvoir and Firestone are in virtual agreement with the patriarchal cultural history they otherwise question. Rich, however, insists that the negative connection between woman and body be broken along other lines. She asks us to think about whether what she calls "flesh-loathing" is the only attitude it is possible to have toward our bodies. Just as she explicitly distinguishes between motherhood as experience and motherhood as institution, so she implicitly asks us to distinguish between embodiment as experience and embodiment as institution. Flesh-loathing is part of the well-entrenched beliefs, habits, and practices epitomized in the treatment of pregnancy as a disease. But we need not experience our flesh, our body, as loathsome.

I think it is not a psychological or historical accident that having examined the way women view their bodies, Rich also focused on the failure of white women to see Black women's experiences as different from their own. For looking at embodiment is one way (though not the only one) of coming to recognize and understand the particularity of experience. Without bodies we could not have personal histories. Nor could we be identified as woman or man, Black or white. This is not to say that reference to publicly observable bodily characteristics settles the question of whether someone is woman or man, Black or white; nor is it to say that being woman or man, Black or white, just means having certain bodily characteristics (that is one reason some Blacks want to capitalize the term; "Black" refers to a cultural identity, not simply a skin color). But different meanings are attached to having certain characteristics, in different places and at different times and by different people, and those differences affect enormously the kinds of lives we lead or experiences we have. Women's oppression has been linked to the meanings assigned to having a woman's body by male oppressors. Blacks' oppression has been linked to the meanings assigned to having a black body by white oppressors. (Note how insidiously this way of speaking once again leaves unmentioned the situation for Black women.) We cannot hope to understand the meaning of a person's experiences, including her experiences of oppression, without first thinking of her as embodied, and second thinking about the particular meanings assigned to that embodiment. If, because of somatophobia, we think and write as if we are not embodied, or as if we would be better off if we were not embodied, we are likely to ignore the ways in which different forms of embodiment are correlated with different kinds of experience.

Rich—unlike de Beauvoir—asks us to reflect on the culturally assigned differences between having a Black or a white body, as well as on the differences between having the body of a woman or of a man. Other feminists have reflected on the meaning of embodiment and recognized the connection between flesh-loathing and woman-hatred, but they have only considered it far enough to try to divorce the concept of woman from the concept of the flesh. In effect, they have insisted that having different bodies does not or need not mean men and women are any different as humans; and having said that, they imply that having different colored bodies does not mean that Black women and white women are any different. Such statements are fine if interpreted to mean that the differences between woman and man, Black and white, should not be used against Black women and white women and Black men. But not paying attention to embodiment and to the cultural meanings assigned to different forms of it is to encourage sexblindness and colorblindness. These blindnesses are vicious when they are used to support the idea that all experience is male experience or that all experience is white experience. Rich does not run away from the fact that women have bodies, nor does she wish that women's bodies were not so different from men's. That healthy regard for the ground of our differences from men is logically connected to—though of course does not ensure—a healthy regard for the ground of the differences between Black women and white women.

"Colorblindness" . . . implies that I would look at a Black woman and see her as white, thus engaging in white solipsism to the utter erasure of her particular reality.[47]

Colorblindness denies the particularity of the Black woman and rules out the possibility both that her history has been different and that her future might be different in any significant way from the white woman's.

VI

I have been discussing the ways in which some aspects of feminist theory exhibit what Adrienne Rich has called "white solipsism." In particular, I have been examining ways in which some prominent claims about the relation between sexism and racism ignore the realities of racism. I have also suggested that there are ways of thinking about women's oppression and about women's liberation that reflect and encourage white solipsism, but that thinking differently about women and about sexism might lead to thinking differently about Blackness and about racism.

First, we have to continue to reexamine the traditions which reinforce sexism and racism. Though feminist theory has recognized the connection between somatophobia and misogyny/gynephobia, it has tended to challenge the misogyny without challenging the somatophobia, and without fully appreciating the connection between somatophobia and racism.

Second, we have to keep a cautious eye on discussions of racism versus sexism. They keep us from seeing ways in which what sexism means and how it works is modulated by racism, and ways in which what racism means is modulated by sexism. Most important, discussions of sexism versus racism tend to proceed as if Black women—to take one example— do not exist. None of this is to say that sexism and racism are thoroughly and in every context indistinguishable. Certain political and social changes may point to the conclusion that some aspects of racism will disappear sooner than some aspects of sexism (see, for example, the statistics Diane Lewis cites in "A Response to Inequality: Black Women, Racism, and Sexism").[48] Other changes may point to the conclusion that some aspects of sexism will disappear sooner than some aspects of racism (e.g., scepticism about the possible effects of passage of the ERA on the lives of Black women in the ghetto). And there undoubtedly is disagreement about when certain changes should be seen as making any dent in sexism or racism at all. But as long as Black women and other women of color are at the bottom of the economic heap (which clearly we cannot fully understand in the absence of a class analysis), and as long as our descriptions of sexism and racism themselves reveal racist and sexist perspectives, it seems both empirically and conceptually premature to make grand claims about whether sexism or racism is "more fundamental." For many reasons, then, it seems wise to proceed very cautiously in this inquiry.

Third, it is crucial to sustain a lively regard for the variety of women's experiences. On the one hand, what unifies women and justifies us in talking about the oppression of women is the overwhelming evidence of the worldwide and historical subordination of women to men. On the other, while it may be possible for us to speak about women in a general way, it also is inevitable that any statement we make about women in some particular place at some particular time is bound to suffer from ethnocentrism if we try to claim for it more generality than it has. So, for

131

example, to say that the image of woman as frail and dependent is oppressive is certainly true. But it is oppressive to white women in the United States in quite a different way than it is oppressive to Black women, for the sexism Black women experience is in the context of their experience of racism. In Toni Morrison's *The Bluest Eye,* the causes and consequences of Pecola's longing to have blue eyes are surely quite different from the causes and consequences of a white girl with brown eyes having a similar desire.[49] More to the point, the consequences of *not* having blue eyes are quite different for the two. Similarly, the family may be the locus of oppression for white middle-class women, but to claim that it is the locus of oppression for all women is to ignore the fact that for Blacks in America the family has been a source of resistance against white oppression.[50]

In short, the claim that all women are oppressed is fully compatible with, and needs to be explicated in terms of, the many varieties of oppression that different populations of women have been subject to. After all, why should oppressors settle for uniform kinds of oppression, when to oppress their victims in many different ways—consciously or unconsciously—makes it more likely that the oppressed groups will not perceive it to be in their interest to work together?

Finally, it is crucial not to see Blackness only as the occasion for oppression—any more than one sees being a woman only as the occasion for oppression. No one ought to expect the forms of our liberation to be any less various than the forms of our oppression. We need to be at least as generous in imagining what women's liberation will be like as our oppressors have been in devising what women's oppression has been.

Women don't lead their lives like, "Well, this part is race, and this is class, and this part has to do with women's identities," so it's confusing.

BEVERLY SMITH

Woman: The One and the Many

I suspect it may be hard not to have the feeling that some philosophical sleight of hand is going on here, that there is something wantonly obscure in piling up argument after argument to the effect that it isn't as easy as one might think to talk coherently about a woman "as a woman," that attempts to isolate gender from race and class don't succeed in doing so. After all, most everyone has no trouble at all answering questions such as "What gender are you?" "What race are you?" and so on. This is not to say that there are not, for example, debates about the "racial" categories on United States census forms. Nor is it to forget that in countries like the United States the pretense of there being no class differences makes it very hard for many people to answer questions about what class they belong to. But I may seem to have forgotten that at least some of these questions about one's identity are easy to answer. I agree: I don't have any trouble answering that I am a woman and that I am white. These appear to be two separate questions, which I can answer separately; my brother answers one of them as I do, the other not. So it seems that I can easily pick out the "woman part" of me and the "white part" of me and, moreover, tell the difference between them.

But does this mean that there is a "woman part" of me, and that it is distinct, for example, from something that is the "white part" of me? If there is a "woman part" of me, it doesn't seem to be the kind of thing I could point to—not because etiquette demands that nice people don't point to their private or covered parts, but because even if I broke a social

133

rule and did so, nothing I might point to would meet the requirements of being a "part" of me that was a "woman part" that was not also a "white part." Any part of my body is part of a body that is, by prevailing criteria, female and white. And now that I have moved surreptitiously from talking about a "woman part" to talking about a "female part," you will remember another reason why pointing to the "woman part" of myself would be no mean feat: being a "woman" is not the same thing as, nor is it reducible to, being a "female." "Women" are what females of the human species become, or are supposed to become, through learning how to think, act, and live in certain ways. What females in one society learn about how they are to think, act, and live, can differ enormously from what females in another society learn; in fact, as we have been reminded often, there can be very significant differences within a given society. Moreover, those females who don't learn their lessons very well, or who resist being and doing what they're taught, or who, as we saw in Aristotle's view, are born into the "wrong" group, may have their credentials as "real women" questioned even while their status as females remains intact. Indeed, unless their female status is assumed, there can be no grounds for wondering whether they are really "women." Being a woman—or a man, for that matter—is a complicated business, and apparently a precarious one, given the number of societal institutions instructing us about how to be women or men and punishing us for failing to act appropriately.

Maybe I could tell you better about that aspect of myself in virtue of which I am called a "woman" and show you how it is different from that aspect of myself in virtue of which I am called "white" by talking about how as a woman I am distinguished from men, while as a white person I am distinguished from, for example, Black people. I can metaphorically point to my womanness by reminding you of how I am different from men, to my whiteness by reminding you of how I am different from Black people. For example, I can attend to the different expectations my parents and teachers had for me and my two sisters, on the one hand, and our two brothers, on the other; or, *à la* Nancy Chodorow, I can try to describe the difference between how we three girls related to our mother and how our brothers related to her, and how that affected our senses of ourselves. And this might appear to have nothing to do with whether I am white or Black, Anglo or Hispana, Christian or Jewish. But it is only because whiteness is taken as a given that there is even the appearance of being able to distinguish simply between a person's being a woman and a person's being a man, and thus of being able somehow to point to the "woman part" of me in isolation from the "white part" of me. Even if the idea is that I am to be distinguished simply from men, it may turn out that

I am distinguished from white men in ways different from the ways in which I am distinguished from Black men. We have discussed this before, but it's worth trying one more approach to it.

Let's suppose I have the chance to stand up on a stage next to James Baldwin. He is a man and I am a woman, but there are other differences between us, including of course the fact that he is Black and I am white. How, then, will contrasting myself to him enable you to see what my "woman part" is and how it is isolatable from my "white part"? Is my difference from him as a woman separable from my difference from him as a white person? To find out whether my gender difference is isolatable from my racial difference from him, it would help to add some more people on the stage. So now Angela Davis joins us. Is there some respect in which I am different from James Baldwin in just the same way Angela Davis is different from him—is there something she and I share such that we are different from him in just the same ways? And now let's add a white man up here—say my brother Jon. Are Angela Davis and I different from Jon in just the same way, since we both are women and he is a man?

Now in what respect could Angela and I be said to be different from Jon in just the same way? Well, we're both called "women" and he is not. But does our being called "women" mean the same thing to us and for us? Are there any situations in which my being white and her being Black does not affect what it means to us and for us to be women? To whom is it not going to make a difference that my "womanness" is the womanness of a white woman, that hers is the womanness of a Black woman? To our mothers? our fathers? our sisters? our brothers? our children? our teachers? our students? our employers? our lovers? ourselves?

If it were possible to isolate a woman's "womanness" from her racial identity, then we should have no trouble imagining that had I been Black I could have had just the same understanding of myself as a woman as I in fact do, and that no matter how differently people would have treated me had I been Black, nevertheless what it would have meant to them that I was a woman would have been just the same. To rehearse this imaginary situation is to expose its utter bizarreness.

The identities of persons are much more complicated than what might be suggested by the simple and straightforward use of terms like "Black," "white," "woman," "man." Conceptual tidiness would suggest that if Angela's a woman and I am too, while James is a man and so is Jon, then unless our language misleads us there must be something Angela and I share that distinguishes us from James and Jon and distinguishes us from them indistinguishably. Similarly, if Angela is Black and so is James, while Jon is white and so am I, then unless our language misleads us there must be something Angela and James share that distinguishes them from Jon and me and distinguishes them from us indistinguishably.

However, as some philosophers have been trying to tell us now for decades, we can't blame language for our failure to examine its use in context. And if we examine the use of "woman" in particular contexts, then we might be encouraged to ask when descriptions of what-it-is-to-be-a-woman really are descriptions of what-it-is-to-be-a-woman-in-culture-X or subculture-Y. Being a woman, as we surely know by now from cross-cultural studies, is something that is constructed by societies and differs from one society to another. Hence unless I know something more about two women than the fact that they are women, I can't say anything about what they might have in common. What is the "womanness" that Angela Davis and I are said to share? Prior to any actual investigation, all we can say for sure is that being a woman is constructed in contrast to (even if the contrast is minimal) being a man (or to some other gender as well—not all cultures are as stingy as those that countenance only "men" and "women").[1] While all women are gendered, and are gendered as women in contrast to men, nothing follows from that alone about what it means to be so gendered. For it is simply a tautology to say that all women are gendered, since women are by definition gendered females. (We are referring to gender and not to sex; not all human females end up gendered as women.)

It is thus evident that thinking about a person's identity as made up of neatly distinguishable "parts" may be very misleading, despite the impetus from philosophers such as Plato and Descartes to so describe ourselves. Just as in their cases we may get the impression that the whole person is a composite of soul (or mind) and body, so in the case of much feminist thought we may get the impression that a woman's identity consists of a sum of parts neatly divisible from one another, parts defined in terms of her race, gender, class, and so on. We may infer that the oppressions she is subject to are (depending on who she is) neatly divisible into racism, sexism, classism, or homophobia, and that in her various political activities she works clearly now out of one part of herself, now out of another. This is a version of personal identity we might call tootsie roll metaphysics: each part of my identity is separable from every other part, and the significance of each part is unaffected by the other parts. On this view of personal identity (which might also be called pop-bead metaphysics), my being a woman means the same whether I am white or Black, rich or poor, French or Jamaican, Jewish or Muslim.[2] As a woman, I'm like other women; my difference from other women is only along the other dimensions of my identity. Hence it is possible on this view to imagine my being the same woman even if my race were different—the pop-

bead or tootsie roll section labeled "woman" is just inserted into a different strand or roll. According to a powerful tradition within Western philosophy (though not limited to it), if my soul is separable from my body,
it might become attached to or lodge in another body; and if my soul is
who I really am, then this new combination of soul and body is still me.
Similarly, if my "womanness" is separable from other aspects of my identity, then I as woman would still be the same woman I am even if I happen
to have been born into a body of a different color, or even a body of the
same color at a different moment in history.[3]

I

There is much new and recently recovered work by and about women, in
history, anthropology, psychology, economics, and sociology, not to
mention literature. It is the result of painstaking and often undervalued
labor. Surely in such investigations we can expect to find people refusing
to let either logical or political assumptions of the kind we discussed in
earlier chapters take the place of good empirical research: rather than assuming that women must have something in common as women, these
researchers should help us look to see whether they do, to investigate not
only the respects in which women of different races, classes, nationalities,
historical periods, religions, sexual orientations, and so forth, are similar
but the respects in which they are different. On the basis of such studies
we may find a way to isolate what is true of women as women.

This way of trying to get at what is true about women is quite different
from the two ways we have already explored: (1) To look within a single
racial or ethnic or religious or cultural group for the effects of gender,
eliminating other differences in an individual's development or treatment.
(2) To examine the effects of gender on women not otherwise subject to
oppression. Both of these methods are based on the unwarranted assumption that what is constant doesn't affect what is variable, that race
or class disappear because they are held constant or because they are not
a factor in a woman's oppression. Neither method requires us to investigate differences among women or to go beyond a single group of women.

This ought to tell us that rather than first finding out what is true of
some women as women and then inferring that this is true of all women
and thus is common to all women, we have to investigate different women's
lives and see what they have in common *other* than being female and
being called "women." Only then (if at all) can we talk about what is true
of any and all of them as women.

Plato, as we saw, thought that only especially gifted thinkers could dis-
cern what differences between men and women, or differences among

men and among women, mattered; only they could know how and why the differences made a difference; and only by virtue of such knowledge were they philosopher-rulers. If we take nothing else away from a reading of the *Republic,* surely we ought to question how the kind of authority about sameness and difference vested in philosopher-rulers ever becomes the bailiwick of any particular person or group (for example, of the justices of the Supreme Court of the United States, who are taken to have not merely the right but the obligation to decide what the relevant similarities and differences are between men and women, whites and Blacks, Christians and Jews, "normal" and mentally retarded people, etc., and what those similarities and differences mean).[4] The philosopher-rulers do not merely notice some interesting features about the world around them when they describe two people as being the same or different in particular ways—for example, when they claim that male and female philosopher-rulers are more alike than male philosophers and male cobblers. Whatever else they are doing, philosopher-rulers are implicitly insisting that this is the way the world really is. Moreover, they think that their actions and those of everyone else ought to be based on a picture of the way things really are and not on some less accurate account.

Reading Plato ought to encourage us to look at the degree of metaphysical and political authority presupposed by those who claim the right to point out commonality, who assert or exercise the privilege of determining just what it means in terms of others' identities, social locations, and political priorities. It is useful to remember, for example, that Plato didn't consult with women around him to find out if they thought they were like men in the significant ways he thought they were; he claimed to know how and to what extent men and women of a given class were similar and what that meant about how their lives ought to be organized. This as much as any other consideration should make us wonder about the extent to which Plato ought to be called a feminist. One can have a theory about the equality between men and women that itself violates the conditions under which real equality can exist: for simply telling a group of heretofore subjugated people "You are like us in the following respects and hence ought to be treated in the following way" is an assertion of the very power and authority that the claims about equality are supposed to make illicit. As James Baldwin said: "There is no reason for you to try to become like white people and there is no basis whatever for their impertinent assumption that *they* must accept *you.*"[5]

It is no wonder, then, that women of color have been distrustful of white women who point to similarities between them when it seems politically expedient to do so and to dissimilarities when it does not.[6] They have wanted to know just why and when white women become interested in similarities and differences among women. At issue is not so much whether there are or are not similarities or differences, but about how white middle-class feminists try to use claims about similarity and differences among women in different directions, depending on what they believe such similarity or dissimilarity implies. For example, as we have seen, sometimes feminists have insisted on the similarity between the treatment of "women" and that of "slaves"; other times they have insisted that the situation of free women and slave women is different enough that the situation of slave women cannot be a useful guide to that of free women.[7] The issue is thus not so much a metaphysical one as a political one. Given the highly charged political atmosphere in which claims about sameness and difference are made, challenged and negotiated, and the consequences of such claims for access to resources, status, and power, we cannot assume that they are simple descriptive reports on the basis of which we can come to see what women of different races, cultures, and so on, have in common, what is true of them as women. Investigations into ways in which women are similar and ways we are different must always be looked at in the light of the following questions: Who is doing the investigating? Whose views are heard and accepted? Why? What criteria are used for similarity and difference? Finally, and most important, what is said to follow from the supposed existence of similarity or difference?[8] Have those under investigation been asked what they think?

Someone might tell me that we have something in common, but even if I agree, I may find that utterly insignificant in terms of my identity and my plans for action. This reminds us that the claim of commonality can be very arrogant indeed: the caller may be attempting to appropriate the other's identity. We are aware of this whenever we find it annoying for a stranger or even an acquaintance to claim something in common with us. In such cases we resent the implication that because we have something in common there is some special connection between us, some reason for spending time together, making plans together.

Nevertheless, not all claims about commonality are arrogant. Let us take for example the following case:

You have described yourself as having certain properties or characteristics by virtue of which you justify the claim to a certain position or status or certain entitlements.

I claim that I am like you in that respect and that I therefore also ought to be enjoying that status or those entitlements.

You have the power and authority to recognize our similarity and your doing so will make a significant difference as to whether my claim is attended to.

139

The history of the civil rights movement and women's rights movements provide familiar examples of this claim. A subordinated people insist that they have characteristics in common with their dominators (e.g., humanity, reason, vulnerability to suffering) and therefore that they are owed a higher regard than presently afforded them by the dominators.

In stark contrast we have the following case:

You have described yourself as having certain properties or characteristics.

You claim that I am like you in having the same characteristics, but you have not consulted me as to whether I think I am like you in this way or whether I attach the same significance you do to having such characteristics.

You have more power and authority than I to make your claims heard and attended to.

White feminists have fallen into this trap whenever they have assumed that women of color are like themselves and hence ought to have the same priorities. Although it is not arrogant, for example, for a Black woman in the United States to claim that she is like me in having characteristics I say entitle me to citizenship, it is arrogant for me to simply declare to the same woman that she is like me and tell her what that means about the two of us. What makes my claim untenable is my presumption that I have the power and the authority to legislate her identity. She makes no such presumptions in her assertion of her rights; she merely refers to my own description of my identity and rights as a basis for asserting her own. Of course none of this means that I can't help but be arrogant in all ways or that she couldn't possibly be in any way. The two cases we've described do not exhaust the possibilities; variations along a spectrum of claims about commonality will be the more interesting cases for feminist examination.

We have begun to realize that I don't necessarily correct my picture of what is true of women "as women" by doing "empirical research" rather than simply generalizing from my own case.[9] For I can't simply "look and see" to find out what we have or don't have in common. First of all, I have to have decided what kind of similarity or difference I am interested in. It makes no sense to ask simply whether women are similar or different—I have to specify in what way they might be similar or different. Moreover, I have to employ criteria of sameness and difference—I have to use some measure by which I decide whether they are the same or different in the specified way. And finally, I have to determine the significance of the similarities and differences I find.

Let us suppose that I am interested in finding out how much economic and political power various groups of women have. Let us also suppose that the criterion for similarity or difference I use is whether women have as much economic and political power as the most powerful men. Using this criterion, I say I find—perhaps I may be challenged by some anthropologists—that there are no significant differences among women with respect to their having that degree of economic and political power. Finally, I judge that being the same in this way is a very significant fact about women, more significant than any other similarity or difference among us. The most important fact about us is what we have in common: namely, that none of us has the power the most powerful men do.

On the other hand, I might employ another criterion. I might ask not simply whether any women have as much power as the most powerful men, but rather investigate the degree to which and ways in which different groups of women have access to such power, even on borrowed terms. Using this criterion I am much more likely to see differences among women; and while I may not be sure just what significance to attach to those differences, I am at least prepared to give them some weight. For example, using the first criterion I cannot attach any significance to the fact that because the wives of white slaveowners in the United States were of a different race and class, they had many more privileges than the Black women who were their slaves (including the privilege of whipping their female slaves at will and with impunity). If my working criterion is the kind of power women lack rather than the degree of power they have, then I have to say that the wives did not have the economic and political power their husbands did, and hence that there is no significant difference between them and the Black slave women. But by the second criterion, I do not discount the power women have (however derivative it might be) in trying to see what women do or do not have in common. I note that while neither the white wife nor the Black female slave had the power the white male slaveowner did, this did not mean they were subject to the same abuses of his power, nor did it mean that the women were equally powerless in relation to each other.

Let us explore a related example. Suppose my criterion for deciding how similar women are with respect to economic and political power is whether they have as much power as men of their own racial, class, or ethnic group. Let us suppose—contrary to some anthropological findings and to the facts of slavery before us—that according to this criterion, all women are the same: none of us has as much or more power than the men of our group. But if we use this criterion for deciding how similar or different we are, then we completely leave aside the differences in power between men of different groups, between women of different groups, and between men of one group and women of another. If we suppose, for example, that upper-class white women in the United States are as subject to the whims of their husbands' desire to abuse them as poor white women

141

are, we leave out of the picture the power upper-class white women and their husbands have over poor white men and poor white women.

The example from Kenneth Stampp discussed in the Introduction brings to mind yet another decision that has to be made when I try to "look and see" what different groups of people have in common: how shall I describe what they share? You will recall that Stampp describes a working assumption of his investigations in this way:

I have assumed that the slaves were merely ordinary human beings, that innately Negroes *are*, after all, only white men with black skins, nothing more, nothing less.[10]

What Blacks and whites have in common, according to Stampp, is an essential "whiteness." Stampp is willing to countenance similarity to members of a different racial group, historically despised by his own, as long as it is on his terms (he gets to decide who is like whom and what that means) and as long as it is favorable to him (it preserves his identity and erases that of the formerly despised group). He is hardly being "color-blind" here, but rather is insisting that Black people aren't the color some of us might have thought; they actually are white.

In short, I may have a great deal at stake when I explore similarities and differences among groups of people. Just what I have at stake may show up at the many points in my investigation at which I must make some crucial decisions: decisions about the kind of similarity or difference I am interested in, decisions about the criteria I will employ to see what similarities and differences there are, decisions about what I take them to mean, decisions about how I describe those similarities or differences. We feminists are no less subject to the biases such decisions can introduce than anyone else is. A description of the common world we share "as women" may be simply a description of my world with you now as an honorary member.

II

Let us return for a moment to the knowledge about our identities that most of us find easy to express. Most of us (in perhaps most societies) are asked at regular intervals to indicate whether we are men or women, what racial or ethnic category describes us, and so on (what we are asked will depend on the society we live in). Indeed, our knowledge of such facts about our identities is called upon all the time—for example, in filling out new patient forms at the dentist's, in choosing which bathroom to enter, in providing information for demographic studies (to say nothing about the information we constantly give out to others about aspects of our identities, through our speech patterns, gestures, accents, inflections, gait, and clothing). No doubt we can lie about these identities—by checking the wrong box, for example. No doubt we can refuse to act the way we might be expected to on the basis of this self-knowledge—my knowing I'm a woman doesn't mean I won't use a bathroom marked "men." But lying and "misbehaving" presuppose the kind of knowledge in question, that is, knowledge of one's gender, one's race, one's ethnicity, one's nationality. What is it I know if I know that I am a woman or a man, Black or Hispana or white, Jewish or Christian, straight or gay or lesbian? Could I be wrong? If others disagree with me, is there a way of deciding which of us is right?

Descartes argued that given good grounds for doubt about anything else he might have come to believe, there was only one thing he could know for certain: that he existed.

This proposition "I am," "I exist," whenever I utter it or conceive it in my mind, is necessarily true.[11]

Indeed, the fact of his doubting was the very condition of his certain knowledge—for doubting (itself a kind of thinking) couldn't take place unless there was someone to do the doubting. To paraphrase Walt Kelly's Pogo: I have met the doubter and he is I. I think, therefore I am. This knowledge of his own existence was something Descartes took himself to have apart from the mediation of his senses (those, he had satisfied himself, were deceptive until proven otherwise) and apart from the mediation of his culture (there was no good reason to believe anything he had been taught).[12] And he was in many ways quite attuned to the reach of his senses and his culture: for having found the nugget of certainty in the fact that he existed, he was very cautious about describing who or what the "I" that exists *is:*

But I do not yet sufficiently understand what is this "I" that necessarily exists. I must take care, then, that I do not rashly take something else for the "I," and thus go wrong even in the knowledge that I am maintaining to be the most certain and evident of all. . . . What, then, did I formerly think I was?[13]

He trots out, only to dismiss on the sceptical grounds he already has laid, several possible candidates for what he is—reasonable animal, man, body, soul. I can't say for certain that I have a face, hands, arms, Descartes reasoned, even though I can say for certain that I exist, because I have said that I have reason to doubt that such things exist.

I bring up Descartes here, not because I think a program of sceptical calisthenics along the lines he proposed is the right antidote for the habits of thought that lie at the root of tendencies toward ethnocentrism in dominant Western feminist thought. But I do find instructive his caution about *what* or *who* he is, as well as his general point about the deceptive ease with which we use words, the facile certainty with which we describe what we might think we know best—ourselves. Descartes—certain as he is about some facts about himself—is concerned about how much our understanding of ourselves is due, not to unmediated introspection, but to concepts and categories we inherit from other people, concepts and categories that presuppose the existence of the very things Descartes thinks we have reason to doubt.[14] I might well be a man, Descartes is saying, but I have to convince myself that I know some other things before I'll agree to this description of myself.

I say that I know I am a woman, I know that I am white, and so on. But if I know that, surely I know what I mean by saying these things. What properties am I ascribing to myself? Are there circumstances under which I might have doubts about what or who I am? Is being a woman something I could cease being? Is being white something I could cease being? What have I learned, when I learn that I am a woman? When I learn that I am white? What have I agreed to, in agreeing to say that I am a woman? In agreeing to say that I am white? What am I refusing, if I were to insist that neither of these terms applies to me?

Imagine a huge customs hall with numerous doors, marked "women," "men," "Afro-American," "Asian-American," "Euro-American," "Hispanic-American," "working class," "middle class," "upper class," "lesbian," "gay," "heterosexual," and so forth. (You may add to or subtract from the number of doors to your heart's content; we'll return in a minute to the question of who decides how many doors there are, what the doors say, and other questions about the legislation and orchestration of identity.) The doors are arranged in banks, so that each person faces first a bank of doors that sort according to gender, then a bank that sort according to race, or alternatively sort first according to race, then according to class, then according to gender, and so on. We'll all give notice of who we are by going through the requisite doors.

Assume that the doors at the first bank are marked

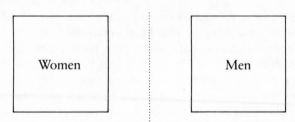

and at the second bank

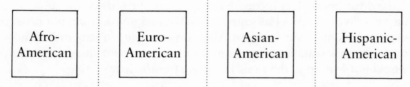

If the sorting done at the first bank is still in effect at the second, then there will have to be two sets of doors at the second, like so:

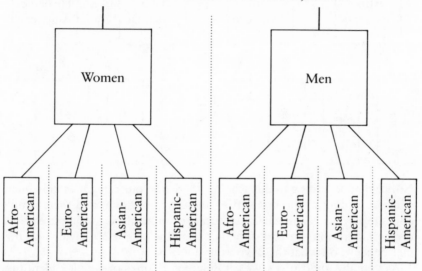

That is, if the original division is maintained between women and men, then Afro-American women and men will not go through the same doors—for there will be two doors marked "Afro-American," one the other side of the door marked "women," the other the other side of the door marked "men."[15] Notice that in this case whatever the Afro-Americans have in common, they will not end up on the other side of the same door; they won't be in the same place. For their Afro-Americanness, whatever that is, will be seen to exist in the context of their being women or men, and more particularly as in some sense subordinate to their being women or men. In accordance with this way of sorting people, there is only one category of "woman," but two categories of each racial or cultural identity.

Let us see what happens if we change the order of the doors or if we do not insist that one sorting have effect on the next: for example, the Afro-American men and women would have ended up on the other side of the same door marked "Afro-American" if after the division into women and men all the people involved in the sorting had come back together again in a big group and started afresh. Though they once would have been divided for another purpose, that fact about them does not show up in the next division. Or let us suppose that the first division was not between men and women but between Afro-American, Euro-American, and so forth. In this situation, Afro-American women and the other women would not end up in the same location after the first sorting.

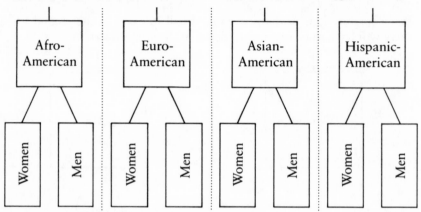

Notice that according to this schema, there are four categories of women, while according to the first sorting there was but one; and there is only one category for each racial or cultural group, while according to the first division there were several. Whether and how people are divided up further depends on what the next set of doors is.

As you already can see, we get different pictures of people's identities, and of the extent to which one person shares some aspect of identity with another, depending on what the doors are, how they are ordered, and how people are supposed to proceed through them. For example, according to the first schema, a woman who is "Asian-American" has more in common with all other women than she does with Asian-American men; while according to the second, Asian-American men and women have more in common than Asian-American women and other women. According to the first schema, I can in some sense think about myself as a woman in isolation from other facts about myself; if I couldn't, I wouldn't know how to go through the doors. Yet according to the second schema, my thinking about myself as a woman is in the context of being Asian-American or Afro-American, or some other racial group.

We will need to know more about these doors: Who makes them, and who guards them? That is, who decides what will be on them, how many there will be, in what order they occur? Who decides which one you are supposed to take if there is any doubt? Is one free to ignore a door or to go around a given set of doors? We surely also need to know what facts about you and your experiences and history make it seem likely—to you and others—that you will go through one door rather than another, or that you will find the order of the doors appropriate to your identity.

Questions will also arise about what the designations on the doors mean. For example, there is a certain ambiguity about the doors marked "men" and "women." That isn't the same as having them marked "male" and "female." [16] Many questions will come up about the accuracy of the designations: What if someone refused to go through a door marked simply "woman" or simply "Asian-American," on the grounds that she found those categories too crude and was suspicious of the point of being cataloged in these ways? Suppose someone didn't know what the point of door-dividing is and was not sure of what the designations mean? Moreover, if I think that things are better behind one door than another, I might try very hard to convince the guards and the people scheduled to be sorted that I ought to go behind that one even though I know it is not the one they expect me to go through. Do some people know better than I what doors I really belong behind? Is there any reason why I should not try to get on the far side of any door I want to? Are the doors there to pinpoint one's "true identity," if there is such a thing? Do people have identities independent of what proceeding through the doors would indicate? Are the doors there mainly to control access to some other place, or some other people? Why are they there? Do I have to go through them? What happens if I try not to? What happens if someone tries to claim an identity as an act of solidarity—by wearing a yellow star or a pink triangle, for example?

The doors imagery helps us to deal with some issues that have been plaguing us throughout this book and helps us also to see the point of questions raised earlier about what it is to have knowledge of one's gender, race, class or any other possible identifier. The alternative schemas (and we have only presented two of indefinitely many) present graphically for us the different things it can mean to talk about what is true of women "as women" and about what women have in common. According to the first schema, what is true of me "as a woman" seems to be what I have in common with all other women in contrast to all other men. According to the second schema, what is true of me "as a woman" would seem to be what I have in common with other women of my ethnic and racial background in contrast to men of the same background. The second schema suggests that one's womanness is to be understood in the context of one's ethnic and racial background, while the first makes it look as if one's womanness can be specified quite independently of such background. According to the second schema, even if a case could be made for there

147

being a "woman part" of each woman that was isolatable from her other "parts," that wouldn't necessarily show that all women have something substantial in common "as women," that the "woman part" would be the same in all cases. In order to know whether all the people who end up behind the doors marked "women" share anything substantial in common, we'd have to know the criteria used for dividing women from men in each case and see if they were similar in all cases (and this, as noted earlier, will require us to decide in what respect and by what criteria we want to see whether they are similar). Of course we could assure that all women have something substantial in common by insisting that anyone who does not have some particular characteristic is not a "woman"; then "all women have something in common" would be as secure, and as trivial, as any other tautology.

The schemas enable us to see how the situation of white middle-class women can be conflated with the situation of "women," thus securing the privileged position of one group of women over others. If we use the first schema, differences among women are recognized but treated as secondary to whatever it is that distinguishes all women from all men. The first schema doesn't tell us what this common distinguishing feature is. But if our description of what distinguishes "women" from "men" in fact ends up being what distinguishes one group of women from the men like them, then what is true of that one group of women will be taken to characterize all women. This is in effect what we saw happening in de Beauvoir's account. If we keep the second schema in mind, we might be less likely to take the case of one group of women for the case of all, since the second schema implies that gender distinctions exist in the context of ethnic and racial distinctions. Indeed, it suggests that the distinctions between any two ethnic or racial groups are more significant (according to those who devise the system) than the distinctions between men and women within any such group. It makes it harder for us to take any particular group of women's experience as representative of all, but surely it does not prohibit us from asking what different groups of women have or might come to have in common.

Since people can be classified and cataloged in any number of ways, overlapping ways, how we catalog them, in particular how we sort out the overlapping distinctions, will depend on our purposes and our sense of what the similarities and differences among them are and how they ought to be weighed. (Think of the different classificatory schemas implicitly proposed by those who insist "I am a woman who is a writer," or "I am a writer who is a woman.") Purposes may clash, indeed may clash somewhat predictably along the lines of certain differences among us; and not all of us have the same degree of power and authority about which schema or schemas are the most appropriate or revealing means of presenting the significance of similarities and differences among people.

By thinking of cataloging schemes as being like doors in an imaginary customs house, or like doors in some version of the immigration bureau that existed at Ellis Island, or like bathroom doors in segregated areas of the United States, we may be more likely to keep in mind the constant human effort it takes to create and maintain classificatory schemes, the continual human battles over which schemes are to prevail, and the purposes of such schemes.

Perhaps we need to add a door that says "officials only" to remind us of another very important difference—that between people who create and maintain the schemes and those simply subject to them. On the other hand, it may well be that those with the most power of all don't have doors—especially not doors labeled "makers and keepers of the doors"— for that would only reveal that the scheme is not a "natural" one and also enable those upset with the scheme to know where to begin to look for its creators and enforcers.[17] This points to another useful feature of the doors analogy: it reminds us how certain human artifacts can come to be regarded as things found or forged in nature, facts to be discovered or unearthed by human investigators. It has been crucial for those who make much of certain differences among humans to portray those differences as givens that humanity disregards at its peril.[18]

Classificatory names on doors have an important kind of official status: while they reflect the particular purposes of powerful members of human communities (purposes that may be shared by less powerful members, a point to which we shall return below), they at the same time obscure those purposes through the suggestion that the categories are uncreated, that they exist in themselves. In this view, each of us is either man or woman, either white or Black or brown, either Jewish or Christian, heterosexual or gay or lesbian, and that like it or not, one or some of those elements of our identities are more fundamentally descriptive of us than others. No doubt it is true that once those categories have been created, and once social and political and economic institutions have been built around them, there will be criteria in accordance with which we can say with assurance into what categories any particular person fits. And even if we had no part in the creation of such categories, if we have learned the ways of our society, we have learned which doors we will be expected to pass through. Indeed, we may joyfully embrace the identities they draw attention to.

Our learning of the categories and where we fit into them is unlikely to include learning about their historical character. That is, it is unlikely that we learn about the point at which a category came into being. (For

example, the creation of "homosexual" as a category of person as opposed to a category of action dates apparently from the late nineteenth
century).[19] It is also unlikely that we learn about the battles over what the
categories mean (for example, battles over definitions among white men
about what constitutes "Negro blood," or over definitions among contemporary Blacks in the United States over what constitutes being "Black").[20]

If we think of such distinctions in terms of the doors, then we might
begin to ask a number of questions that would challenge the assumption
that the distinctions we make among people are simple and straightforward responses to the distinctions found among them in nature. (It
also helps to challenge a somewhat more complicated assumption: that
the categories are indeed created for human purposes, but not for those of
any particular group—as if all humans have the same authority over the
creation and maintenance of the categories.) First of all, the door imagery
implies some ambiguity about whether the process of going (or being
made to go) through the doors represents a recognition of differences
among people or a creation of them. Insofar as there are criteria for the
appropriateness of particular people passing through particular doors,
and insofar as those who pass through and those who monitor their passage seem to have no questions about the passage, it looks as if the doors
simply represent a moment at which people are processed in accordance
with characteristics that inhere in them. Moreover, the monitors or guards
seem to be there, not to keep making up categories, but to make sure that
the people whom the guards know (and whom the guards assume know
they know) to belong to one category rather than another go through the
right door. A further but only occasionally called-upon role of the monitors is to decide about borderline cases.

On the other hand, the process by which people are channeled into one
category rather than another can be seen as creating distinctions. We
need to ask why people are being processed through these doors, whether
social and political positions and privileges are at stake in this processing.
We need also to inquire whether (and how) those subject to such processing ever challenge the categories or their significance. It is important to
know whether they are punished for questioning the appropriateness of
the categories or challenging the authority of those who seem to have
most power over the maintenance of them. Whether categories come into
and go out of existence, and if so, why. We must ask whether there are
battles over what the categories ought to be, or over what they mean, or
over who gets to decide these issues.

We may also want to know more about just how people are processed
through the doors: by this we mean to ask not simply whether people
resist going through or help others who resist going through; but also

whether if they do resist they are forced through anyway. It is not enough to know whether people do something without resistance to decide whether they are made to do it. For we can come to do without apparent coercion what we were encouraged to do and punished for not doing from an early age. We have to ask what happens when we do not do what we are expected to. I should be wary of describing my actions as "willing" if I would have been punished for not acting in that way. The existence of known punishments for failure to do something strongly suggests that one is being made to do that thing—that in the absence of such punishments one probably wouldn't do it.

In light of such considerations we might go back to some questions raised earlier in this chapter about what one knows when one answers such questions as "Are you a man or a woman?" "Are you white or Black or . . . ?" To answer the first by saying "I am a woman" is to agree to what one understands to be the criteria for being a woman and to say that one meets those criteria. But one could be challenged either on the grounds that one isn't using the right criteria or on the grounds that one doesn't meet them. And insofar as the doors analogy helps us to see the extent to which gender identity is, not only as de Beauvoir argued the ongoing creation of a society (women are made, not born), but something over which some members of society have more authority than others, my claim about being a woman may well be challenged by those who have that authority. Sojourner Truth had to argue for the proposition that she was a "woman." Someone who refuses to indicate whether one is a "woman" or a "man," or someone who refuses to specify their "race" or "ethnicity" on a census form, may be punished by those who distribute such forms. Some women may be told by white feminists that they aren't properly distinguishing their voices as "women" from their voices as "Afro-Americans" or "Jews" or members of the "working class."[21] Jan Morris decided that rather than contest the meaning of "woman" or "man" she would change her bodily appearance and her gestures and "lifestyle" so that she would be counted as a "woman."[22] (I don't know what it says on her passport about her sexual identity, or who exactly is in the position to decide what she is entitled to put there, but I feel certain she uses bathrooms marked "women" and presents herself in social life as a woman—indeed, as an upper-middle-class white Englishwoman.)

Given the possibility of questions about and challenges to the categories, it may be more important to ask, not what I know when I answer such questions about my identity, but what I acquiesce in, what I do not resist, when I agree to answer them. I am agreeing to some schema of identity, forged in accordance with some individual's or some group's or some society's classificatory purposes. Unless I register some kind of protest or qualification, I accept (willingly or not) the appropriateness of the classification and the significance attached to it. So, for example, I might gladly use the word "woman" to refer to myself but try in concert with others to resist what I take to be the prevailing meaning of the term or the prevailing significance attached to it. Or I might think it important to resist a term altogether—for example, "handicapped." I might think it important to embrace joyfully a term such as "lesbian" or "Black" and to try with others to invest it with new meaning.

Insofar as we don't regard the kinds of exercises in which we are asked to indicate our gender, race, and so on, as problematic, we may have forgotten to ask how we came to use those categories to refer to ourselves or to others. It may seem to us as if who we are, who others are, and what we do and don't have in common are matters of simple observation. Perhaps because we learn the categories so early and are continually asked to reflect our knowledge of them, they seem unproblematic. Ease of application of the categories can be confused with justified certainty about how "natural" they are.

Furthermore, if we think about identities and points of similarity and difference as things that are always being negotiated and challenged, we may think more about ways in which these categories depend upon the particular purposes of those who create and maintain them. This is not to say that it is easy to identify those who create and maintain them. It often seems as if none of us created these categories but all of us help to maintain them. But insofar as we feel moved to do battle over them, we exhibit both a sense of being subject to them against our will and a sense of being able to do something about the power they have over the articulation of our identities and thus over our social and political positions to the extent that they depend on those identities.

In some ways it ought to be quite surprising that describing who we are and how we are like and unlike others is not always the straightforward process it appears to be. For first of all, the ability to compare and contrast things by seeing what categories they do or don't fit into is crucial to thinking and to using language. Second, in societies in which great significance is attached to sexual, racial, and class categories, we learn early and well which of those categories we and everyone around us belong to. Indeed, most of the time we probably are showing ourselves and others which of these categories we belong to, even when we are not explicitly saying so. Unless categorization is made problematic for us, we are not likely to raise questions about the categories we use; and it seems likely that the more a society has invested in its members' getting the categories right, the more occasions there will be for reinforcing them, and the fewer occasions there will be for raising questions about them.[23]

As noted right at the beginning of this book, feminists have rightly been concerned with how philosophers and other thinkers have spoken with great authority about the differences between men and women and what social and political significance those differences have. We have tried to lay bare how neatly their classificatory schemes conflate being a man with being human, how in subtle or not so subtle ways they show us that women are inferior specimens of humanity. But we feminists have not been free of classificatory schemes either—how could we be?—and many of us have not been attentive to the political priorities and race and class privileges imported by the schemes we use. The imagery of the doors can help us review some of the ways in which this importation works.

III

According to Plato, in order to create and maintain the best possible state it is absolutely crucial that someone know the "proper divisions and distinctions" among its various members.[24] Such a person would know that the distinction between philosopher-rulers and cobblers is much more significant than that between male and female. Thus Plato might arrange the doors in the following fashion:

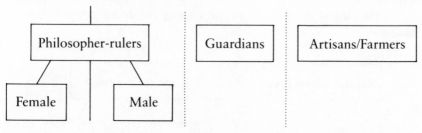

The purpose of such a division is the recognition of differences necessary for the creation of a just state. The divisions will be maintained by the philosopher-rulers with the aid of the guardians; and if child-rearing is done the way Plato prescribes, everyone will acquire the habits and desires appropriate to one's role, perpetuating the structure of the society. That is, people will come to understand that they wouldn't be better off trying to do the work assigned another group, that real happiness lies in knowing what one's nature is and doing the kind of work appropriate to it.

Where would Plato place slaves in this arrangement? Their position seems to be so taken for granted by Plato that they are hardly mentioned. In terms of the doors imagery, this is like finding no door with the term by which you expect to be called (whether or not you contest it). We may well wonder whether, whatever the difficulties about being classified in a

153

particular way, there are worse difficulties in store for those not deemed worthy of the notice classificatory schemes provide.

Nor does the above schema capture everything Plato says about women. It does seem accurate as a representation of what Plato said about the possibility of female philosopher-rulers and their position vis-à-vis male philsopher-rulers as well as males belonging to other groups. But it leaves out what he took to be typical of Athenian women. We know he did not think of them as belonging to the same category as women who would be philosopher-rulers; the distinction between such women and other women was as important for Plato as that between males who would be philosopher-rulers and males who would be artisans or farmers. For Plato, the distinction between men and women is phrased in terms of distinctions among philosopher-rulers, guardians, artisans. Women who are philosopher-rulers have an entirely different nature from those who are not, even though all women are alike in their bodily configuration. So were we to speak as if gender is the primary consideration in Plato's views of "women," we would not simply give an inaccurate account of his views; we would give notice that the only women worth knowing about are those belonging to a particular group. We would take Plato's views about an elite group of women to be all there is to his views about women.

On the face of it, Aristotle might arrange the doors in the following manner:

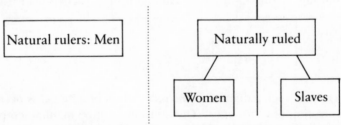

The distinctions between the rulers and the ruled are simply those intended by nature, according to Aristotle; and any well-ordered community will respect them, since they correspond to the different functions different people are fit to perform in the community.

But as we saw, there is something misleading about this way of representing Aristotle's views. First of all, there is the somewhat nagging problem of whether Aristotle thought there were some men who were by nature neither natural rulers nor naturally ruled. But more important for our purposes, the category "slaves" obscures the fact that even on Aristotle's own reckoning some of those slaves were female. So Aristotle, like Plato, really has two different categories of females or women. Indeed, in effect he puts females in two different gender categories: females with the gender "woman" and females with no gender at all. A slave woman trying to go through the door Aristotle marked "women" wouldn't be allowed through; she would have to go through the one marked "slave," along with males who are slaves.

As with Plato, so with Aristotle: We cannot fully represent his views about the significance of sex or gender by using the schema according to which the most significant distinction among people is that between men and women. It would be misleading to imply that we could get at his views about women by focusing simply on the distinctions he draws between men and women of a particular group. Moreover, it would show that we had decided that what he says about female slaves isn't important in trying to come to understand his views about the significance of sex and gender, that we only need to understand what he says about "free" women.

The tension we explored in de Beauvoir's account of the condition of women can be represented usefully through the analogy of the doors. On the one hand, de Beauvoir says much to suggest that in order to understand the condition of women we have to look at them in the context of the various racial and class groups to which they belong. That is, we have to look at the relative privileges they have vis-à-vis one another, which might be done in the following way:

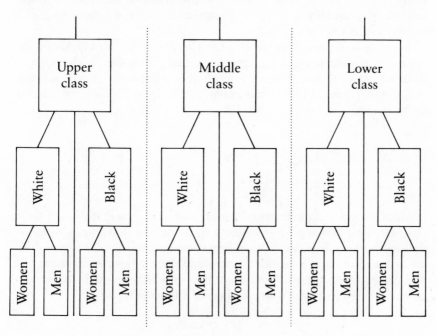

This is a way of representing her claim that in order to describe sexual privilege properly we have to keep the race and class of the men and women constant.

On the other hand, she also describes as the condition of women something that might best be represented by the schema in which the most important distinction is that between men and women. More accurately, given the contrasts she draws early in the book, it looks as if the first bank of doors includes not simply two categories

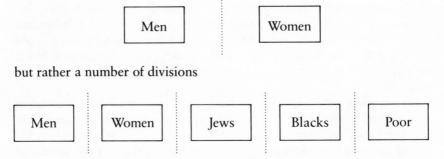

but rather a number of divisions

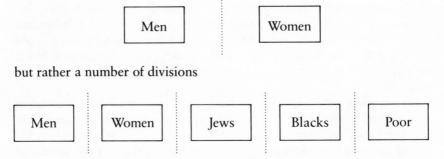

and so forth. Indeed, this latter schema best represents her conflation of the condition of "women" with that of white, middle-class, Christian women, for when she talks generally about relations between "men and women" she can only be referring to men and women who are not Jewish or Black or poor.

Which schema best represents what Chodorow has to say about distinctions among humans and the significance they have? The kind of similarity and differences she is interested in is the sense of self and relational stance toward others that humans develop; the significant division in this regard, she says, is

Or does she? Her claim is actually more cautious: It is that though there are interesting and important differences in the way different cultures assign work, they all assign it according to gender and in all cases women are assigned the major work of parenting.[25] Hence her view is more like that represented in the schema according to which we ought to look at gender differences in the context of other differences.

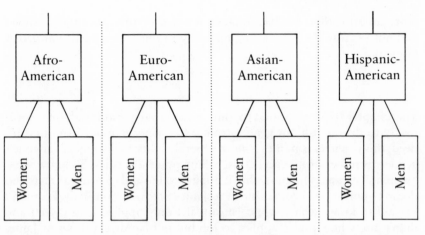

However, Chodorow implies that for the purpose of her study we can ignore the cultural differences: for the same thing that is true of the relationship between men and women of one group will be true of that between men and women of any other group. Mothers always do most of the parenting, and they do it always in the context of sexism. In this sense, the distinction between the first and second schemas collapses. And when it does, we lose sight of important features of the context of gender relations only visible in the second schema—namely, that women mother in a social and political context in which they not only are distinguished from men, but are, along with men of their same cultural background, distinguished from men and women of other cultural backgrounds.

It is also revealing to try to use the doors to represent Chodorow's fledgling account of the relation between sexism and other forms of oppression such as racism and classism. According to such an account, we recall, the attitudes that men have toward women as Other provide the model for the attitudes they come to have toward everyone else. Thus the relation between men and women in any one group is the same as the relation between any one group of men and women to any other group of men and women when one group is racist or classist toward the other. But this would mean that the relationship between whites and Blacks is in important ways the same as that between white men and white women, as well as that between Black men and Black women. As mentioned in chapter 4, and as we shall see in more detail still in chapter 7, for a variety of reasons this is an odd position to hold. It also suggests that white men and white women have the same attitude toward Black men and Black women as white men have toward white women (and as Black men have toward Black women). But if that is the case, Chodorow ought to pay more attention than she does to racist and classist attitudes among women and not portray them as belonging solely to men (or a particular group of men).

IV

This chapter tries to respond to quite reasonable questions about our capacity to distinguish our gender from other aspects of our identities. Indeed, this capacity is part of a more general ability to distinguish anyone's gender from her or his race, class, or any other identities. To know what "woman" means is to know that it applies to me and to Angela Davis and doesn't apply to my brother Jon or to James Baldwin. (Similarly, I couldn't be said to know what "white" means if I only applied it to myself and didn't know how it also applies to Jon but not to Angela Davis or James Baldwin.) The question for us is not whether we have such capacities but what, if anything, follows from them.

It certainly doesn't follow that there is an essential "womanness" that Angela and I share and that Jon and James lack. That is, what makes it true that Angela and I are women is not some "woman" substance that is the same in each of us and interchangeable between us. Selves are not made up of separable units of identity strung together to constitute a whole person. It is not as if there is a goddess somewhere who made lots of little identical "woman" units and then, in order to spruce up the world a bit for herself, decided to put some of those units in black bodies, some in white bodies, some in the bodies of kitchen maids in seventeenth-century France, some in the bodies of English, Israeli, and Indian prime ministers.

Indeed, positing an essential "womanness" has the effect of making women inessential in a variety of ways. First of all, if there is an essential womanness that all women have and have always had, then we needn't know anything about any woman in particular. For the details of her situation and her experience are irrelevant to her being a woman. Thus if we want to understand what "being a woman" means, we needn't investigate her individual life or any other woman's individual life. All those particulars become inessential to her being and our understanding of her being a woman. And so she also becomes inessential in the sense that she is not needed in order to produce the "story of woman." If all women have the same story "as women," we don't need a chorus of voices to tell the story.

Moreover, to think of "womanness" in this way obscures three related facts about the meaning of being a woman: first of all, that whatever similarities there are between Angela Davis and me, they exist in the context of differences between us; second, that there is ongoing debate about what effect such differences have on those similarities (different arrangements of the doors express different positions on this matter); third, not all participants in that debate get equal air time or are invested with equal authority.

The problem with the "story of man" was that women couldn't recognize themselves in it. So those who produce the "story of woman" want to make sure they appear in it. The best way to ensure that is to be the storyteller and hence to be in a position to decide which of all the many facts about women's lives ought to go into the story, which ought to be left out. Essentialism works well in behalf of these aims, aims that subvert the very process by which women might come to see where and how they wish to make common cause. For essentialism invites me to take what I understand to be true of me "as a woman" for some golden nugget of womanness all women have as women; and it makes the participation of other women inessential to the production of the story. How lovely: the many turn out to be one, and the one that they are is me.

The juice from tomatoes is not called merely juice. *It is always called* TOMATO *juice.*

GWENDOLYN BROOKS

Now You See Her, Now You Don't

Let us return to Uncle Theo at the beach, still thoroughly overwhelmed by the manyness of the pebbles, their physicality, their appalling randomness, their threat to any order or intelligibility in a chaotic world of particulars. He can barely sit on the pebbles, let alone give them (or see any point in giving them) more than a cursory examination. I have suggested that much of dominant Western feminist thought has shared Uncle Theo's dismay and discomfort with manyness, that it has been uneasy about the enormous variety of women and women's experiences. We can sketch this plethoraphobia as a series of related questions: Is there a oneness in all this manyness? Is there something all women have in common despite (or maybe even because of) their differences? A thread running through all our accounts of our lives? An underlying identity as women? Shared conditions of oppression? If not shared conditions of oppression, at least a shared oppressor? A shared psychological stance toward the world and the people in it? A shared viewpoint of some sort? Shared vulnerabilities or liabilities? Shared commitment to social and political change of a certain kind? We'd have to have more than superficial knowledge about one another to answer these questions—and, as discussed in chapter 6, an awareness that we are not likely to come to investigations of one another's lives free of unchallengeable preconceptions about what count as similarities and differences among us and what they mean.

The sheer variety of women poses enormous epistemological problems: as de Beauvoir noted, the fact that we all are women does not mean that we are all open books to each other, that we can easily come to know and understand one another, especially (though not only) in light of differences of race, class, religion, ethnicity, nationality, erotic orientation. It is one of the main tenets of most versions of feminism that women's lives and thoughts and works have been obscured or erased by the men who control the cultural tools for noting and recording such things. Even though we may question the accuracy of the controllers' record and even though we realize there are other ways of coming to know about each other than those enshrined in those records, it would be presumptuous for us to assume that we understand each other. We can't assume we do simply because we are women, even though many women report finding it easy to understand what other women quite different from them are talking about. It is not hard to confuse this relief that we may be able to connect in some way with a conviction that we know a great deal about each other and share a common struggle. Struggles among us are always a possibility—but not, as I shall argue, undesirable.

Indeed, it is the sense of the need to find a common ground that makes the metaphysical and epistemological issues described above felt as issues at all. For the possibility of a coherent feminist politics seems to require a singleness of voice and purpose. A plea made in the name of a movement is different from a single individual's plea only because the movement can be said to function in behalf of great numbers of people; but the point of having numbers is lost if each of the many is saying something quite different. As we have noted frequently, differences among women seem threatening to the possibility of a coherent women's movement.

While it is true that one of the results of racism and other forms of oppression is our profound lack of knowledge of one another across racial and other lines, this doesn't mean that such ignorance is symmetrical. In relationships of oppression, oppressors typically only come to "know" what they feed themselves through vicious stereotypes, and the oppressed are forced by circumstance to learn much more about their oppressors than their oppressors do about them (none of this is to say that what is learned is free from distortion).[1] As feminists such as bell hooks and Marilyn Frye have reminded us, the ignorance of white women, for example, about Black women is not passive.[2] We might add to this that not all knowledge is chosen, nor actively or happily acquired: surely there are things those who are oppressed would rather be learning than what to expect from the monsters today and how best to resist it. (And of course contrary to what oppressors like to believe—must believe—those they oppress *do* think about something other than their oppressors.) Because women live in a world in which there is not only sexism but racism, classism, and other forms of oppression, some of the differences among women carry with them differences in privilege and power. Such differences may become problematic for the privileged women as the occasion for fear, shame, and guilt. In such circumstances the "problem of difference" is really the problem of privilege.

I

Indeed, some ways in which we have expressed our need to talk about differences reveal the privileges meant to be called into question. What am I really saying when I say something like "Feminist theory must take differences among women into consideration," or "We need to hear the many voices of women," or "Feminist theory must include more of the experiences of women of different races and classes"? In recent years such expressions have been heard again and again in feminist classrooms and at feminist conferences. Let us take a close look at them.

1. "Feminist theory must take differences among women into consideration." This axiom doesn't make sense unless there is already something called "feminist theory" that makes reference to some women; the women not yet referred to are thus the "different" ones. Given the history of dominant Western feminist theory, it is not white middle-class women who are different from other women, but all other women who are different from them. So the attempt by insiders to "bring in" outsiders employs language that reflects and preserves the outsiders' status as outsiders. But there is more at issue here than language that reinstates the very distinctions it purports to undo. The language reflects the pervasiveness of institutional means for maintaining the distinctions; privilege is more than skin deep. Furthermore, to say that feminist theory must take differences into consideration makes sense only to the extent that what has been counted as "feminist theory" does not include the feminist theory done by Black women, Hispanas, Indian women, Arab women, and others. Finally, what is meant by "take into consideration"? The phrase reveals the freedom of feminist theory, or rather of its makers, to think or not to think about what is being brought to their attention, to do with it what they will. The phrase does nothing to undermine their power and authority to control the conditions under which "differences" will be brought up. It suggests a hearing in which existing social and political inequalities between the theorists and those being asked to make their case will not be challenged. In short, it, as well as the propositions we examine below, suggests a setting of tolerance, which requires looking but not necessarily seeing, hearing but not necessarily listening, adding voices but not chang-

ing what has already been said. We shall return to the topic of tolerance a bit later.

2. "We need to hear the many voices of women." Unless "we" also ask ourselves certain hard questions, this proposition, however earnestly stated, simply reflects and perpetuates our privileges. Who are "we" here, what is the need, and what will the hearing involve? "We" are of course those who have been heard from, who have been calling the shots in feminism, who now recognize a need that can only be satisfied by hearing from other women. What is the need? Is it to give legitimacy to a movement that already reflects the priorities of women not yet heard from? Is it to make other women feel as if they count, regardless of how well we listen or what we decide to do with what we hear? Does the fact of our having a need mean they ought to satisfy it? Is the reason we haven't heard them before that they haven't spoken, or that we haven't listened?[3] Is hearing from them the same thing as talking with them? Are we really willing to hear anything and everything they might have to say, or only what we don't find too disturbing? Are we prepared to hear what they say, even if it requires learning concepts or whole languages that we don't yet understand?

3. "Feminist theory must include more of the experiences of women of different races and classes." In addition to relying on the telltale concept of "difference," this proposal uses the language of "inclusion," which is always highly revealing of the power of those who might "include" others. Like "taking into consideration," "including" points to the freedom of the agent in question to take it or leave it. It's as if there is someone who has a pile of things she has brought together; she might put something else in the pile, she might not. It's up to her. It's her privilege to add new things or not add new things, even to throw things out if she no longer wants to include them. The power to include implies the power to exclude: if feminism hadn't the power to exclude certain women before, it wouldn't make sense now to appeal to its power to include them. It's as if to say: "I've made a home here, and now I'd like to welcome you in. It's not our home—yours and mine—but my home. But you are welcome into it." This does nothing to suggest that feminist theory will have to change in any significant way, only that it has to be more "inclusive," which could mean simply adding on more stories and investigations without saying anything about how the significance of the new additions will be assessed. Welcoming someone into one's own home doesn't represent an attempt to undermine privilege; it expresses it.

The pebbles elicited strong symptoms of plethoraphobia in Uncle Theo, but he certainly didn't feel fear or shame or guilt about unjustifiably taking one pebble to be representative of all. He simply felt overwhelmed by their multiplicity and heterogeneity. But people aren't pebbles, and hence there has been a deep concern among some contemporary white middle-class feminists that we have handily forgotten about the race and class privileges that we have and that earlier feminists had. We often express this concern by insisting—typically in language like that we have just examined—that feminism be broader based, that it not show the traces of race and class privilege in its terminology, its focus, its priorities. We've left something very important out, and it is high time, we say, to put it in. Our leaving it out is the reflection of our privilege. In many ways this book is about whether attempts to talk about "difference" simply preserve the privilege they were supposed to challenge. It has been about how deep such privilege goes.

Noticing how privilege redeposits itself in our language may not be too much cause for alarm. After all, however privilege-reflecting they are, efforts like those described above nevertheless begin a process by which we can reveal and remove the unnecessary biases (as opposed to the necessary commitments) of feminism. But throughout this book we've also examined deeper places where white middle-class privilege lurks—for example, in principled arguments against taking the situation of slave women to be of theoretical significance for the feminist investigation of gender; in attempts to study race and class that do nothing to dislodge white middle-class women as the focus of feminist theory and that take the race and class privilege of such women to be of no theoretical significance for feminist theory. Encountering these expressions of privilege has seemed cause for alarm, since to challenge them challenges what seem to be necessary commitments of feminism—the focus on women as women, the isolation of gender from race and class. We have seen reason to question whether these commitments are fully compatible with paying proper regard to differences among women. Let us review briefly where we have located these lodging-places for white middle-class privilege, then turn to whether their exposure and removal is in fact disastrous for the feminisms in which they live.

II

Feminists have undertaken examinations of the role of gender in women's lives in order to expose the ways in which men's treatment of gender differences has contributed to the oppression of women (it thus continues to be a source of surprise that feminist investigations of gender could express any form of privilege, since they are undertaken to undermine some version of it).[4] And we have rightly complained that many people who look at the oppression connected with race, class, erotic orientation, religion, ethnicity, or nationality do so without touching at all on gender (or rather by focusing on only one gender). Feminism has been preoccupied with gender, and in order to talk about what gender is and how being a woman affects women, it has seemed necessary and extremely useful to make the following assumptions:

1. Women can be talked about "as women."
2. Women are oppressed "as women."
3. Gender can be isolated from other elements of identity that bear on one's social, economic, and political position such as race, class, ethnicity; hence sexism can be isolated from racism, classism, etc.
4. Women's situation can be contrasted to men's.
5. Relations between men and women can be compared to relations between other oppressor/oppressed groups (whites and Blacks, Christians and Jews, rich and poor, etc.), and hence it is possible to compare the situation of women to the situation of Blacks, Jews, the poor, etc.

It is unnecessary here to rehearse the many different arguments throughout this book intended to show how the phrases "as a woman" and "oppressed as a woman," and attempts to isolate gender from race and class, typically operate to obscure the race and class identity of white middle-class women. Such attempts treat the womanness of all other women as if it were simply the same version of womanness as that of white middle-class women. If a woman's womanness distinguishes her not only from men but from Blacks, Jews, and "others," then such womanness has to be that of women who are not Black, or Jewish, or "other." With their axiomatic strength, the assumptions described in 1–5 together lead inevitably to a focus on women who are not subject to any other form of oppression than sexism, that is, women who are white and middle-class.

However, despite feminism's focus on gender, it nevertheless has not left race and class out of its descriptions of the social, political, and economic worlds in which women live, nor has it ignored how such factors affect various women's lives. (This is already indicated to some degree in points 3 and 5 above, both of which mention race and racism, class and classism.) Feminism has included examination of the roles of race and class in several ways:

6. It has recognized differences among women in saying that gender is the same but our race and class identities are not.

7. It talks not just about a woman's gender but also about her race and class; not just about sexism but about racism and classism too.
8. It has explored differences by investigating what women of different races and classes have and do not have in common.

Largely owing to the prodding of women left out of their accounts, mainstream feminists since de Beauvoir have noticed that feminism must talk about race and class (among other things) in addition to gender. But white middle-class privilege, as de Beauvoir herself pointed out, is typically a hardy shrub, and it doesn't disappear because reference is made to the existence of aspects of women's identities other than gender, or to forms of oppression other than sexism. Privilege has been able to find new and ever more subtle places to root. Concessions to the multiplicity of women nevertheless preserve the privileged focus on white middle-class women. Although it may look as if we are going to take differences among women seriously if we acknowledge that some women are Black, some are white, some are rich, some are poor, if we insist that nevertheless they all are the same as women, that differences among women reside in some non-woman part of them, then these differences will never have to make a difference for feminism. For if it's the "woman" part of any woman that counts, and if differences among women can't lodge there, then differences among women finally don't really matter.

As we saw, de Beauvoir and others assume that we have the clearest examples of the oppression women face as women when they are not subject to any other form of oppression. If that is so, it must be unproblematic what the "woman" part of white middle-class women is— for by hypothesis the oppression such women face as women is so clear. This means that these women provide the model of womanness for all others, so that insofar as what Black women suffer resembles what white middle-class women do, we can tell what they suffer "as women"; insofar as they suffer what Black men do, we can tell what they suffer "as Blacks." If white women and Black women are just the same as women, if the sexism they endure is just the same as sexism, their being white or Black makes no difference to their being women, no difference to what they endure because of their sex.

In short, if we assume there are differences among women, but at the same time they are all the same as women, and if we assume the woman part is what we know from looking at the case of white middle-class women, then we appear to be talking about differences among women even though we actually are talking only about white middle-class women. This is how white middle-class privilege is maintained even as we purport to recognize the importance of women's differences. Such privilege will thrive as long as there are lots of ways of appearing to talk about differences among women without really doing so.

Moreover, "adding on" race and class means in effect "adding on" women who are not white and middle-class. To add race and class is to talk about the racial and class identity of Black women, or of poor women, but not about the racial and class identity of white middle-class women. Talking about racism and classism thus ends up being talk about something experienced by some women rather than something perpetuated by others: racism and classism are about what women of color and poor women experience, not about what white middle-class women may help to keep afloat. Given the assumption at work in feminist theory that gender identity exists in isolation from race and class identity, proposals to include "different" viewpoints amount to keeping race and class peripheral to feminist inquiry even while seeming to attend to them.

In an earlier chapter, I described the phrase "as a woman" as the Trojan horse of feminist ethnocentrism, for its use typically makes it look as if one can neatly isolate one's gender from one's race or class. If this weren't so, how could it ever have seemed logical for some women to say to others: "No, don't tell me about what it is like to be Hispanic, just what it is to be a woman"[5] or "Let's just focus on women's issues, not on Arab-Israeli issues." Have white women ever asked themselves to distinguish between being white and being a woman?

Debates over what being a "woman" means, and over what constitute women's issues as opposed to other kinds of issues, can't be resolved by references to a clearly understood and agreed upon metaphysical difference between one's gender and one's race or class. As the above examples indicate, insisting on the distinction between these things has served only to avoid such debates or to put a quick end to them, leaving a particular view in place. If we remember de Beauvoir's comment that women are made, not born, and that it is part of the ongoing work of a society to make sure that women are made, we can see feminist debates as a continuation of that work, with women at the fore of the social and political struggles over what it is to be a woman. We may not agree over what it means to be a woman and hence on what "women's issues" are. But that would be nothing new; societies and subgroups within societies distinguish themselves in part by how they define what it is to be a man or woman. We can't insist that "being a woman" is in some sense defined by one's culture and then use the phrase in a way meant to deny cultural content. We need to unpack what it means to talk about oneself "as a woman," not use the phrase to suggest that there is no unpacking to do, or that even after unpacking we'd find that underneath all their cultural differences women are the same.

In the chapters on Plato and Aristotle, we saw ways in which the phrases, assumptions, and points of focus with which we approach the issues of gender and race (points 1–8 above) work to make us mistakenly think that a philosopher's account of one group of women applies to women in general. Since Plato and Aristotle clearly divide humanity not only into male and female but simultaneously into groups according to something like race and class, they end up referring or alluding to the existence of different groups of women. Hence a feminist account of philosophers' views about "women" ought to investigate whether their treatment of different groups of women is the same; if we then choose to focus on one group rather than others, we ought to explain why.

In examining how assumptions 1–8 would lead us astray in a complete account of what Plato and Aristotle said about women, we can begin to see that if we challenge one of those assumptions, we may be led to raise questions about another. For example, if we remember that Plato argued for the equality of "men" and "women" in the context of arguing for the inequality between these men and women and everyone else, male or female, then we can see a challenge to assumption 3—that we can talk about gender independently of race and class. This, then, may make us see why assumption 5—that the situation of women ought to be compared to that of other groups—is also misleading. Insofar as Plato insisted that the distinction between philosopher-rulers and cobblers was more important than that between men and women, he made it clear that from his point of view (at least in book 5 of the *Republic*) the distinction between men and women has to be talked about in the context of the class the men and women belong to (contra assumption 3). Hence, contra 5, it makes no sense to compare women to other oppressed groups of people since women are always part of each such group: comparisons between "women" and "X's" should always make us ask, what about women who are X's?

Moreover, it became clear that we couldn't accurately describe either Plato's or Aristotle's view of gender if we assumed, as in point 6, that women have the same gender even if they are of different classes or races. Plato's female philosopher-rulers were not feminine or womanly in the way he took typical Athenian women to be. Their education was meant to ensure that they became, instead, manly—like male philosopher-rulers. Aristotle, we recall, thought the distinction between women and slaves was a very crucial one. Since some of those slaves were female, Aristotle in effect held that there were at least two different genders females could become, depending on whether their function was to be a "woman" or to be a "slave." Only barbarians would fail to make the distinction (again, a reminder of how crucial gender distinctions can be to the maintenance of class and race distinctions). It became especially clear in the case of Aristotle that he treated gender identity as the function of the combination of sexual identity and "race" identity. So for him, a difference in "race identity" has to mean also a difference in gender identity; it is not something different from gender identity.

In short, we learned that if we take points 1–8 as axioms of feminist inquiry, we not only give a distorted account of Plato's and Aristotle's views about women, but focus our attention on one group of women rather than another—in particular, on women of the ruling classes rather than on slaves or women belonging to what Plato called "the masses."

In examining why de Beauvoir ended up focusing on white middle-class women despite much in her own account that implied their case was hardly representative of all women, we saw that she took as axiomatic several of our assumptions above: that gender is isolatable (point 3), that "women" are to be contrasted to "men" (point 4), and that "women" can be compared to "Blacks" or "Jews" or other oppressed groups (point 5). She assumed that sexism is most obvious and hence best studied in the case of women not otherwise subject to oppression. We noted at that point that assumptions or axioms work best to preserve the privilege of a certain group if they lead to a favored focus on that group without seeming to do so.

For a feminist theory to end up focusing on one group of women without saying that that is what it is going to do is no mean feat. For example, a discussion promising to deal with how "women" fare in the U.S. military shouldn't end up, logically speaking, being simply about white women; but if the group called "women" is contrasted to the group called "Blacks" (as in assumption 5), it becomes clear that "women" really has meant "white women" all along. But why wasn't that said explicitly? Both because it didn't need to be—we expect mainstream newspapers to indicate a woman's race if, and only if, she is not white—and because it needed *not* to be noted, lest the normative status white women have as "women" be eroded. Black women's being Black somehow calls into question their counting as straightforward examples of "women," but white women's being white does not. As long as "women" are compared to "Blacks," a decision will have to be made about whether to classify Black women as "Black" or as "women," but not about whether to classify white women as "white" or as "women." That is why it seemed so axiomatic to de Beauvoir and others to take the oppression white middle-class women are subject to as the paradigmatic example of sexism.

It is notable that if de Beauvoir had paid attention to her own stricture that descriptions of sexual hierarchy only make sense if we presuppose

169

that the men and women in question are of the same race and class, then she would have had to understand assumptions 1–4 in a different way and assumption 5 just wouldn't make sense. For—referring now to our first four assumptions—if women are to be contrasted to men of their own race and class, then to talk about their situation or oppression "as women" would be to talk about their situation as women of their particular race and class; and while their gender identity would indeed be treated "in isolation" from their race and class identity, that would mean only that our focus would not be on racial and class differences between men and women but on gender differences between them. As we saw, that hardly means that the racial and class identity of the men and women in question has no effect on their gender relations. As to assumption 5, if it doesn't make sense to talk about relations between men and women unless they are of the same race and class, then it can't make sense to compare the relations between "women" and "men" to that between whites and Blacks, Christians and Jews, and so on, for to do so requires that we forget about the race and class of the "men" and "women." For example, if the men and women in question are Black, then we are asked to compare their relations to that between whites and Blacks. Moreover, we are asked to ignore the fact that among the groups to which "women" are contrasted are the women in those other groups. De Beauvoir's comment that men and women can only be compared within a cultural group should serve to remind latter-day feminists that all cultural groups always have both men and women.

In Chodorow's work we saw the promise of an account that would both give due attention to gender and show how gender issues are connected to, even if separable from, race and class issues. Chodorow says at the beginning of *The Reproduction of Mothering* that we can't assume that sexual relations are the same across societies (or presumably even across racial and class lines within societies), but she believes there are some universal truths about them; specifically, she accepts points 1–4 on the isolation of gender. Her examination of gender relations nevertheless holds very important implications for understanding race and class relations, for it tells us that the sexist attitudes boys develop in their early relation to their mothers expand into the kinds of attitudes characteristic of racists and classists. From her account, it looked as if examining gender in isolation from race and class, examining sexism in isolation from racism and classism, not only does not have to make us disregard racism and classism but in fact enables us to understand their origin or at least their maintenance.

However, in the final analysis, her account of gender identity and her explanation of the relation between sexism and other forms of oppression proved impossible. Chodorow makes it look as if a woman's mothering takes place in a social context that is simply sexist (leaving unexamined and unexaminable how the existence of racism and classism affect a mother's engenderment of her children). She makes it look as if a boy's acquiring a masculine gender identity involves simply the notion that men are superior to women, whoever the men and women are; that a girl's acquisition of a feminine gender identity involves simply the notion that women are inferior to men, whoever the men and women are. But, as we saw, if this is the case, it is awfully difficult to explain how white male racists come to believe that they are superior to Black men and that Black men are not superior to white women; it is equally difficult to explain how white female racists come to believe that they are superior to Black men and to Black women. Indeed, it becomes impossible to explain why some men are the perpetrators, others the victims, of racism and classism; and it also becomes impossible to give any theoretical significance to the development of racist and classist attitudes among women.

In chapter 5 we saw how a number of attempts to contrast being a "woman" with being "Black" in the United States, to contrast sexism and racism, end up making the situation of white middle-class women paradigmatic for an examination of sexism and preclude the examination of Black women, not only from inquiries about sexism, but also from inquiries about racism. Feminists ignore their own expressed need to "explore differences among women" in not even thinking about Black women or in simply assuming that Black women are not significantly different from white women. This tells us that not caring whether Black women's situation is in fact like that of white women has the same effect as assuming that it is so different as not even to be considered.

In chapter 6 we became aware of the ways in which white middle-class privilege can be preserved even as one engages in "empirical investigation" into what women do and do not have in common. Depending on how they are made, comparisons among women may operate to obscure the privilege some women have over others. As bell hooks puts it:

Feminist emphasis on "common oppression" in the United States was less a strategy for politicization than an appropriation by conservative and liberal women of a radical political vocabulary that masked the extent to which they shaped the movement so that it addressed and promoted their class interests.[6]

III

Modern feminist theory is faced with a dilemma: will throwing out the bathwater of white middle-class privilege involve throwing out the baby of feminism? Moreover, though there are many versions of feminism (which vary according to the analysis of the nature of oppression, its causes, and what is necessary to end it), the dilemma applies to all versions—for all versions seem to rely on fundamental phrases such as "as a woman"; on attempts to isolate gender from race and class; and on attempts to deal with race and class by adding the separate elements together to produce the sum of gender, race, and class identity.[7] If we can't isolate gender from race or class, if we can't talk about the oppression women face as women, or about the experience of women as women, isn't feminism left without a foundation, without a specific focus?

I would argue against this bleak outlook—though we should not be surprised if certain assumptions at the heart of much feminist theory will have to be discarded or revised if the experiences of women of color are to be taken as seriously as those of white middle-class women. The end of privilege means the end of institutional support for one's concerns above those of others, the end of one's being able to discount, however unintentionally, the experiences and perspectives of others. It's only from a position of privilege that it would seem that the end of focus on white middle-class women has to mean the end of feminism.[8]

I would not argue that feminism can give up talking about gender. But we do need to keep in mind the full force of the idea that gender is a social construction, a very important social construction. It is because she said this so well that de Beauvoir has been important to feminist theory. She pointed out that the construction of differences between men and women—both the creation of the meaning of gender differences and the molding of individuals in accordance with those differences—are ongoing projects of societies and involve the active work and cooperation of men and women.

But de Beauvoir told us more than that societies make females into women. She also pointed out, only to terrifically underplay, the fact that different societies and different groups within societies use their constructions of the difference between men and women as part of giving definition to themselves. This is what de Beauvoir was getting at when she discussed—much too briefly—the ways in which powerful race or class privilege is revealed whenever women with such privilege insist that the kind of relation they have to the men of their race and class is superior to the kind found between men and women of other races and classes. Thus some of these women have been willing and eager to maintain the sexual status quo within their own race and class in order to preserve race and class privilege.[9]

Both Plato and Aristotle point to the importance of distinctive gender relations for the meaning of difference between societies or between

172

groups within a given society. Among the philosopher-rulers in Plato's *Republic*, men and women are and are to be treated as equals. This distinguishes the ideal state described in the *Republic* from lesser polities, in which people do not even know enough to call upon the capacities and talents of their best women. The point is even clearer in Aristotle: in the best-ordered state, but not among barbarians, there is a difference between "women" and "slaves" (male and female). Moreover, male citizens are naturally superior to their wives; male slaves are not.

In light of the importance distinctive gender relations can have to the expression of cultural and class and racial differences, the suggestion by Chodorow and others that oppressive gender relations are the model for oppressive relations between races and classes is ill-conceived. For if one important way a group may distinguish itself from another (especially a "lowly" other) is by the "propriety" of its gender relations, it is unlikely that the group will characterize its relations to other groups in the imagery of its own gender relations. The point can be made graphically in this way:

$$\frac{S_1}{(m/w)_1} \qquad \frac{S_2}{(m/w)_2}$$

One society, S_1, defines itself in part by the shape it gives to relations between men and women, $(m/w)_1$; similarly, society S_2 sees its nature in its own gender relations $(m/w)_2$. Let us suppose that S_1 takes itself to be superior to S_2 and takes that superiority to consist in part in the way it shapes its gender relations. If that is the case, S_1 is certainly not going to treat $(m/w)_1$ as the model for the relation S_1/S_2: for that would imply that members of S_2 are capable of having an $(m/w)_1$ relationship, indeed of having it with members of S_1. But part of S_1's sense of superiority to S_2 is that S_2 can't give rise to a relationship like $(m/w)_1$, and that a member of S_1 would surely never enter into one with a member of S_2.

A variation on the doors imagery from chapter 6 can further clarify the point. Let's imagine that there is a door marked $(m/w)_1$ and that only people who belong to S_1 will be allowed to go through it—two by two. By this they will indicate their superiority to all other groups of people (it is not hard to imagine who made the doors in this case). No member of S_1 is going to want to go through that door with a member of S_2. Yet that is what we must suppose would happen if the relationship $(m/w)_1$ is the model for the relationship S_1/S_2.

It's no wonder that Chodorow's suggestion comes to ruin against the history of racism in the United States. For while the nature of gender relations among whites involves the idea of the superiority of white men to white women, this is supposed to ensure (among other things) the reproduction of lily-white children. The racial similarity of the white men and women is crucial to the notion of appropriate gender relations—including the superiority of the men to the women—applying to them. But the superiority of whites to Blacks requires racial difference and does not describe a relation between people meant to ensure the production of white children. On the contrary, it is supposed to prevent whites and Blacks from having anything like the relation between white men and white women.

Of course $(m/w)_1$ and S_1/S_2 (as conceived by S_1) do have some similarities—in particular, both involve relations of superiority/inferiority. But not all such relations are the same, though that is obscured by claims such as "women are treated like slaves." Even Aristotle, who created a multitude of distinctions between those who naturally rule and those who naturally are ruled, insisted that the grounds for superiority were different in each case. The relation between a "man" and a "woman" (i.e., a citizen and his wife) was quite different, he thought, than that between a "man" and his "slave," and only barbarians don't know and can't live out the difference.

None of this is to diminish the importance of studying gender. Sexist gender relations cannot be taken as the model for other oppressive relations, but the study of gender relations is absolutely essential to the study of class and race relations because it is pivotal to the study of how societies define and distinguish themselves.[10] Feminism thus doesn't have to give up contrasting men and women, or in some sense isolating gender from race and class. Indeed, if we are going to talk convincingly and clearly about the difference gender makes, we better be able to isolate it from the difference race and class make, and we can best do this by talking about gender relations between men and women of the same race and class. This is not to argue that the race and class of the men and women in question are irrelevant to the shape of gender relations between them. It is to argue that feminism must specify which men and women it is talking about, and that it must stop using language that suggests that a white middle-class woman's position vis-à-vis her white middle-class husband is no different that her position vis-à-vis men from other groups.

Nor do feminists have to give up all-encompassing phrases like "as a woman." But we do need to explore what such phrases mean to women in all their heterogeneity (for reasons which by now should be clear, I suggest dropping the word "difference" except under special conditions). If we can say with de Beauvoir that societies create women out of females (making gender out of sex), and that different societies do this differently, indeed in part define their differences by how they do this, we can say that in an important sense there are a variety of genders. Plato and Aristotle certainly treated women as if they belonged to different genders.

I find myself backing away from this even as I say it, and I suspect many readers do too. But why? First of all, perhaps, is the worry that saying this is too reminiscent of *Animal Farm*—that once the notion of different genders, of different kinds of women, is introduced, then a ranking inevitably follows. Just as some humans are more human than others (which Plato and Aristotle held), so, it is feared, some women are more "woman" than others. My gender is bigger, is better, than your gender. But as we've seen, spotting differences among women is no more likely to involve making invidious distinctions among us than refusing to note differences (or noting them but insisting they have no significance). The desire to deny differences among women may be an expression of a desire not to expose one's status as the norm from which others differ, or it may be an insistence that all women are after all basically just alike—underneath, everyone is just like me.

The notion of many genders also may seem repellent because it appears to make feminism unwieldy and maybe even incoherent. All along we thought feminism made sense because all women were affected by their gender identity and in light of this might come to see the extent to which they all were made to suffer for it. But if there are different genders, the case about women "as women" turns out to be many different cases—as different as the different kinds or genders women are. What then of the possibility of a unified voice for women "as women"? Isn't our shared gender identity precisely where we'd hope to find the foundation for such a voice?

Worse still, it begins to look as if the differences among us are not simply connected to our different racial or class or national identities, but to our gender identities as well. We saw this most starkly in Aristotle, where it became clear that not only was gender not isolatable from "race," but precisely because gender was a function of "race," females of different "races" also were of different genders. Such a view seems both to undermine the notion that gender is a primary component of a person's identity and that women of different genders have anything in common. Isn't this a tough row to hoe for feminism?

No, for in fact the study of gender reaches much further than previously imagined. The idea that gender is constructed and defined in conjunction with elements of identity such as race, class, ethnicity, and nationality rather than separable from them helps explain why gender ought to be studied in connection with every academic discipline and not

175

only in women's studies departments. If we really could understand gender in isolation from race and class (where that means we don't have to consider race and class at all, rather than we have to keep race and class constant and describe our results accordingly), gender would be less important than it actually is in our lives. For one thing, as long as we think both that gender identity is describable without reference to race and class (and is experienced and understood independently of them) and that feminism is centrally about gender and sexism, whatever else it might be about, then studies of race and class, racism and classism, have to remain peripheral to feminism. On the other hand, if gender is neither experienced nor describable independently of race and class, then race and class become crucial to feminism.

It is not a loss in any way for feminism that in Aristotle, for example, there are at least two gender identities assigned females, depending on their "race." Indeed, we saw that by inquiring seriously into how Aristotle distinguishes between "women" and "slaves" (male and female) we have a clearer view of what Aristotle took to be important distinctions between those who are natural rulers and those naturally ruled. In short, in examining Aristotle's view about gender relations in detail we threw light on what otherwise might have not appeared to be related to gender at all.

Moreover, it is not a threat to the coherence of feminism to recognize the existence of many kinds of women, many genders. It may in fact help us to be more willing to uncover the battles among women over what "being a woman" means and about what "women's issues" are. It may make us more ready to recognize that our engaging in these battles is a sign of our empowerment, not something that stands in the way of such empowerment. Yes, we may want and need to make a united case against a hostile world. But it is also necessary and hence a healthy sign that we battle over what that case should be, rather than relegating the making of it to the usual spokeswomen. (If a hostile world can't keep all women quiet, it will settle for some women keeping others quiet. Why should feminist theorists do the work of silencing women?)[11] What could be a better sign of any woman's sense of empowerment than her desire and willingness and ability to speak up about what being a "woman" means? Why is Sojourner Truth so powerful a figure, after all? And why should we expect that women would not want and need to engage in such debates, given the recognition that gender is a social and political construction and given the feminist hope that women will have more and more to say about the ways their lives and the meaning of their lives are constructed and lived? Finally, any case made in behalf of a heterogeneous group of women will be stronger the clearer it is that it is the product of an exploration of the complexity of the situations of women. It must make visible that we make a common struggle, if at all, in and through our differences from one another, not around them.

IV

We have seen how fundamental assumptions of feminist theory help to disguise the conflation of the situation of one group of women with the situation of all women. But it isn't likely that the situation of Black women in the United States will be taken by mainstream feminists to be representative of or identical to the situation of all women. Why is that? If by hypothesis all women are women and experience the same oppression as women whatever else differentiates them (if by hypothesis gender is isolatable from race, sexism from racism), *any* group of women could be taken to be representative of or identical to all. We have had not only to make clear why that hypothesis is wrong, but also to flag the race and class of white middle-class women as clearly as the race and class of other women are flagged. (There is always the danger that in explicitly identifying their race, by saying "as white middle-class women," they might also be flaunting it; but that doesn't remove the need to do so, since the earlier way of flaunting it was to appropriate the term "woman" for white women alone.) Our discussion in section III above of how our old assumptions can be used without the inevitable focus on white middle-class women suggests the following ways to ensure that their race and class identity is no more protected from view than that of any other women:

When referring to women or to relations between men and women, note the class and race of the men and women in question. The situations in which those are relevant considerations far outweigh those in which they aren't.

Take the full implication of what gender is and be prepared to talk about women's different genders.

Keep in mind that gender relations and gender identity can be important ways in which societies and subgroups distinguish themselves and hence that one's gender identity locates one in a particular society or group. (For example, in thinking about your own early lessons about what "girls" do, what "girls" are, try filling in the blanks: Did you grow up with the idea that nice _____ girls, unlike those nasty _____ girls, don't _____?)

Assume that debates and discussions and confusions about what it means to be a "woman" and what "women's issues" are, are exactly what we ought to expect if we believe that gender is socially and politically constructed. Hence

177

there is no reason to take any woman's description of what it is to be a "woman" as definitive of what is true of all women "as women."

But there are not only privilege-preserving categories, assumptions, and methodological strategies for the investigation of gender. There are also privilege-preserving postures, which we touched on early in this chapter. Let us return to them.

One reason feminist theory by and for white middle-class women hasn't said much about the variety of women's experiences is sheer ignorance. When such ignorance is combined with the power and authority to decide what it is important to know, important to hear about, it not surprisingly leads to a situation in which a white woman at a conference on "women's history" can blithely refer to hearing about women of color as "an extra burden."[12]

Thus if lack of knowledge and unwillingness to hear from "different" women reveal and sustain the white middle-class privilege enshrined in dominant Western feminist theory, then it may seem important for white feminists to call upon the resources of their imagination and their capacity for tolerance. However, we will find that this view involves privilege-preserving postures, revealing no desire to gain knowledge or to have such knowledge make a difference to one's privileged standing.

Imagination

It certainly seems that if feminist inquiry and feminist political action are to have any coherent base at all, we have to have a solid answer to the following questions: What do I and can I know about women from whom I differ in terms of race, culture, class, ethnicity. (This question leaves out other closely related and also necessary questions such as what I in fact know about myself or about other women from whom I do not differ in terms of race, culture, etc.) We know that racism and other forms of oppression result in (as well as require) lack of knowledge, especially a lack in the oppressors of real knowledge of the oppressed. I cannot provide here an account of what I take real knowledge to be, but I do want to say here that the acquisition of such knowledge requires a kind of apprenticeship; and making oneself an apprentice to someone is at odds with having political, social, and economic power over them. What happens when oppressors want to undo racism or other oppression; how do they go about acquiring knowledge about others, knowledge whose absence is now regretted.

There are lots of different and mostly compatible answers to this question; read books, take classes, open your eyes and ears or whatever instruments of awareness you might be blessed with, go to conferences planned and produced by the people about whom you wish to learn and manage not to be intrusive, and so on. These answers must be accompanied by caveats: given the history of racism and other forms of oppression, be careful about what books you buy, what classes you take; think about the limits there presently are on what you are prepared to see or hear; examine your own motivations for wanting to understand others' lives.[13] However, another answer to the question of how one acquires knowledge of others is to use one's imagination:

I haven't been through what those whom I now wish to know about have been through; indeed, one of the central features of oppression is that the oppressors make the oppressed go through what they hope never to have to go through. Part of what it means for there to be cultural differences is for there to be different experiences of what may appear to be similar kinds of events: birth, death, eating, cooking, working, loving, having kin, being friends. Given these differences, even given oppressive institutions that mangle them, I nonetheless can try—I must try—to enter imaginatively into the worlds of others. Imagination isn't enough, but it is necessary. Indeed, it is a crucial starting point: because I have not experienced what the other has, so unless I can imagine her having pain or her having pleasure I can't be moved to try to help put an end to her pain or to understand just what her pleasures are. Against the odds I must try to think and feel my way into her world, a world that I do not know now, and surely cannot come to know overnight; and so, given what I do know, I try to imagine what her world is like. Imagination in this context thus marks at one and the same moment my similarity to another woman and my difference from her: it is because we both are human, maybe even because we both are women, that I dare to imagine, am required to imagine, that we share something in common—e.g., that it is horrible to be subject to physical or psychological violence. Precisely because as far as I know we are quite different from each other, I must use my imagination to try to enter her world, try to see the world the way she sees it.

If we reflect a moment on why imagination may seem necessary in this situation—where a member of an oppressor group is trying to learn about a member of the oppressed group—we can see why it is also dangerous. If we already knew a lot about each other, I wouldn't have to use my imagination in this way to enter into your world, any more than I would have to, to understand my own. But if I only rely on my imagination to think about you and your world, I'll never come to know you and it. And because imagining who you are is really a much easier thing for me to do than find out who you are (this of course is true about my relationship to myself, too, a different though interestingly related matter), I may persist in making you an object simply of my imagination even

179

though you are sitting right next to me. So while I need to think imaginatively about you, if I am to think about you at all, nevertheless your palpable existence does not mean I'm ready to give up my imaginative ruminations about you for the more direct access that your presence, your speech, your anger, your laughter might provide. Just because you are there doesn't mean I'll perceive you. If I start trying to perceive you, rather than simply (or elaborately) imagining you, I'm going to have a much harder task.[14]

What is the difference between really seeing you and simply imagining you, and why and how is the one much more exacting of the would-be knower than the other is? In sketching out answers to these questions, I am going to draw on the work that first provoked them in this form for me: Jean-Paul Sartre's *Psychology of Imagination.*[15] I do this not because I am a great fan of Sartre's, nor because I know a lot about existentialism, but because the distinction he draws between imagining and perceiving someone or something provides such a useful description of the task awaiting those of us eager to learn about the lives of those from whom we differ,[16] and alerts us to the enticements of a poor substitute for that task.

Sartre claims that one of the pleasures—a suspect one, to be sure—of imagining someone or something is that there is never anything recalcitrant, resistant, or unwanted about the image, for you never find anything in an image except what you put there. You don't investigate or interrogate an image to find out about it; there is nothing to learn from it because it only contains what you posit as being in it. Objects of the imagination only exist insofar as they are thought of, and they can be destroyed by the simple act of turning away from them in consciousness. On the other hand, Sartre says, if I am not imagining someone but actually perceiving her, I must make myself an apprentice, for there is an infinite amount to learn from a real object or a real person: "There is always, at each and every moment, infinitely *more* than we see; to exhaust the wealth of my actual perception would require infinite time" (11). Real things and real people are "brimming over" in the sense that there is so much to learn about what they are and what their relationships to other things and people are. By comparison images are impoverished because whatever is true of them is what I posit as true of them; I can't go wrong. To cite a homely example from Sartre:

When I perceive Peter I can always approach him close enough to see the grain of his skin, to observe his enlarged pores, and even the theoretical possibility of my examining his microscopic cells and so on to infinity. This infinity is implicitly contained in my actual perception, it overflows it infinitely by everything I can specify about him at each moment. It is this which constitutes the "massiveness" of real objects, but the nature of Peter as an image is to be thinned. (189)

Real objects and persons make demands on me as a perceiver that imaginary objects and persons cannot make on me when I am simply imagining: "I can stop the existence of the unreal object [the imaginary object] at any moment, I am not dragged along despite myself to the specification of its qualities: it exists only while I know it and want it" (190). When I am perceiving someone, I must be prepared to receive new information all the time, to adapt my actions accordingly, and to have my feelings develop in response to what the person is doing, whether I like what she is doing or not. When simply imagining her, I can escape from the demands her reality puts on me and instead construct her in my mind in such a way that I can possess her, make her into someone or something who never talks back, who poses no difficulties for me, who conforms to my desires much more than the real person does. (It will perhaps come as no surprise that Sartre describes imaginative thinking as "imperious" and "infantile" [177].)

Students of the imaginative capacities of human beings may disagree with some of Sartre's claims about imagination or, what amounts to the same thing, insist that while the kind of thinking he describes no doubt goes on, that is not what they would call imagination. While one's imagination can be impoverished, they might insist, it need not be defined as the capacity for producing only impoverished views of people and things. Let that debate develop as it may. What is important for our purposes is the kind of distinction Sartre is drawing, whatever he chooses to name the things so distinguished. For in drawing the distinction between imagining and perceiving he alerts us to the strenuousness of knowing other people, even people very much like ourselves. Such knowledge is all the more demanding the less we actually know about others and the stronger the sense of urgency to know. At the same time, that very sense of urgency may induce us to bypass the slow and often painful labor of real perception and rush to the easy gratification of imaginatively constructing other people and their lives. Sartre's analysis of perceiving as opposed to imagining others tells us that really knowing others has to loosen whatever grip we might have thought we had on them. We can tell that we are imagining and not perceiving others, in Sartre's terms, if we've decided once and for all what those people really are like; if we conclude that nothing in our lives has to change once we've listened to their words; if we think we have reached or can reach a point beyond which we will cease to be surprised by what we learn; if we think that knowledge can only and immediately make things easier or nicer for us; if we fail to realize that white women marginalize women of color as much by the assumption that as women of color they must be right as by the assumption that they must be wrong.[17]

I think it important to note too that the attitudes Sartre describes as constitutive of an imagining consciousness are fully compatible with tolerance. Tolerance is thus the least of the virtues of people who really want to learn about others and about their lives: to tolerate someone is simply to let her have her say; I needn't listen to her, I needn't respond to her, I needn't engage with her in any way at all. All I have to do is not interfere with her. Prior to and after I've allowed her to make her presence known, I can blot her out of my consciousness. It is as if I have simply imagined her being there.

Tolerance

Let us remind ourselves what imagination and tolerance are being conceived as an answer or response to. The "problem of difference" in recent feminism, we've suggested, should be understood to be a reflection of the problem of privilege: one group of women have taken their own situation to be that of "women in general," and now, in order not to have an account of "the condition of woman" that is as exclusionary as masculinist accounts of "the situation of man," differences among women must be noted and discussed. Having claimed the field, white middle-class women must start recognizing and hearing from women quite different from themselves. This we will do with a certain amount of reluctance (even if only in the privacy of our own headrooms), since having defined the issues facing "women" in a particular way, and having fought hard against the odds to make progress on them, the issues of women "different" from us will appear to be yet "another burden."[18] Nevertheless, if privilege is expressed in having one's voice be the only one heard out of a vast wilderness of heretofore silenced voices, indeed in having the power to mute or disregard the others, then allowing others to speak seems just the right thing to do.

However, as we have begun to see, tolerance can itself be an expression of privilege, and for that reason it is not necessarily something that undermines privilege. The locution "Yes, I'll tolerate you" leaves me the same. If one is in a position to allow someone else to do something, one is also in a position to keep that person from doing it. To tolerate your speaking is to refrain from exercising the power I have to keep you from speaking. In tolerating you I have done nothing to change the fact that I have more power and authority than you do. And of course I don't have to listen to what you say.

It is of the nature of privilege to find ever deeper places to hide. As suggested earlier, if the feminist attempt to deal with "difference" means simply the attempt to include the lives and concerns of some women without seriously challenging white middle-class privilege, then all the talk in the world about "difference" is simply disingenuous. Tolerance is easy if those who are asked to express it needn't change a whit.

On the other hand, it is true that the opening up to other voices, other viewpoints, which tolerance at least makes possible, may do something to begin to challenge the privilege of my position. If the mere hearing of other voices weren't possibly the thin edge of the wedge of challenge, no one would ever demand that others tolerate her or her point of view. But as long as I am simply tolerating your viewpoint, not actively seeking it out and taking seriously how it represents a critique of my own—indeed not wondering what it means to you apart from its representing a critique of me—I have not given any indication that I might be prepared to change my privileged position. This is especially clear if on examination of what I am now "allowing" you to say, it turns out that there are limits on what I will allow you to talk about or how I allow you to talk about it. For example, I might only let you speak or continue listening to you as long as you don't make me too uncomfortable. Tolerance perhaps may mark the beginning of the end of ignorance, but it is a double-edged virtue and may work against the acquisition of knowledge.

V

Privilege finds another perhaps unlikely-looking roost in the particular kind of despair that may follow upon the realization that feminism's statements about "women in general" or "the situation of women" have been unfounded generalizations from the lives of white middle-class women. For it may seem as if it is impossible, given the heterogeneity of women and women's situations, to make any well-founded yet nontrivial statements about all women. If that is impossible, however, its impossibility does not follow simply from the fact that such statements cannot be based on the situation of white middle-class women. That is, it doesn't automatically follow that no generalizations about women are possible. To assume otherwise is again an expression of the kind of privilege we have been examining, for it amounts to my claiming that if there is any general case to be made, it can only be the one made on the basis of my case. It is a way of trying to ensure that if I get dislodged from center stage, no one or nothing else is going to replace me. It is as if to say: if I can't win the contest, we'll just have to stop the contest. Either my position is authoritative or no position is. If I've been wrong, nobody can be right. If what we know now, about women like me, isn't sufficient to ground a case about "women in general," then nothing we can come to know will be either.

In short, there are two quite different ways to ensure that my picture of the world remains unchallenged. One is to present my particular picture as *the* picture: that is, to present it as if it were what everyone sees or would see if they were clear-headed enough. The other is to insist, after accepting the justice of complaints that I have failed to see how much about me my picture is, that any other picture is going to have just the same problems as mine.

In the first case my picture remains unchallenged insofar as all other pictures are described as too specific and biased, and mine is taken to have the requisite generality and objectivity. My picture, I say, is that of woman as woman, while that of my Black colleague is that of Black woman as woman or Black woman as Black or Black woman as Black woman. (There is, as Allan Bloom put it recently, the study of "man as man," and then there is the study of the Black experience. No matter the extent to which the first is the study of white men; as long as it is seen— as Bloom insists it must be—to be the analysis of "man as such," the study of Black men and women will get at best second billing.) [19] But in the event that someone calls my bluff and insists that all along the picture I've been giving of "woman" is actually of white middle-class woman, I've a second line of defense to make sure my picture is not seriously challenged: if my picture is biased, so is everyone else's, in just the same way and to just the same degree. So if in the first case no one can challenge me because I must be right, in the second case no one can challenge me because we are all equally wrong (or what amounts then to the same thing, equally right). If I can't maintain my position of privilege by being the sole arbiter of truth, I at least can insist that no one is. This is quite different from admitting to the possibility not only that I am wrong but that someone else might be right. I want to make sure that my inaccurate picture gets lost in the sea of all the other inaccurate pictures, rather than being compared to another more accurate account. This is a reverse of the *Animal Farm* trick, according to which we're all human (or all women), but I'm more human (or more woman) than you. Here we have: we all make mistakes but mine are no worse and no less corrigible than yours. Or alternatively, we all know truths but mine is the true truth, but if what I say turns out *not* to be true, then nothing anyone else says can be true either. I may not be right, but there's nothing against which I can be judged to be wrong, or anyway "more wrong" than anyone else.

Imagining isn't the same thing as knowing, nor tolerance the same as welcoming; neither show curiosity and openness to learning what may be disadvantageous to one's closely guarded position of privilege. Neither solution to my ignorance requires a change in my privileged position. I know at some level that if I am clever enough about how I conceive a problem, I don't have to change at all in order to find a solution.

Recent calls within dominant Western feminist theory to "include" women of color, poor women, and others either not mentioned at all or kept at the very periphery of feminist inquiry spring from the need white middle-class women quite rightly feel that we must come to know women from whom we differ in terms of race, culture, class, ethnicity. But I have been trying to suggest that our recognition of this need must be matched by an awareness of how the legacies of our privilege appear in the ways we may try to satisfy that need: in our confusing imagining women with knowing them; in priding ourselves on tolerance; and in appropriating others' identities through our desperate rush to find similarity.

Moreover, we cannot assume that our need is or ought to be a project foremost in the minds and hearts of all of those women about whom we hope to know more. Such a need cannot by definition be satisfied without making oneself an apprentice in some ways to other women. Doing that, I've suggested, requires that we not make others simply the objects of our imagination. But of course it also requires that those we wish to know themselves wish to be known, or anyway wish to be known in the ways in which we wish to know them. We cannot demand that they make themselves available to be known simply because we have a need that has to be satisfied. That is not apprenticeship but imperialism. There surely is evidence that those about whom we wish to know do wish to be known. I hope here to have suggested ways in which we ought not to abuse the gifts of others that have been made available to us.

VI

When I said in the Introduction that I thought the phrase "as a woman" was the Trojan horse of feminist ethnocentrism, part of what I meant was that this apparently necessary tool of all feminist inquiry and activity has carried a heavy political load. This is perhaps surprising, because the phrase looks so very innocent; but that's how Trojan horses work. The more innocent they look the more damage they can do. One of the things we can learn from close readings of Plato and Aristotle is how metaphysical distinctions that seem politically innocent are in fact ideologically charged: in Plato and Aristotle, distinctions between soul and body, as well as between rational and irrational parts of the soul, are highly politicized. In much feminist theory, we have chopped women up metaphysically into parts: the part of me in virtue of which I have a particular gender identity, the part of me in virtue of which I am of a particular race, and so on—as if a person's identity were like a patchwork quilt, made up of separable pieces, each with an identity, a history, and a meaning all its own; or as mentioned earlier, as if identity were like a tootsie roll, or a pop-bead necklace, made up of detachable parts. Just as Plato gives pride of place to one part over another—soul over body, reason over emotion—so dominant feminist theory locates a women's true identity in a metaphysical space where gender is supposed to be able to roam free from race and class. I have tried to explain why though doing this appears to be necessary for feminism, it has the effect of making certain women rather than others paradigmatic examples of "woman"—namely, those women who seem to have a gender identity untainted (I use the word advisedly) by racial or class identity, those women referred to in newspapers, magazines, and feminist journals simply as "women," without the qualifier "Black" or "Hispanic" or "Asian-American" or "poor." What is in fact a function of the privilege of white middle-class women is being passed off as a metaphysical truth: that is, that we can talk about a woman "as a woman" without explicitly or implicitly alluding to her race or class.

I am not saying that we ought never to think about or refer to women "as women" or to men "as men." I am only insisting that whenever we do that we remember which women and which men we are thinking about. Feminists have rightly insisted that to talk simply about relations between whites and Blacks, between rich and poor, between colonizer and colonized, masks gender distinctions within each group: for example, the problem with an explanation of inequality based simply on class ignores inequalities based on gender. But for similar reasons, talking simply about relations between men and women masks race and class distinctions among men and among women. Thus to refer to the power "all men have over all women"[20] makes it look as if my relationship to the bank vice president I am asking for a loan is just like my relationship to the man who empties my wastebasket at the office each night; similarly it makes it look as if their relationship to me is no different from their relationship to the woman who cleans the halls of the administration building. Whenever we feel tempted to talk about women "as women," we might remember what the poet Gwendolyn Brooks once said in a somewhat different context:

The juice from tomatoes is not called merely *juice*. It is always called TOMATO juice.[21]

Even the most literal reading of Brooks ought to make us ask whether we're more careful about what we order in a restaurant than we are in thinking of women as the particular women they are.

It surely would lighten the tasks of feminism tremendously if we could cut to the quick of women's lives by focusing on some essential "woman-ness." However, though all women are women, no woman is only a woman. Those of us who have engaged in it must give up the hunt for the generic woman—the one who is all and only woman, who by some miracle of abstraction has no particular identity in terms of race, class, ethnicity, sexual orientation, language, religion, nationality. (Anonymous, by the way, was not a generic woman.)

Don't misunderstand me: I've never met a generic woman I didn't like. But I wouldn't want my brother, or my sister, to marry one. And I certainly wouldn't want to be one: generic women don't eat rice and beans, collard greens, samosa, challah, hot dogs, or Wonder Bread; even in Cambridge, Massachusetts, I've never seen one eating a croissant. And while it is true that generic women don't have bad breath, that is hardly any consolation, I should think, for having no breath at all.

The founder of the institute that made completion of this project possible is not a generic woman—nor is the grateful fellowship recipient who sat in her office having nongeneric thoughts about the possibility of generic women. It was not a generic man or a generic woman who came by each night to clean up that office, so that the next day the intrepid scholar wouldn't be disturbed by the smell of yesterday's banana or the sight of coffee stains on styrofoam. It was not a generic woman who made at least three hundred trips through the swamps and woods of the southeastern United States rescuing her people from slavery. It was not generic women who daily created ways to maintain some shred of dignity beneath the heels of Nazi boots. It is not generic women who week after week in the Plaza de Mayo bear witness for their disappeared ones. Our mothers, our daughters, our sisters, our lovers, are not generic women.[22] There are no short cuts through women's lives.

Notes

Introduction

1. Actually Plato may have been doubtful about whether there was a Form of pebblehood. In the *Parmenides* (130c ff.), Socrates is described as thinking that "it would surely be too absurd to suppose" that "hair or mud or dirt or any other trivial and undignified objects" have a Form. See *The Collected Dialogues of Plato,* edited by Edith Hamilton and Huntington Cairns (New York: Pantheon, 1961). All references to Plato are from this edition and are cited parenthetically in the text.

2. Iris Murdoch, *The Nice and the Good* (Middlesex: Penguin, 1969), 158–59.

3. We could be many and yet be clones of one another, in which case the only difference among us would be numerical.

4. As we shall see throughout the book, there is considerable debate among women—some of whom identify themselves as feminists, others of whom are wary of doing so even though they share many struggles with self-identified feminists—about whether women have something in common and, if we do, what that means. Black activist, singer, and cultural historian Bernice Johnson Reagon argues that "the women's movement has perpetuated a myth that there is some common experience that comes just cause you're women" ("Coalition Politics: Turning the Century," in *Home Girls: A Black Feminist Anthology,* edited by Barbara Smith [New York: Kitchen Table/Women of Color Press, 1983], 360). Black writer and teacher bell hooks maintains that "the idea of 'common oppression' was a false and corrupt platform disguising and mystifying the true nature of women's varied and complex social reality" (*Feminist Theory: From Margin to Center* [Boston: South End Press, 1984], 44).

189

5. Bishop Berkeley probably would have insisted that we can't think about pebbles in general without thinking about a particular pebble and letting it stand for the others. Responding to what he took to be the view of John Locke, Berkeley said: "The idea of man that I frame to myself must be either of a white, or a black, or a tawny, a straight, or a crooked, a tall, or a low, or a middle-sized man. I cannot by any effort of thought conceive the abstract idea" of a man who is "neither white, nor black, nor any particular color" (*Principles of Human Knowledge,* paragraphs 9–10, in *Berkeley's Complete Works,* vol. 1, edited by A. C. Fraser [Oxford: Clarendon Press, 1891]). For an illuminating account of the relation between Locke's and Berkeley's positions, see Margaret Atherton, "The Inessentiality of Lockean Essences," *Canadian Journal of Philosophy* 14, no. 2 (1984):277–93.

6. See, for example, Christine Garside Allen, "Plato on Women," *Feminist Studies* 2, no. 2–3 (1975): 131–38; Julia Annas, Plato's *Republic* and Feminism," *Philosophy* 51 (1976): 307–21; Anna Dickason, "Anatomy and Destiny: The Role of Biology in Plato's View of Women," in *Women and Philosophy,* ed. C. Gould and M. Wartofsky (New York: Putnam, 1976), 45–53; Susan Moller Okin, *Women in Western Political Thought* (Princeton: Princeton University Press, 1979); Martha Lee Osborne, "Plato's Unchanging View of Women: A Denial that Anatomy Spells Destiny," *Philosophical Forum* 6, no. 2–3 (1974): 32–35; Lynda Lange, "The Function of Equal Education in Plato's *Republic* and *Laws,* in *The Sexism of Social and Political Theory: Women and Reproduction from Plato to Nietzsche,* ed. Lorenne M. G. Clark and Lynda Lange (Toronto: University of Toronto Press, 1979), 3–15; Elizabeth V. Spelman, "Woman as Body: Ancient and Contemporary Views," *Feminist Studies* 8, no. 1 (1982): 109–31; Jane Flax, "Political Philosophy and the Patriarchal Unconscious: A Psychoanalytic Perspective on Epistemology and Metaphysics," in *Discovering Reality: Feminist Perspectives on Epistemology, Metaphysics, Methodology, and the Philosophy of Science,* ed. Sandra Harding and Merrill Hintikka (Dordrecht: Reidel, 1983); Genevieve Lloyd, *The Man of Reason* (Minneapolis: University of Minnesota Press, 1984); Arlene W. Saxonhouse, *Women in the History of Political Thought: Ancient Greece to Machiavelli* (New York: Praeger, 1985); Jean Bethke Elshtain, *Public Man, Private Woman: Women in Social and Political Thought* (Princeton: Princeton University Press, 1981), 19–54; Dorothea Wender, "Plato: Misogynist, Phaedophile, and Feminist," in *Women in the Ancient World: The Arethusa Papers* (Albany: SUNY Press, 1984), 213–28.

7. For example, Alice Rossi noted in her introductory essay to John Stuart Mill and Harriet Taylor's *Essays on Sex Equality* (Chicago: University of Chicago Press, 1970) that major collections of Mill's works typically do not include *The Subjection of Women* (see page 5 and especially note 3). Similarly, although Descartes defended a strong distinction between mind and body, and as we shall see, versions of this distinction have played an important role in attitudes about women, "woman's nature" or differences between men and women were not central among his concerns. See *Passions of the Soul,* trans. E. S. Haldane and G. R. T. Ross (New York: Cambridge University Press, 1911), 2: 90. However, as Genevieve Lloyd has reminded us, Descartes did seem to think that the method for

clear thinking he outlined did not require the kind of schooling typically denied women of his time (see Lloyd, *The Man of Reason*). Perhaps, then, Descartes said next to nothing about women because he saw no reason for his purposes to distinguish between men and women—a possibility that will be discussed in more detail shortly.

8. Friedrich Nietzsche, *Beyond Good and Evil* (Middlesex: Penguin, 1973), para. 232. A single quote of course can't tell us the whole story about Nietzsche's views of women. For a helpful account, see "Nietzsche's Ambivalence about Women" by Christine Garside Allen, in *The Sexism of Social and Political Theory*, ed. Clarke and Lange.

9. Immanual Kant, *Observations on the Feeling of the Beautiful and Sublime*, trans. John T. Goldthwait (Berkeley: University of California Press, 1960), 81.

10. A number of feminists have argued that their misogyny seeps into their work on other matters. See, for example, Evelyn Fox Keller, *Gender and Science* (New Haven: Yale University Press, 1985); Flax, "Political Philosophy and the Patriarchal Unconscious"; Lloyd, *The Man of Reason;* Jean Grimshaw, *Philosophy and Feminist Thinking* (Minneapolis: University of Minnesota Press, 1986).

11. This is a reminder that those who counsel reconstruction may simply assume that what the philosophers in question said about "man" was so on the mark and so attractive that it would be a good thing for women to be described in the same way. (We would do well to remember that feminist button of yesteryear: "Women who want to be equal to men lack ambition.")

12. "This fellow was quite black from head to foot, a clear proof that what he said was stupid" (*Observations,* 113). Of course Kant thought that behaving morally was not easy for anyone, but he didn't seem to think that having white skin and being male posed a constitutional obstacle to performing one's duty.

13. See, for example, Theaetetus 175e, in which we are reminded that the philosopher "is nursed in freedom and leisure" and "may be excused if he looks foolish or useless when faced with some menial task, if he cannot tie up bedclothes into a neat bundle or flavor a dish with spices and a speech with flattery." In this connection, see M. M. Austin and P. Vidal-Naquet: "To our way of thinking there is a flagrant contradiction between the freedom of some and the servitude of others. But the Greek point of view was different: the freedom of some could not be imagined without the servitude of others and the two extremes were not thought of as contradictory, but as complementary and interdependent" (*Economic and Social History of Ancient Greece* [Berkeley: University of California Press, 1977], 19).

14. Betty Friedan, *The Feminine Mystique* (New York: Norton, 1963).

15. Quoted in *off our backs,* July 1986, 3.

16. See Audre Lorde, "An Open Letter to Mary Daly," in *Sister Outsider* (Trumansburg, New York: Crossing Press, 1984), 66–71.

17. Ellen Carol DuBois, *Feminism and Suffrage* (Ithaca: Cornell University Press, 1978), 178.

18. See, for example, Judith Rollins, *Between Women: Domestics and Their Employers* (Philadelphia: Temple University Press, 1985).

19. See María C. Lugones and Elizabeth V. Spelman, "Have We Got a The-

ory for You! Feminist Theory, Cultural Imperialism, and the Demand for 'The Woman's Voice,'" *Women's Studies International Forum* 6, no. 6 (1983): 573–81.

20. This is so despite the fact that Plato in some places argued for a kind of equality between men and women of a certain class.

21. Contemporary concepts of "class" and "race" don't easily fit the kinds of distinctions Plato and Aristotle had in mind. See, for example, Austin and Vidal-Naquet, *Economic and Social History,* and M. I. Finley, *Ancient Slavery and Modern Ideology* (Hammondsworth: Penguin, 1983).

22. See Spelman, "Aristotle and the Politicization of the Soul," in *Discovering Reality,* ed. Harding and Hintikka, 17–30.

23. See chapter 5. However, given the racism within the suffrage movement, and the sexism within the abolition movement, it is clear that too much can be made of that link.

24. In a particularly thoughtful and helpful article on the treatment of "different" children in schools, Martha Minow has described "the dilemma of difference": "Identification or acknowledgement of a trait of difference, associated by the dominant group with minority identity, risks recreating occasions for majority discrimination based on that trait. Nonidentification or nonacknowledgement, however, risks recreating occasions for discrimination based on majority practices, such as tests, norms, and judgments forged without regard for difference, or with regard solely for the perspective, needs, and interests of the dominant group. Because minority differences have been made to carry implications for a person's worth and status a minority member may be reluctant to expose or emphasize such difference. Yet nonexposure can subject the minority to evaluation by allegedly neutral criteria that in fact implement the majority values and view" ("Learning to Live with the Dilemma of Difference: Bilingual and Special Education," *Law and Contemporary Problems* 48, no. 2 [1985]: 160).

25. The prime example is, of course, George Orwell's *Animal Farm* (New York: Harcourt, Brace, 1946).

26. Kenneth Stampp, *The Peculiar Institution: Slavery in the Ante-Bellum South* (New York: Knopf, 1956), vii–viii.

27. A recent account of the history of reactions to *The Peculiar Institution* appears in August Meier and Elliott Rudwick's *Black History and the Historical Profession 1915–1980* (Urbana: University of Illinois Press, 1986), 137–40 and 240–47.

28. On this issue, see Lugones and Spelman, "Have We Got a Theory for You!"

29. Ultimately I shall argue that being white and being woman is in fact a seamless whole—but that on the same grounds, being Black and being woman is a seamless whole, being Hispanic and being woman is a seamless whole, and so on. The particular woman I am is constructed and is experienced in concert with my racial, ethnic, and class identity.

30. Barbara Omolade, "Black Women and Feminism," in *The Future of Difference,* ed. Hester Eisenstein and Alice Jardine (New Brunswick: Rutgers University Press, 1985), 248.

31. For questions about whether sexual distinctions are any less conventional

than gender distinctions, see Andrea Dworkin, *Woman Hating* (New York: E. P. Dutton, 1974), 175 and 183.

32. Richard Halloran, "Women, Blacks, Spouses Transforming the Military," *New York Times*, 25 August 1986, A1 and A14. In the article, the "women" referred to are white, the "Blacks" referred to are men. Since "women" and "Blacks" are being contrasted, it makes no sense to describe the situation of Black women as a composite of the situation of "women" and "Blacks." In the caption to a chart depicting the "percent of blacks and women in the armed forces" per year, we are told that "figures for blacks include both men and women." So perhaps the idea is that the situation for Black women is not different from that of Black men, but no explanation is offered.

33. In some recent widely reported cases, two Black women—Eula Love in Los Angeles, and Eleanor Bumpurs in New York—were shot dead by heavily armed police officers at close range. It is hard to imagine that a white woman would have been killed for waving a kitchen knife, but in both cases that was the alleged ground of the threat the Black woman posed to the officers.

Chapter 1: Hairy Cobblers and Philosopher-Queens

1. There is evidence that Pythagoras treated women as the equals of men, but as Sarah Pomeroy argues, "this phenomenon was unique in the Greek world of the sixth and fifth centuries B.C." (*Women in Hellenistic Egypt* [New York: Schocken, 1984], 65). There is considerable debate about the meaning of the portrayal of women in classical literature. See, for example, Sarah B. Pomeroy, *Goddesses, Whores, Wives, and Slaves: Women in Classical Antiquity* (New York: Schocken, 1975); Eva Cantarella, *Pandora's Daughters: The Role and Status of Women in Greek and Roman Antiquity* (Baltimore: Johns Hopkins University Press, 1987); M. R. Lefkowitz, *The Lives of the Greek Poets* (Baltimore: Johns Hopkins University Press, 1981); Martha C. Nussbaum, *The Fragility of Goodness: Luck and Ethics in Greek Tragedy and Philosophy* (Cambridge: Cambridge University Press, 1986).

2. Plato thus inverts what appears to us as a paradoxical situation in the Athenian society of his time: Democratic reforms in Athens in some ways lowered the status of many women (on this, see Pomeroy, *Goddesses, Whores, Wives, and Slaves*, 57–58, and Ellen M. Wood and Neal Wood, *Class Ideology and Ancient Political Theory: Socrates, Plato, and Aristotle in Social Context* [New York: Oxford University Press, 1978], 49–50), but Plato in effect raises the status of some women in the process of constructing a very undemocratic society.

3. Plato has most recently been described as a feminist by Nussbaum in *The Fragility of Goodness*, 4n.

4. For a useful summary of the meaning of "nature" or *phusis*, see Okin, *Women in Western Political Thought*, 51 ff.

5. See G. Vlastos, "Does Slavery Exist in Plato's *Republic?*" *Classical Philology* 63 (1968): 291–95.

6. Plato uses *psuchē* here, which usually is translated as "soul."

7. Soul (*psuchē*) and nature (*phusis*) are different concepts, but as we saw earlier, in the context of the inquiry into whether men and women have different natures, having the same soul settles for Plato the question of whether people have the same nature. See *Republic* 454d.

8. Plato does sometimes speak of a mortal part of the soul; see, for example, *Timaeus* 61d.

9. See G. Vlastos, "The Individual as an Object of Love in Plato," in his *Platonic Studies*, 2d ed. (Princeton: Princeton University Press, 1981), 40: "Body-to-body endearment is one of [the] normal features [of Platonic love], though always subject to the constraint that terminal gratification will be denied."

10. As Nussbaum points out, this message from the *Symposium* (210bff.) is in effect reassessed in the *Phaedrus* (*The Fragility of Goodness*, 220ff.)

11. While it is true that sometimes he argues to the effect that it is wasteful not to make use of women's capacities—see, for example, Annas, "Plato's *Republic* and Feminism"—his argument presupposes his being able to see that women have such capacities.

12. See A. W. H. Adkins, *From the Many to the One* (Ithaca: Cornell University Press, 1970), 148: "The whole well-being of the *polis* depends on the ability of the rulers to distinguish these natural kinds."

13. See Erving Goffmann, *Asylums* (Garden City, N.Y.: Anchor Doubleday, 1961): "A basic social arrangement in modern society is that the individual tends to sleep, play, and work in different places, with different co-participants, under different authorities, and without an over-all rational plan. The central feature of total institutions can be described as a breakdown of the barriers ordinarily separating these three spheres of life. First, all aspects of life are conducted in the same place and under the same single authority. Second, each phase of the member's daily activity is carried on in the immediate company of a large batch of others, all of whom are treated alike and required to do the same thing together. Third, all phases of the day's activities are tightly scheduled, with one activity leading at a prearranged time into the next, the whole sequence of activities being imposed from above by a system of explicit formal rulings and a body of officials. Finally, the various enforced activities are brought together into a single rational plan purportedly designed to fulfill the official aims of the institution" (6). Total institutions are incompatible with the family (11). When spheres of life are "desegregated," a person's conduct "in one scene of activity is thrown up to him . . . as a comment and check upon his conduct in another context" (37).

14. Wood and Wood, *Class Ideology*, 53–54. See also Ernest Barker, *The Political Thought of Plato and Aristotle* (New York: Dover, 1959), 139.

15. While the philosopher-rulers of the *Republic* have to be able to distinguish between the well- and ill-born, the philosophers of the *Theaetetus* wouldn't bother: "Whether any fellow citizen is well- or ill-born or has inherited some defect from his ancestors on either side, the philosopher knows no more than how many pints of water there are in the sea" (173d). This suggests some ways in which the life of a philosopher who is not a ruler is quite different from the life of one who is; we might say that philosopher-rulers have to be interested in the particular historical identity of people in a way that mere philosophers are not.

16. Although Plato objects to certain types of men—sophists, tyrants, and so forth—his disdain for women is always expressed as disdain for women in general and not for any subgroup of women. Moreover, one of the ways he shows his disdain for certain types of men is to compare them to women. Children, slaves, and brutes also sometimes reveal the malfunctioning of the appropriate soul/body relation.

17. In passages like this we see Plato assuming that a certain kind of body implies the presence of a certain kind of soul. This is at odds with his explicit view elsewhere that what is really important about someone is that the person has a soul, no matter what kind of body she has.

18. In the *Phaedo* (82a ff.), Socrates suggests that those who have led wantonly reckless and lawless lives are likely to come back as wolves, hawks, and kites, while those with the "ordinary goodness" of "self-control and integrity . . . will probably pass into some other kind of social and disciplined creature like bees, wasps, and ants, or even back into the human race again, becoming decent citizens."

19. For elaboration on the extent and significance of Plato's misogyny, see Spelman, "Woman as Body," 109–31.

20. In the *Menexenus* Socrates also expresses admiration for Aspasia as "an excellent mistress in the art of rhetoric" (235e). But there is serious doubt about whether Plato is the author of this dialogue. Moreover, Diotima may be a fictitious person.

21. In the examples from the *Laws* (944e) and *Timaeus* (42b–c, 91a), there is the suggestion that people are sentenced by the gods; in the Myth of Er at the end of the *Republic,* it is implied that people choose their next lives.

22. As should be clear already, Plato refers to the significance of reincarnation in a number of places throughout the dialogues; he doesn't always include ending up in a female body in his lists. See, for example, *Phaedrus* 248d ff.

23. The point is made less forcefully in the *Laws* (655a), when the Athenian legislator and Clinias agree that "a manly soul struggling with distress and a cowardly soul in the same or equal straits" will not express themselves in similar "postures . . . utterances . . . complexions." Later the Athenian suggests that a soul's "successive conjunction first with one body and then with another" is due to the power and responsibility of a god or gods "to shift the character that is becoming better to a better place, and that which is growing worse to a worser, each according to its due, that each may meet with its proper doom" (903d–e). See also Adkins, *From the Many to the One,* 134.

24. Necessary as long as you are alive; Plato would seem to believe that you don't need it after your soul is separated from your body, in death.

25. Barker, *Political Thought,* 145.

26. Annas, "Plato's *Republic* and Feminism," 183.

27. In connection with this, see Lynda Lange, "The Function of Equal Education in Plato's *Republic* and *Laws,*" in *The Sexism of Social and Political Theory,* ed. Clark and Lange, 3–15.

Chapter 2: Who's Who in the Polis

1. See, for example, Okin, *Women in Western Political Thought;* Saxonhouse, *Women in the History of Political Thought;* Spelman, "Aristotle and the Politicization of the Soul." See also notes 34–36, 39, 42, and 46 below.

2. The shift in terminology here from "women" and "men" to "male" and "female" is significant (see pp. 41–43 below).

3. See, for example, *Politics,* book 1, chap. 2; book 3, chap. 8; *Ethics* 1170b13: What "living together means in the case of human beings" is "conversing and exchanging ideas"; it does not mean "being pastured like cattle in the same field."

4. *Polis* is not univocal in meaning: see, for example, H. D. F. Kitto, *The Greeks* (Hammondsworth: Penguin, 1951), 64–79; Barker, *Political Thought,* 411ff.

As is well known, there is some ambivalence in Aristotle about just what activities constitute the most noble of all human activities. Is a life of contemplation, away from the fray of politics, a nobler life, finally, than one in which one does the kind of thinking and acting characteristic of the statesman? (See, for example, Thomas Nagel, "Aristotle on Eudaimonia," and J. L. Ackrill, "Aristotle on Eudaimonia," both in *Essays on Aristotle's Ethics,* ed. Amélie Oksenberg Rorty (Berkeley: University of California Press, 1980), 7–14 and 15–33). Either form of the noble life is made possible by the existence of the household, in which everyday necessities are taken care of by those who are not capable of leading the highest form of human life. (On this point, see below.)

5. In the well-ordered state, Aristotle says, "farmers, artisans and laborers of all kinds" (*Politics* 1329a36) ought not to be slaves but neither ought they to be citizens. Aristotle thus thought it a grave mistake for Athens to include traders, artisans, and workers in the citizen assembly (on this see Austin and Vidal-Naquet, *Economic and Social History,* 107).

6. From *The Complete Works of Aristotle,* ed. Jonathan Barnes (Princeton: Princeton University Press, 1984), vol. 2. All references to works by Aristotle are to this two-volume set and will be cited parenthetically in the text.

7. Austin and Vidal-Naquet note the existence in Athens of laws trying to undermine such judgments about the meaning and effects of plying a trade (*Economic and Social History,* 107). M. I. Finley notes the difference between Benjamin Franklin's concern about slavery threatening the virtue of the children of white slaveowners because it offered them idleness, and ancient moralists' ideal of freedom from industry (*Ancient Slavery,* 100).

8. Referring to the woman as "free" seems bizarre, since women surely were not the social or political equals of free men and since Aristotle says that it is the "mark of a free man not to live at another's beck and call" (*Rhetoric* 1367a32). Nevertheless, as discussed below, some women were slaves, others were not slaves, that is, were free.

9. This is somewhat misleading, since soul and body aren't so distinct in Aristotle as in Plato. See, for example, *De Anima* 403a15, 412b6, 414a20.

10. Aristotle waffles a bit about for whose sake the master rules the slave. See, for example, *Politics* 1255b14. His struggles to find the appropriate language for

describing the kind of rule of husband over wife, master over slave, may have to do with his using terminology geared to describe a variety of possible relationships in the polis in order to talk about relationships within the household.

11. In this passage, Aristotle uses completely separate words to refer to females and female slaves: *thēlu* for "female" and *doulē* for "female slave" (the latter being simply the feminine version of *doulos;* Aristotle often uses the neuter *doulon*).

12. Thus though the soul is intended by nature to rule the body, in corrupt or evil men it appears that the body rules the soul. See, for example, *Politics* 1254a35–37.

13. For a recent argument that Aristotle probably thought that no enslaved people of his own time met the criteria he lays out for a people being natural slaves, see Wayne Ambler, "Aristotle on Nature and Politics: The Case of Slavery," *Political Theory* 15, no. 3 (1987): 390–410. Ambler, like many authors referred to below, speaks as if "female" and "slave" were mutually exclusive categories.

14. According to Austin and Vidal-Naquet, the Periclean law of 451–450 decreed that in order to be a citizen one's parents both had to be citizens; relations between citizens and slaves were not legally sanctioned (*Economic and Social History,* 89).

15. Aristotle says little if anything about public slaves, that is, slaves who did not work only in the household.

16. See Austin and Vidal-Naquet, *Economic and Social History,* 184: "The distinctions between men and women, and adults and children, are relevant for the author of the *Politics* only within the body of free citizens."

17. See *Politics* 1258b37–40: "Those occupations are most truly arts in which there is the least element of chance; they are the meanest in which the body is most maltreated, the most servile in which there is the greatest use of the body, and the most illiberal in which there is the least need of excellence." Also see *Rhetoric* 1361a8 ff., where it is said that the excellences of women include "self-command and an industry that is not sordid." In Demosthenes there is an account of a man whose citizenship was questioned because his mother was engaged in the unbecoming trade of selling ribbons in market (quoted in Austin and Vidal-Naquet, *Economic and Social History,* 178 ff.).

18. Aristotle doesn't really say very much about free men and women of the metic class.

19. See, for example, *Generation of Animals* 728a17 ff., 732a1 ff., 775a15.

20. As Finley (*Ancient Slavery,* 118) and others remind us, stigma did not attach to skin color in ancient Greece.

21. Has women's capacity to reproduce ever been taken to be significant in isolation from the kind of children they can produce? To what extent has men's concern about women's reproductive capacities been a concern about producing children of their own kind? We need to explore the extent to which the sexism at work in the attempt to control women's bodies through legislation about contraception, abortion, and so on, is linked to explicit or implicit eugenics projects.

22. See note 9 above.

23. Or, for that matter, of children vis-à-vis fathers.

24. Cf. *Nicomachean Ethics* 1102b30, in which that irrational part or element of the soul called the desiderative or appetitive is said to be "submissive and obedient" to the rational part.

25. Austin and Vidal-Naquet say that the idea here is that "a woman is capable of deliberation but cannot give the force of law to her deliberations" (*Economic and Social History,* 183). See also Saxonhouse, *Women in the History of Political Thought,* 74. As Martha Nussbaum points out, this most likely is not what Aristotle meant, even if that is what the Greek seems to mean (see *The Fragility of Goodness,* 499). Aristotle is not concerned about obstacles that prevent the realization of women's well-thought-out deliberations, but about a kind of incapacity in women's reasoning ability.

26. Fathers are to rule children, because although children—male children, presumably; more specifically, male children who are not born of natural slaves— have the capacity to deliberate that is associated with the rational element of the soul, this capacity is immature (*Politics* 1260a6–15).

27. "The difference between ruler and subject is a difference in kind, which the difference of more and less never is" (*Politics* 1259b36–37).

28. As evident in the passage from the *Politics* comparing women and slaves (1252b1–7), Aristotle seemed to take barbarians to be natural slaves (although Ambler, "Aristotle on Nature and Politics," argues against this view). Thus, while he didn't think one's status as slave was reflected in bodily appearance, he perhaps did take one's speech as an important clue: a barbarian was "a man whose speech was unintelligible and sounded like 'bar-bar-bar'" (M. I. Finley, *The Ancient Greeks* [Hammondsworth: Penguin, 1963], 18).

29. Aristotle mentions that some women are "exceptions to the order of nature" and may be more fit for command than their husbands (*Politics* 1259b2–3).

30. On this see Spelman, "Aristotle and the Politicization of the Soul," 17–30.

31. Aristotle suggests that while most states of the soul take place in and involve a body (e.g., *De Anima* 403a15, 412b6, 413a4), there is no connection between any activity of reason and bodily activity. See, for example, *Generation of Animals* 736b29, and *De Anima* 413b26, 430a16 ff.; see also Lange, "The Function of Equal Education in Plato's *Republic* and *Laws,* 6. If there is a kind of reason that needn't be embodied in order to exist, having a male body could not be a necessary condition for its presence.

32. It also would be misleading to say that Aristotle's views about the biological differences between men and women are parallel to his views about the psychological differences between them. The psychological differences complicate and confuse the biological ones because of Aristotle's insistence on the distinctions both between "men" and "women" and between "master" and "slave." If not all males are natural rulers, something other than reproductive biology is going to have to ground the distinction between them and those who are the naturally ruled; if nature distinguishes between "women" and "slaves," something other than reproductive biology is going to have to ground the distinction between the women who are appropriate companions for natural rulers and those who are fit to be slaves.

33. As noted earlier, Aristotle doesn't talk much about a class of free men and women who are neither citizens nor slaves. There was such a class in Athens, but it does not fit neatly into Aristotle's categories: the dichotomy of the rulers and the ruled is supposed to be exhaustive, and it may be unclear where free men and women belong. Aristotle does say at one point that a person is by nature a master or a slave but not by nature an artisan or a farmer (*Politics* 1260b3 ff.), leaving it unclear how we could tell whether artisans are by nature rulers or ruled.

34. As we note below, the kind of work one did was not always a reliable indicator of a man's status as free or slave in Classical Athens, even though those free men who were citizens may have shared Aristotle's concern about the bad effects of engaging in certain kinds of activities. Free women and slave women spent much time together and may have done some of the same kind of work: "Women of the upper class, excluded from the activities of males, supervised and—when they wished—pursued many of the same tasks deemed appropriate to slaves. [Slave and free women] spent much time together and their lives were not dissimilar" (Pomeroy, *Goddesses, Whores, Wives, and Slaves,* 71). Hannah Arendt refers to work showing "that women and slaves belonged and lived together, that no woman, not even the wife of the household head, lived among her equals—other free women—so that rank depended much less on birth than on 'occupation' or function" (*The Human Condition* [Garden City, N.Y.: Doubleday Anchor, 1959], 321). Now if these characterizations of the lives of free and slave women are accurate, does that mean that there was no significant difference in their position, no matter Aristotle's views on the matter? The messages from Pomeroy and Arendt are confusing: Pomeroy says that perhaps the lives of free and slave women were not dissimilar even though she has just said that the free women were in a position to supervise the slaves and that whether they performed the same tasks depended on whether they wanted to. Surely, then, their work conditions could not be said to be the same. Arendt says in one breath that free women do occupy a particular rank, and then in the next suggests that really their rank depended on the kind of work they did, as if being free really didn't finally matter. It seems obvious from these very brief attempts to describe the relative positions of free and slave women that we need to give much more attention to the matter than we have heretofore. Moreover, if there is no significant distinction between the treatment of free and slave women, then there is something quite odd about the claim that we can best understand the position of "women" by focusing on free rather than on slave women.

35. Spelman, "Aristotle and the Politicization of the Soul," 17–30.

36. Okin, *Women in Western Political Thought,* 86.

37. Ibid., 89, 90.

38. Ibid., 87.

39. Pomeroy, *Goddesses, Whores, Wives, and Slaves,* 60.

40. Ibid., 58.

41. Ibid., 58, 59.

42. Grimshaw, *Philosophy and Feminist Thinking,* 41.

43. Another way of asking this question: What would happen if we took the primary reference of the word "woman" to be slave women, not free women?

Whenever we talked about the status of free women, we'd have to make sure to include the qualifier "free." Why can't I say "whenever I use the word 'woman' without a qualifier, I am referring to slave women; so whenever I want to refer to free women I will use 'free women'"? What kind of implicit rules for the use of the unqualified "woman" am I breaking?

44. A note on terminology: there is no easy way to categorize that aspect of a person's identity by virtue of which, according to Aristotle, one is free or slave. Both "class" and "race" are likely to be misleading. Slaves in ancient Greece can't be said to constitute a class in terms of their position in relations of production or in terms of shared consciousness. In Aristotle's time, the kind of labor one did was not always a reliable indicator of one's status as a citizen, free noncitizen, or slave (see, e.g., M. I. Finley, *Economy and Society in Ancient Greece* [New York: Penguin, 1983], chap. 7 and passim). This is a fact of Greek life that might have been of concern to Aristotle, since, as we've seen, he thinks that with the difference between master (citizen) and slave ought to go the difference between kinds of activities people are engaged in (whether he would insist on this distinction between free and slave is not clear). But "class" better describes Aristotle's discussion of relations among citizens (as, for example, in book 5 of the *Politics*) than those between citizen and slave (see Austin and Vidal-Naquet, *Economic and Social History*, 22).

Moreover, reference to "racial" differences is likely to lead to misunderstanding as well, because as we saw above, Aristotle didn't think the distinction between master and slave or between free and slave corresponded to a difference in skin color or any other physical difference. On the other hand, as we've also seen, Aristotle thought of natural slaves as distinctly and irretrievably different from natural rulers—as if they were a different breed of humans. Hence some scholars, such as Finley, insist on the word "racism" to describe the "ideological expressions . . . formulated around 'barbarians'" such as we find in Aristotle (*Ancient Slavery*, 118). "Race," then, is probably less misleading than "class." I shall use "race" in quotation marks to refer to that dimension of the identity of persons by which, according to Aristotle, rulers/citizens and their wives are distinguished from those males and females who are "by nature" slaves.

45. Janet Radcliffe Richards, *The Sceptical Feminist* (Boston: Routledge and Kegan Paul, 1980), 5.

46. Cantarella, *Pandora's Daughters*, 39.

47. Ibid.

48. See footnote 44 above for an explanation of why "racism" is used in this context.

49. I've actually suggested that there may be two different accounts in Richards and Canterella of the position of slave women. One could be described as follows:

4. The treatment of some women has to do only with their "race," with their being slaves; sexism is not a factor here, because it is not as women that slaves are excluded from the polis.

The other is suggested in my extrapolation on p. 49:

5. The treatment of some women has to do with their gender and their "race"; their treatment is a combination of their status as slaves and of their being women.

Now we need to notice that propositions 4 and 5 contradict each other if they are taken to apply to the same women. That is, we can't say (even apart from the question of what Aristotle's opinion on the matter is) that the treatment of slave women in Aristotle has to do *both* with their gender and "race" and *simply* with their "race"; we can't say that they were subject *both* to sexism and "racism" and *only* to "racism." Which will it be? If we go with proposition 5 and say that they were excluded on both counts, then we lose the rationale for focusing on free women: if any and all women are excluded from the polis as women, then we can take any woman as an example. If we go with point 4 and say they were excluded on the single count of "race," then we can't maintain the idea that there is a form of oppression to which all women are subject as women. Alice Paul insisted that the disenfranchisement of Black women was due to their race rather than their sex, even though she also assumed that suffrage was a "purely feminist" issue around which women could unite despite their differences. See Nancy Cott, *The Grounding of Modern Feminism* (New Haven: Yale University Press, 1987), 70–71.

50. This argument obscures the existence of those who are neither male nor female.

51. The males and females who are slaves are from Aristotle's perspective without a gender identity (or anyway without the gender identity of "man"or "woman"). Cf. Angela Davis's description of Black female slaves as "genderless" in chapter 1 of *Women, Race, and Class* (New York: Random, 1981).

Chapter 3: Simone de Beauvoir and Women

1. Simone de Beauvoir, *The Second Sex,* translated and edited by H. M. Parshley (New York: Knopf, 1953). References are to this edition and are cited parenthetically in the text.

2. See, for example, Judith Okely, *Simone de Beauvoir* (London: Virago, 1986).

3. This is not to say that feminists have not found reason to disagree with her. For a recent extended critique, see Mary Evans, *Simone de Beauvoir: A Feminist Mandarin* (London and New York: Tavistock, 1985).

4. See chapter 1. Though her terminology is certainly different from Aristotle's, there are echoes here of his distinction between a group of cattle grazing and a vibrant human polis.

5. The translator here renders *l'existence* as "existing" and *la vie* as "living." "Living" carries more weight for contemporary English speakers than mere "existing."

6. De Beauvoir does say quickly in passing that only feminists have done this (xviii–xix).

7. But she also insists for example, that "woman's 'character' [is] to be explained by her situation" (588).

8. These points ought to remind us of some issues raised in connection with Plato and Aristotle in earlier chapters. When looking at Plato we asked whether

we should be satisfied that someone is a feminist if he holds only that women of one class are the social and political equals of men of that class, meanwhile holding that the men and women of that class are to dominate all other men and women. With Aristotle we asked whether it wasn't true that the sexism experienced by free women was a function of their "race" identity.

9. The idea that white middle-class women might be more reluctant than other women to battle sexism—if doing so is to cost them the privileges they have over white working-class women and all women of color—appears to conflict with what has become a historical truism: that the nineteenth- and twentieth-century women's movements in England, Europe, and the United States were founded and maintained by white middle-class women. Two questions immediately arise: Did they perceive their activity to be something that would involve giving up race or class privilege? Was what they were fighting for in fact something that would lead to loss of privilege whether or not they so perceived it? Were white female abolitionists actually fighting to end race privilege? Did they think it could be ended without ending sex privilege in the white population? In any event, if middle-class women were as reluctant as de Beauvoir says, what might this tell us about those middle-class women who were not reluctant?

10. Contemporary feminists now stick in the qualifying adjective "white," as if that took care of the problem. But if it matters whether a man is white, it surely also matters—even if not in the same way—that a woman is white.

11. On this see Ann Firor Scott, *The Southern Lady: From Pedestal to Politics* (Chicago: University of Chicago Press, 1971).

12. But it is not as if she thinks women are more clearheaded in their thinking than men. On the contrary: "Not accepting logical principles and moral imperatives, skeptical about the laws of nature, woman lacks the sense of the universal; to her the world seems a confused conglomeration of special cases" (580). Women are right to look at particular real cases, but they are more likely to believe in "the tittle-tattle of a neighbor than in a scientific explanation" (580).

13. In fact, the existentialist point is probably even stronger: we shouldn't even assume that sameness of race or class or ethnicity will make a significant impact on the shape of someone's life, because it is always up to them what they make of their lives. This point, however, would surely complicate de Beauvoir's insistence that sameness of sex does make a difference.

14. Okely, *Simone de Beauvoir*, 105.

15. There is a distinction between (a) explicitly claiming superiority over others and the right thereby to dominate them, and (b) paying attention to one's own situation and ignoring that of others. But in societies with a history, for example, of race and class exploitation, such attention is both symptomatic and supportive of explicit claims to race and class domination.

16. See, for example, the discussion of Richards and Cantarella in chapter 2.

17. As Margaret Simons has pointed out, the English translation of *The Second Sex* does not include all of the original French version. See "The Silencing of Simone de Beauvoir: Guess What's Missing from *The Second Sex*," *Women's Studies International Forum* 6 (1983): 559–64.

18. We return to this issue in chapters 6 and 7.

Chapter 4: Gender in the Context of Race and Class

1. As we saw, this didn't mean what it may suggest—that for different races and classes the sexism is always the same.

2. Notice how different this is from saying that whether one is *female*|is unaffected by what race or class one is.

3. Among the philosophers and political theorists who have incorporated Chodorow's work into their own analyses are Jane Flax, "Political Philosophy and the Patriarchal Unconscious: A Psychoanalytic Perspective on Epistemology and Metaphysics," Nancy C. M. Hartsock, "The Feminist Standpoint: Developing the Ground for a Specifically Feminist Historical Materialism," Naomi Scheman, "Individualism and the Objects of Psychology," and Sandra Harding, "Why Has the Sex/Gender System Become Visible Only Now?"—all in *Discovering Reality,* ed. Harding and Hintikka. See also Isaac D. Balbus, *Marxism and Domination* (Princeton: Princeton University Press, 1982). Chodorow's work also has been incorporated into the literary criticism of Judith Kegan Gardiner, "On Female Identity and Writing by Women," *Critical Inquiry* 8, no. 2 (1981): 347–61, and of Elizabeth Abel, "(E)Merging Identities: The Dynamics of Female Friendship in Contemporary Fiction by Women," *Signs* 6, no. 3 (1981): 413–35. Students of psychoanalysis such as Jessica Benjamin and Evelyn Fox Keller have found Chodorow's work helpful in explaining their own positions, Benjamin in "Master and Slave: The Fantasy of Erotic Domination," in *Powers of Desire: The Politics of Sexuality,* ed. Ann Snitow, Christine Stansell, and Sharon Thompson (New York: Monthly Review Press, 1983), 280–99; Keller in "Gender and Science," *Psychoanalysis and Contemporary Thought* 2, no. 3 (1978): 409–33. Chodorow's work has also influenced the far-reaching work of Carol Gilligan, *In a Different Voice* (Cambridge: Harvard University Press, 1982). Chodorow's book and earlier articles were the subject of a critical symposium in *Signs* 6, no. 3 (1981), with comments from Judith Lorber, Rose Laub Coser, Alice S. Rossi, and a response from Chodorow. Iris Young recently has expressed doubts about the wisdom of Flax's, Hartsock's, and Harding's use of Chodorow, in "Is Male Gender Identity the Cause of Male Domination?" in *Mothering: Essays in Feminist Theory,* ed. Joyce Trebilcot (Totowa, N.J.: Rowman and Allanheld, 1983). In the *Mothering* volume also appears Pauline Bart's highly critical review of Chodorow's book, a review first found in *off our backs* 11, no. 1 (1981). Adrienne Rich has pointed out the heterosexist bias in *The Reproduction of Mothering* in "Compulsory Heterosexuality and Lesbian Existence," *Signs* 5, no. 4 (1980): 631–60. As discussed below, Gloria Joseph has addressed the fact of the absence of a discussion of race and racism in accounts like Chodorow's.

4. Nancy Chodorow, *The Reproduction of Mothering: Psychoanalysis and the Sociology of Gender* (Berkeley: University of California Press, 1978). All references are to this edition and are cited parenthetically in the text.

5. Chodorow, Reply to "On *The Reproduction of Mothering:* A Methodological Debate," with Judith Lorber, Rose Laub Coser, and Alice S. Rossi. *Signs* 6, no. 3 (1981): 502, 503. Hereafter referred to as "Reply."

6. Chodorow, "Gender, Relation, and Difference," in *The Future of Differ-*

ence, ed. Hester Eisenstein and Alice Jardine (New Brunswick, N.J.: Rutgers University Press, 1985), 3–19. Reprinted from *Socialist Review* 9, no. 46 (1979): 51–69.

7. See note 3 above, specifically articles by Bart, Rosaldo, Young, and Rich. See also comments by Mark Poster in *Sociology and Social Research* 63 (1979): 394–96.

8. This chapter can be seen in part as one way to carry out Michelle Rosaldo's suggestion that we look at sexual inequality in light of its connections to other forms of inequality in any society. See "The Use and Abuse of Anthropology: Reflections on Feminism and Cross-cultural Understanding," *Signs* 5, no. 3 (1980): 389–417.

9. Chodorow, "Gender, Relation, and Difference," 12.

10. For discussion of this, see Iris Young, "Is Male Gender Identity the Cause of Male Domination?"; Roger Gottlieb, "Mothering and the Reproduction of Power," in *Socialist Review* 77 (September/October 1984).

11. Chodorow, "Reply," 514.

12. For a recent account of Emmet Till's murder, see Juan Williams, *Eyes on the Prize* (New York, Viking, 1986), 41 ff.

13. In the *Signs* article again, she says that "in order to insure his sense of self" the boy first tries to dominate his mother; but this then "extends to women, and is then generalized to include the experience of all others as objects rather than subjects" ("Reply," 503). Her use of the quotation from Lévi-Strauss suggests that it is through such a process of generalization that "slavery and class domination" might be explained in large part by reference to sexual domination.

14. Sandra Harding, "What Is the Real Material Base of Patriarchy and Capital?" in *Women and Revolution,* ed. Lydia Sargent (Boston: South End Press, 1981), 139, 153.

15. Extrapolating from the work of John L. Hodge (*Cultural Bases of Racism and Group Oppression,* co-written with Donald K. Struckmann and Lynn Dorland Trost [Berkeley: Two Riders Press, 1975], 9–10), I take there to be three main elements in full-blown cases of sexism: (1) the belief that one sex is different from another; (2) the belief that by virtue of such difference one sex is superior to another; (3) institutions that support points 1 and 2. Similar conditions must exist for full-blown cases of racism, classism, and so on.

16. Evelyn Fox Keller is ambivalent about this. Sometimes in her work on the development of the sense of gender she refers simply to men and women, fathers and mothers; other times she indicates that what our attention needs to be drawn to is a particular group of men: "To explore the relations among autonomy, power, and gender . . . requires an examination of the central role played by the stereotypic white middle-class father in the child's consolidation of gender and autonomy" (*Gender and Science,* 108).

17. The account also ignores the fact that in order to think about belonging to a "race" and also be racists men have to be able to think of themselves in connection with some group of others (i.e., women of their own "race") even while thinking about themselves as separate from another group of others (i.e., men and women of the other "race").

18. See Chodorow, "Reply," 502, 503.

19. See, for example, Claudia Koonz, *Mothers in the Fatherland: Women, The Family, and Nazi Politics* (New York: St. Martin's Press, 1987).

20. We return to these concerns in chapter 7.

21. For a recent attempt to explain how Descartes can avoid this criticism, see Norman Malcolm, "Descartes's Proof that His Essence Is Thinking," *Philosophical Review* 74, no. 3 (1965): 315–38.

22. See Iris Young, "Is Male Gender Identity the Cause of Male Domination?" for a discussion of the distinction between gender differentiation and male domination.

23. Mary Burgher, "Images of Self and Race in the Autobiography of Black Women," in *Sturdy Black Bridges,* ed. Roseann P. Bell, Bettye J. Parker, and Beverly Guy-Sheftall (Garden City, N.Y.: Anchor, 1979), 115.

24. Nikki Giovanni, *Gemini* (New York: Penguin, 1976), 24.

25. Barbara Cameron, "Gee, You Don't Seem Like An Indian From the Reservation," *This Bridge Called My Back,* ed. Cherríe Moraga and Gloria Anzaldúa (Watertown, Mass.: Persephone Press, 1981), 46–47.

26. Cherríe Moraga, "La Güera," in *This Bridge Called My Back,* 28.

27. Gloria Joseph, *Common Differences: Conflicts in Black and White Perspectives* (with Jill Lewis) (Garden City, N.Y.: Anchor, 1981), 80.

28. Daryl Dance, "Black Eve or Madonna? A Study in the Antithetical Views of the Mother in Black American Literature," in *Sturdy Black Bridges,* 127. Here Dance is referring to *Black Rage,* by William H. Grier and Price M. Cobbs (New York: Basic Books, 1968), 61.

29. Ibid., 128.

30. Dorcas Bowles, "In Search of an Ethnic Self" (Northampton, Mass.: School for Social Work, Smith College, n.d.).

31. In the *Signs* symposium on Chodorow (note 2 above), Judith Lorber quotes Mary Lyndon Shanley on the apparent universality of emotion: "Hunger is hunger, pride is pride, and love is love—but these feelings, while universal, are evoked, expressed, and experienced differently in different societies" (see Mary Lyndon Shanley, "The History of the Family in Modern England," *Signs* 4, no. 4 [1979]: 750).

32. Dance, "Black Eve," 129, quoting John A. Williams, *Sissie* (New York: Farrar, Strauss, 1963), 38–39. See also the conversation between Hannah and Eva in Toni Morrison's *Sula* (New York: Bantam, 1975), 58–60.

33. Lillian Smith, *Killers of the Dream* (New York: Norton, 1949), 82.

34. Ibid., 87.

35. Ibid., 89. Some of the most moving parts of Smith's memoire/essay are her descriptions of the white children's confusion over the double messages of "Christian" parents about the importance of fellow feeling among all humankind. But the children were powerless to act on their perceptions, and on their more truly Christian affections. This is a reminder of how misleading it is for Chodorow to describe the mother/children domestic "sphere" as characterized by the absence of authority relations.

36. From Moraga and Anzaldúa's introduction to part 2 of *This Bridge Called My Back,* 23.

37. See Alison Jaggar's *Feminist Politics and Human Nature* (Totowa, N.J.: Rowman and Allanheld, 1983) for an especially useful account of socialist feminism.

38. This has been suggested by Barbara Ehrenreich and Deirdre English in *Complaints and Disorders: The Sexual Politics of Sickness* (Old Westbury, N.Y.: Feminist Press, 1973), 11–12. See also Rosaldo, "The Use and Abuse of Anthropology."

39. See Jaggar, *Feminist Politics,* 99 ff. for a review of reasons some feminists take sexual identity also to be in some important sense a cultural creation.

40. For a recent account of this, see Barbara Christian, "Shadows Uplifted," in *Black Women Novelists: The Development of a Tradition, 1892–1976* (Westport, Conn. Greenwood Press, 1980).

41. Jacqueline Jones, *Labor of Love, Labor of Sorrow: Black Women, Work, and the Family, from Slavery to the Present* (New York: Vintage, 1986), 41–42.

42. See, for example, ibid., chap. 1.

43. See ibid., 25–26.

44. See, for example, Minrose C. Gwin, "Green-eyed Monsters of the Slavocracy: Jealous Mistresses in Two Slave Narratives," in *Conjuring: Black Women, Fiction, and Literary Tradition,* ed. Marjorie Pryse and Hortense J. Spillers (Bloomington: Indiana University Press, 1985), 39–52.

45. In *Labor and Monopoly Capital* (New York: Monthly Review Press, 1974), Harry Braverman described "problems" among workers that industrial engineers were called in to try to deal with: "The problems addressed are the problems of management: dissatisfaction as expressed in high turnover rates, absenteeism, resistance to the prescribed work pace, indifference, neglect, cooperative group restrictions on output, and overt hostility to management" (141). "The hostility of workers to the degenerated forms of work which are forced upon them continues as a subterranean stream that makes its way to the surface when employment conditions permit, or when the capitalist drive for a greater intensity of labor oversteps the bounds of physical and mental capacity. It renews itself in new generations, expresses itself in the unbounded cynicism and revulsion which large numbers of workers feel about their work, and comes to the fore repeatedly as a social issue demanding solution" (151).

46. Thanks to Helen Longino, Monica Jakuc, and Marilyn Schuster for helpful comments on a very early draft of this chapter.

Chapter 5: Gender & Race

1. This chapter is a slightly revised version of my "Theories of Race and Gender: The Erasure of Black Women," in *Quest: a feminist quarterly* 5, no. 4 (1982): 36–62.

2. Halloran, "Women, Blacks, Spouses Transforming the Military." See also Introduction, note 32.

3. See also Gloria T. Hull, Patricia Bell Scott, and Barbara Smith, eds., *All the Women Are White, All the Blacks Are Men, But Some of Us Are Brave: Black Women's Studies* (Old Westbury, N.Y.: Feminist Press, 1982).

4. See Eleanor Flexner, *Century of Struggle* (New York: Atheneum, 1972), especially chapter 13, on the inhospitality of white women's organizations to Black women, as well as Aileen S. Kraditor's *The Ideas of the Woman Suffrage Movement, 1890–1920* (Garden City, N.Y.: Doubleday, 1971). See also DuBois, *Feminism and Suffrage;* Sara Evans, *Personal Politics* (New York: Vintage, 1979), on sexism in the civil rights movement; Dorothy Sterling, *Black Foremothers* (Old Westbury, N.Y.: Feminist Press, 1979), 147, on Alice Paul's refusal to grant Mary Church Terrell's request that Paul endorse enforcement of the Nineteenth Amendment for all women; Davis, *Women, Race, and Class;* Bettina Aptheker, *Women's Legacy: Essays on Race, Sex, and Class in American History* (Amherst: University of Massachusetts Press, 1982); Paula Giddings, *When and Where I Enter: The Impact of Black Women on Race and Sex in America* (New York: Morrow, 1984).

5. Adrienne Rich, "Disloyal to Civilization: Feminism, Racism, Gynephobia," in her *On Lies, Secrets, and Silence* (New York: Norton, 1979), 299 and passim. In the philosophical literature, solipsism is the view according to which it is only one's self that is knowable, or it is only one's self that constitutes the world. Strictly speaking, of course, Rich's use of the phrase "white solipsism" is at odds with the idea of there being only the self, insofar as it implies that there are other white people; but she is drawing from the idea of there being only one perspective on the world—not that of one person, but of one "race." (For further comment on the concept of race, see references in note 24 below.)

6. Ibid., 306.

7. Audre Lorde, "Man Child: A Black Lesbian Feminist's Response," *Conditions* 4 (1979): 35. My comments about racism apply to the racism directed against Black people in the United States. I do not claim that all my arguments apply to the racism experienced by other people of color.

8. See Margaret A. Simons, "Racism and Feminism: A Schism in the Sisterhood," *Feminist Studies* 5, no. 2 (1979): 384–401.

9. A somewhat similar list appears in Alison M. Jaggar and Paula Rothenberg's introduction to part 2 of *Feminist Frameworks,* 2d ed. (New York: McGraw-Hill, 1984), 86.

10. Kate Millett, *Sexual Politics* (New York: Ballantine, 1969), 33–34.

11. Simons, "Racism and Feminism."

12. Millett, *Sexual Politics,* 33–34.

13. Elizabeth F. Hood, "Black Women, White Women: Separate Paths to Liberation," *Black Scholar,* April 1978, 47.

14. This is precisely the position we found Richards attacking in chapter 2 above.

15. Shulamith Firestone, *The Dialectic of Sex* (New York: Bantam, 1970), 108.

16. Ibid., 117–18.

17. Ibid., 115. Emphasis in the original.

18. Ibid., 116.

19. Richard A. Wasserstrom, "Racism and Sexism," in *Philosophy and Women,* ed. Sharon Bishop and Marjorie Weinzweig (Belmont, Cal.: Wadsworth, 1979), 8. Reprinted from "Racism, Sexism, and Preferential Treatment: An Approach to the Topics," *UCLA Law Review* (February 1977): 581–615.

20. Ibid.

21. Laurence Thomas, "Sexism and Racism: Some Conceptual Differences," *Ethics* 90 (1980): 239–50.

22. I shall here leave aside the question of whether Thomas succeeds in offering a description of sexism that is not of something morally objectionable (see B. C. Postow's reply to Thomas, "Thomas on Sexism," *Ethics* 90 [1980]: 251–56). I shall also leave aside the question of to whom such a description is or is not morally objectionable, as well as the question of how its moral objectionableness is to be measured.

23. Thomas, "Sexism and Racism," 239 and passim.

24. Thomas says that "one very important reason" for this lack of analogy is that racial identity, unlike sexual identity, is "more or less settled by biological considerations" (ibid., 248). If Thomas means by this that there are such things as "races," and that the question of what race one belongs to is settled by biology, one must point out in reply that it is far from clear that this is so. See Ashley Montagu, "The Concept of Race: Part 1," *American Anthropologist* 64, no. 5 (1962), reprinted in *Anthropology: Contemporary Perspectives,* ed. David E. Hunter and Philip Whitten (Boston: Little, Brown, 1975), 83–95; and Frank B. Livingstone, "On the Nonexistence of Human Races," *The Concept of Race,* ed. Ashley Montagu (New York: Collier, 1964), reprinted in Hunter and Whitten. The existence of racism does not require that there are races; it requires the belief that there are races.

25. This is the kind of superiority that, as we saw in chapter 3, de Beauvoir described.

26. *Philosophical Forum,* 9, no. 2–3 (1977–78): 113.

27. See Carol Christ and Judith Plaskow Goldenberg, "For the Advancement of My Career: A Form Critical Study in the Art of Acknowledgement," *Bulletin of the Council for Religious Studies* (June 1972), for a marvelous study of the literary form of the "acknowledgement to the wife." See also the gruesomely delightful "Collecting Scholar's Wives," by Marilyn Hoder-Salmon, in *Feminist Studies* 4, no. 3 (n.d.): 107–14.

28. Thomas, "Sexism and Racism," 242–43.

29. Linda Brent, "The Trials of Girlhood," in *Root of Bitterness,* ed. Nancy F. Cott (New York: Dutton, 1972), 201.

30. Angela Y. Davis, "Reflections on the Black Woman's Role in the Community of Slaves," *Black Scholar* 3 (1971): 7.

31. Barbara Smith, "Notes For Yet Another Paper on Black Feminism, or Will the Real Enemy Please Stand Up," *Conditions* 5 (1979): 123–32. See also "The Combahee River Collective Statement," *Capitalist Patriarchy and the Case for Socialist Feminism,* ed. Zillah Eisenstein (New York: Monthly Review Press, 1979), 362–72.

32. Gerda Lerner, ed., *Black Woman in White America* (New York: Vintage, 1973), 15.

33. Davis, "Reflections on the Black Woman's Role," 7. Davis revises this slightly in *Women, Race, and Class.*

34. Mary Daly, *Beyond God the Father* (Boston: Beacon Press, 1975), 56–57.

35. Ibid.

36. Nikki Giovanni, "Nikki Rosa," in *The Black Woman,* ed. Toni Cade (New York: New American Library, 1980), 16.

37. Paule Marshall, "Reena," in *The Black Woman,* 28.

38. Pat Parker, *Womanslaughter* (Oakland: Diana Press, 1978), 13.

39. Spelman, "Woman as Body."

40. De Beauvoir, *The Second Sex,* xii, 57.

41. Ibid., 119.

42. Friedan, *The Feminine Mystique,* 247–77.

43. Firestone, *The Dialectic of Sex,* chap. 10.

44. Winthrop P. Jordan, *The White Man's Burden* (New York: Oxford University Press, 1974), chap. 1.

45. Smith, *Killers of the Dream,* 83–98.

46. Adrienne Rich, *Of Woman Born* (New York: Norton, 1976).

47. Rich, "Disloyal to Civilization," 300.

48. Diane Lewis, "A Response to Inequality: Black Women, Racism, and Sexism," *Signs* 3, no. 2 (1977): 339–61.

49. Toni Morrison, *The Bluest Eye* (New York: Pocketbooks, 1972).

50. See, for example, Carol Stack, *All Our Kin* (New York: Harper and Row, 1974).

Chapter 6: Woman: The One and the Many

1. See, for example, Robert B. Edgerton, "Pokot Intersexuality: An East African Example of the Resolution of Sexual Incongruity," *American Anthropologist* 66, no. 1 (1964): 1288–99.

2. Many thanks to Barbara Cottle Johnson for the pop-bead imagery.

3. A white woman might think her gender is thoroughly distinct from her race because she appears to experience sexism in isolation from racism: she is subjected to sexism but not to racism. (I say "appears" because we cannot understand the sexism she experiences without understanding its connection to the racism she does not.) It does not follow from that apparent isolation that her gender is distinct from her race; but neither does it follow, from the fact that a woman experiences sexism *and* racism, that her gender is distinct from her race. We discussed reasons for this earlier in chapter 2 and they are explored further below.

It is important to note that this composite, collection-of-parts view of personhood, as well as its accompanying view of political activity, is held implicitly by a wide range of feminist political and social theorists—not only those who treat gender as distinct from and isolatable from racial, ethnic, or other identity, but those who treat racial, class, and ethnic identity as isolatable from gender identity.

4. For extremely illuminating accounts of the role of the judiciary in making such decisions, see Martha Minow, "When Difference Has Its Home: Group Homes for the Mentally Retarded, Equal Protection, and Legal Treatment of Difference," *Harvard Civil Rights Civil Liberties Review* 22, no. 1 (1987), 111–89; and her "Foreword: Justice Engendered," in "The Supreme Court 1986 Term," *Harvard Law Review* 101, no. 1 (1987): 10–95.

5. *The Fire Next Time* (New York: Dell, 1962), 19. James Baldwin died while I was writing this book.

6. See Lorraine Bethel, "What Chou Mean *WE*, White Girl?" in *Conditions 5* (1979): 86–92.

7. See the discussion of Richards and Cantarella in chapter 2.

8. See Minow references in note 4 above.

9. I hardly begin to dip into the issues raised by reflection on what actual or desirable social science methodology is.

10. Stampp, *The Peculiar Institution*, vii–viii.

11. René Descartes, *Meditations on First Philosophy,* in *Descartes: Philosophical Writings,* translated and edited by Elizabeth Anscombe and Peter Geach (London: Nelson, 1969). Meditation 2: 67. Further citations are from this edition.

12. See Descartes, *Discourse on Method.*

13. Meditation 2: 67.

14. That is, he would agree with the later Wittgenstein (see, for example, *The Philosophical Investigations* [New York: Macmillan, 1953]) to some extent that the language we use to talk about ourselves is itself an intersubjective product and project and that therefore if we want to locate a kind of knowledge that does not depend on such products and projects we can't use language that imports them. Descartes does not realize how this undermines the method of the *Meditations.*

15. This pattern of sorting was not used by those who constructed segregated bathrooms in the United States.

16. This reminds us to ask whether the kinds of questions we referred to earlier that we are so adept at answering are questions about our sexual identity or our gender identity. It is worth thinking about why many bathroom doors are marked "men" and "women" rather than "male" and "female," since applications and census forms typically use the latter and seem to have to do simply with sexual identity. (Forms that ask one to pick from among "Mr.," "Mrs.," "Miss," and now "Ms." have more to do with gender identity and social role than sexual identity, since there are only two sexes referred to.) Perhaps it is because bathrooms have a lot to do with the maintenance of gender identity, insofar as they are places where females are expected to engage in the titivating activities necessary for maintaining one's womanly appearance—brushing one's hair, putting on makeup, adjusting one's skirt, attending to small children, spraying on perfume, and so forth.

In regard to accuracy of designation, one knows why doors are marked "men" and "women," and one knows what is in store behind those doors—even if one thinks bathrooms ought to be co-ed. I also note that it is perfectly within the rules about bathroom doors that humans below a certain age can go into either—or rather, that little boys can go into rooms marked "women" even though little girls don't usually go into rooms marked "men."

17. It is not without reason that trustees of colleges and universities typically don't have campus offices.

18. Sociobiology is perhaps the most recent field to define human differences in this way. For another illustration of the creation of difference in the guise of discovering it, see the legal and medical documents collected by Michel Foucault together with the memoirs of a nineteenth-century French hermaphrodite in *Herculine Barbin* (New York: Random, 1980).

19. For a recent discussion of this, see Ian Hacking, "Making Up People," in *Reconstructing Individualism,* ed. Thomas C. Heller, Morton Sosna, and David E. Wellerby (Stanford: Stanford University Press, 1986), 222–36. See also "On 'Compulsory Heterosexuality and Lesbian Existence': Defining the Issues," a collection of comments by Ann Ferguson, Jacquelyn N. Zita, and Kathryn Pyne Addelson, *Signs* 7 (1981): 158–99.

20. See, for example, "Woman Seeks Change in Racial Designation," *The New York Times,* Friday, 28 November 1984, A28. Also see Michael Omi and Howard Winant, "By the Rivers of Babylon: Race in the United States," parts 1 and 2, *Socialist Review* 71 and 72 (1983).

21. See Lugones and Spelman, "Have We Got a Theory for You!" 573–81.

22. Jan Morris, *Conundrum* (New York: Signet, 1974).

23. There will be tension between these two things, since being too obvious about reinforcing categories may make people suspicious.

24. *Republic* 454a; see chapter 1 above.

25. See chapter 4 above on what she takes to be universal about gender relations.

Chapter 7: *Now You See Her, Now You Don't*

1. See, for example, Sherley Anne Williams, "Meditations On History," in *Midnight Birds,* ed. Mary Helen Washington (Garden City, N.Y.: Anchor/ Doubleday, 1980), 200–48; Sarah Patton Boyle, *The Desegregated Heart* (New York: Morrow, 1962).

2. bell hooks, *Feminist Theory,* 11 and passim; Marilyn Frye, "On Being White," in *The Politics of Reality* (Trumansburg, N.Y.: Crossing Press, 1983), 110–27.

3. "In more recent years, racism has become an accepted topic in feminist discussions not as a result of black women calling attention to it (this was done at the very onset of the movement), but as a result of white female input validating such discussions, a process which is indicative of how racism works" (hooks, *Feminist Theory,* 51).

4. Indeed, some feminists have thought that the creation and maintenance of gender differences has been so crucial to female oppression that they take the elimination of such differences to be necessary to the elimination of sexism; for a useful discussion of this, see Jaggar, *Feminist Politics,* 254, 317, and passim.

5. Note that if we used "Hispana" here, the oddity of the request would be even more apparent.

6. hooks, *Feminist Theory*, 5–6.

7. Iris Young has pointed out that socialist feminists typically have talked about the relation between class and gender in an additive fashion, and thus have tended "to claim that *qua* women we are in an identical situation whatever our historical location or situation" ("Beyond the Unhappy Marriage: A Critique of the Dual Systems Theory," in *Women and Revolution,* ed. Lydia Sargent [Boston: South End Press, 1981], 55).

8. Similarly, it is only from such a vantage point that the beginning of an "autonomous women's movement" is said to be marked at the point at which the women's movement severed its ties to the abolitionist and trade-union movements (see, for example, DuBois, *Feminism and Suffrage,* chap. 6). To say this may seem to be saying merely that the movement had to be controlled by women who were setting their own agenda, as opposed to having men in other movements telling them what to do. But it is also to say that as soon as the movement gave up concern about abolition and the situation of workers, it could really focus on "women's issues"—which is to say that the condition of Black women slaves, and of women of any color in the work force, were not "women's issues."

9. As we noted in chapter 5, the work of Mary Daly reminds us that it is also an expression of privilege for white middle-class women to assume that women of other races and classes couldn't possibly see anything positive in their identities and could only welcome the end of such distinctions—as if the only distinction between white and Black worth attention is that Blacks have less social, economic, and political power than whites.

10. This I think is one of the implications of the early work of Gayle Rubin. See "The Traffic in Women," in *Toward an Anthropology of Women,* ed. Rayna Reiter (New York: Monthly Review Press, 1975), 157–210.

11. See Lugones and Spelman, "Have We Got a Theory for You!"

12. See Introduction, 8.

13. See Lugones and Spelman, "Have We Got a Theory for You!" and Lugones, "On the Logic of Pluralist Feminism" (unpublished manuscript, 1988).

14. "White/Anglo women do one or more of the following to women of color: they ignore us, ostracize us, render us invisible, stereotype us, leave us completely alone, interpret us as crazy. All of this *while we are in their midst*" (María C. Lugones, "Playfulness, 'World'-Travelling, and Loving Perception" [unpublished manuscript, 1986]).

15. Jean-Paul Sartre, *The Psychology of Imagination* (Secaucus: Citadel Press, n.d.).

16. Note the difference between saying "the lives of those from whom we differ" and "the lives of those who differ from us."

17. See Spelman, "Combating the Marginalization of Black Women in the Classroom," in *Gendered Subjects,* ed. Margo Culley and Catherine Portuges (Boston: Routledge and Kegan Paul, 1985), 240–44.

18. This is clear from the "extra burden" example and many others, and it is

expressed as principled argument by Janet Radcliffe Richards (see chap. 2): feminists might be interested in what happens to Black women under slavery, for example, but it is not central to their work as feminists.

19. Allan Bloom, *The Closing of the American Mind* (New York: Simon and Schuster, 1987), 95.

20. See, for example, Catherine A. MacKinnon, "Feminism, Marxism, Method, and the State: An Agenda for Theory," *Signs* 7, no. 3 (1982): 517.

21. Quoted by Dick Lourie in *Triquarterly* 23, no. 24 (1972): 81.

22. Thanks to Sweet Honey in the Rock for "mothers, daughters, sisters, lovers."

Index

Beauvoir, Simone de (*continued*)
67; Otherness in, 74; sex and gender in, 66–69, 72, 172; transcendence vs. immanence in, 61, 65, 73–74
—sexism in: explanation of, 61–62; and other forms of oppression in general, 58, 60, 61, 62–66, 71, 74–77, 115; and racism and classism, 62–66, 68–69; 72, 166, 170
—woman in, 62–66, 148, 155–56, 160–61, 166; the creation of, 66–69, 72, 151, 167, 174; nature of, 58, 59; as Other, 60, 61, 67, 69, 73–75; the real vs. the ideal, 69–71
Benjamin, Jessica, 203 n
Bloom, Allan, 184
Body, the, 126–28; in Aristotle, 10–11, 39, 44–45, 185; in Firestone, 126, 128, 129; and racial definition, 134; in Rich, 129–30; and sexual identity, 151; and subjectivity, in de Beauvoir, 67, 69, 72, 126–27, 128; views of, and racism, 126–28, 129; woman's relation with, 126–28
—and the soul, 137; in Aristotle, 10–11, 39, 44, 185; in Plato, 10, 13, 22, 23–25, 30–32, 185, 186
Bowles, Dorcas, 99
Boyle, Sarah Patton, 211 n
Braverman, Harry, 206 n
Brent, Linda, 122
Brooks, Gwendolyn, 160, 186
Bumpus, Eleanor, 193 n
Burgher, Mary, 97–98

Cameron, Barbara, 98
Cantarella, Eva, account of slave women, 50–51, 52, 53–54, 55–56, 193 n
Capitalism, 87, 108, 109
Chodorow, Nancy, 16, 80–113; capitalism in, 108, 109; class differences in, 87–88, 93–95; families in, role of, 85–86; femininity in, 82–84, 85, 86–88, 94, 171; mothering in, 82–89, 96–99, 108–9, 110–11, 171; Otherness in, 85; private and public spheres in, 108–10; relational capacities in, gender-based, 82, 84, 107–11; sexism in, and other forms of oppression, 84–85, 88, 89–94, 171;

the sexual division of labor in, 82, 83, 87, 108; woman as Other in, 92–93
—gender and selfhood in, 82–84, 86–87, 94, 97, 108; and racism and classism, 134, 157–58, 170–71
—masculinity in, 83–84, 86–87, 88, 93–95; and affective ties, 108–10; and the belief in male superiority, 95, 96–99, 108, 171
Christ, Carol, 208 n
Christian, Barbara, 206 n
City-state. *See* Polis
Civil rights movement, 11, 115, 116, 140
Class: differences, in Chodorow, 87–88, 93–95; identity, 10, 94–95, 104
Classism, 11, 14, 52, 110, 116; and sexism, 51, 155–56
—and racism: in Chodorow, 134, 157–58, 170–71; in de Beauvoir, 62–66, 68–69, 72, 166, 170; and feminism, 35, 112–13, 165–66. *See also* Sexism, and other forms of oppression
Commonality, 13, 138–40
Connection. *See* Relational capacities, gender-based

Daly, Mary, 8, 123–25, 212 n
Dance, Daryl, 99
Davis, Angela, 122, 123, 135–36, 158, 159, 207 n
Demosthenes, 64
Dickson, Anna, 190 n
Descartes, René, 95, 96, 136, 143–44, 210 n
Difference, 4, 140, 164; the assertion and denial of, and domination, 11–12; and gender, in Chodorow, 84. *See also* Women, commonalities and differences between
Diotima, 29–30
DuBois, Ellen Carol, 191 n, 207 n, 212 n
Dworkin, Andrea, 193 n

Edgerton, Robert B., 209 n
Elshtain, Jean Bethke, 190 n
ERA (Equal Rights Amendment), 131
Essentialism, 159
Ethnicity, 111, 143, 151, 165, 178
Ethnocentrism, 13, 110, 167, 185

216

Index

Index

182–83; and feminist theory, three axioms regarding, 162–64
—and slavery: in Aristotle, 37–56, 154–55, 168, 176; Cantarella on, 50–51, 52, 53–54, 55–56; Richards on, 50, 51, 52, 53–54, 55–56
—white middle-class, 3, 139, 166, 202 n; as the focus of feminist theory, 164, 171–72; privilege of, 3–5, 75–77, 177–78, 183; racial and class identity of, 112; and the situation of "women" in general, 77, 148. *See also* Aristotle, views on women; Male/female relations; Plato, views on women

Wood, Ellen M., 193 n, 194 n
Wood, Neal, 193 n, 194 n

Young, Iris, 203 n, 204 n, 205 n, 212 n

Zita, Jacqueline, 211 n